CRASH COURSE

Michael Prince

CRASH COURSE

THE WORLD
OF AIR SAFETY

GRAFTON BOOKS
A Division of the Collins Publishing Group

LONDON GLASGOW
TORONTO SYDNEY AUCKLAND

For BM

Grafton Books
A Division of the Collins Publishing Group
8 Grafton Street, London W1X 3LA

Published by Grafton Books 1990

British Library Cataloguing in Publication Data

Prince, Michael
  Crash course: the world of air safety.
  1. Aviation. Safety aspects
  I. Title
  363.124

ISBN 0–246–13577–8

Phototypeset by Input Typesetting Ltd, London
Printed in Great Britain by
Butler & Tanner Ltd, Frome, Somerset

CONTENTS

ABBREVIATIONS

ALPA (USA): The Air Line Pilots' Association of the United States: looks after the interests of commercial pilots.

ANC: Air Navigation Commission: part of the International Civil Aviation Organization. The Commission comprises fifteen people experienced in aeronautics. Their duty is to recommend international standards and procedures for safety and efficiency in air navigation.

ATC: Air Traffic Control: collectively, the men and women throughout the world who route aircraft safely on the ground and in the air.

ATS: Air Traffic Services: includes air-traffic control, weather forecasting and reporting, and aeronautical information. Dates back to 1919 when an international agreement was reached for the standardization of navigation lights, rules of the air and signals to be adopted at airfields.

BALPA: British Air Line Pilots' Association: looks after the interests of British pilots, especially regarding the hours to be worked and raising questions of safety regarding new aircraft.

CAA: Civil Aviation Authority: the governing body of airline operation in the United Kingdom.

FAA: Federal Aviation Administration: America's equivalent of Britain's CAA.

IAPA: International Airline Passenger Association: formed in 1960 in the United States as a pressure group to influence airlines regarding consumers' needs. Membership was 110,000 in 1988 and the organization had offices in eight countries, including Britain.

IATA: International Air Transport Association: involved in the negotiation of tariff and scheduling agreements and also legislation affecting the carrying of dangerous goods, aircraft maintenance, security and the training of flight crews. The administrative headquarters are in Geneva, Switzerland, while the technical research is undertaken in Montreal, Canada.

ICAO: International Civil Aviation Organization: specialist agency of the United Nations with more than 150 member states. Involved in world-wide safety initiatives, even in countries which are not represented.

IFALPA: International Federation of Air Line Pilots' Associations: formed in 1948, the membership includes more than 60 national pilots' associations. It is non-political and, therefore, attracts pilot groups from all over the world. Some 80 per cent of IFALPA's work involves safety measures.

IFATCA: International Federation of Air Traffic Controllers' Associations: a body to promote the professional interests of air-traffic controllers.

NTSB: National Transportation Safety Board: investigates accidents in the United States and sends experts to crash scenes all over the world to help draw conclusions from disasters and to pave the way for greater safety.

PHOTO CREDITS

INTRODUCTION

When Pan Am Flight 103 crashed at Lockerbie in south-west Scotland on 21 December 1988, it changed everything.

Overnight, the blasé globe-jetter became an anachronism, to be replaced by the white-knuckle brotherhood, characterized by nervous twitches and over-sensitive ears tuned to the cadence of aircraft engines.

Earlier check-in times, overt security, elaborate boarding and baggage procedures, together with more vigorous passenger screening, made sure flying would never again be taken for granted. Executive travellers, the backbone of the business, began asking themselves whether their next scheduled trip really was necessary.

In the United States, distances dictated that air travel would never be replaced as the mainstream means of inter-city journeys. And holidaymakers, with time strictly rationed, continued to take the quickest route to their destination. For almost everybody, however, the pain and frustration were growing less bearable by the day. Those cynics who predicted that Lockerbie would soon become a forgotten statistic, allowing air transport to regain its credibility, miscalculated the depth of the public's disquiet.

Indeed, a survey commissioned nine months after Lockerbie by *Executive Travel*, a London magazine, showed that safety had become the most important criterion for the busy air-travelling executive. Eighty-five per cent of the 7300 business people who were questioned in the United Kingdom favoured even tighter security, regardless of the inevitable delay incurred. They admitted shunning airlines which had been targeted by terrorists, including Pan Am, Air India and Japan Airlines.

If the newspapers could be believed, it was a source of amazement that any flight ever reached its destination. The catalogue seemed as repetitive as it was endless – of ageing aircraft, daily dodgem manoeuvres in the sky, engines dropping off, gaping holes materializing in the fuselage at high altitude, air-crews falling asleep at the controls, pilots resorting to drink and drugs to enable them to sustain their workload, maintenance engineers indulging in industrial sabotage, planes drifting hundreds of miles off course and even landing at wrong airports, and negligent manufacturers.

'Fear of flying' courses, from New York to Tokyo, have been over-subscribed ever since Lockerbie. At a London Heathrow seminar for phobics, a bar owner complained to a roomful of fellow sufferers that there were three stages of flying which distressed him: 'The take-off, the landing, and the bit in between!' His public self-analysis was greeted with thunderous applause. A pilot tried to calm everyone by saying that nail-biting and white knuckles represented 'low-grade' panic. The *really* frightened tended to faint, suffer fits and heart attacks, even die. To be frightened, he said, was much more dangerous than flying itself, a statement which appeared only to intensify the general fear.

Maurice Yaffe, a British therapist specializing in the treatment of flying phobia, believed it imperative that phobics identified their fear: is it claustrophobia, a terror of heights, or the loss of control of one's own destiny? One woman confided that it was more 'the little things' which panicked her, such as 'engines failing, mid-air collisions, bombs exploding, tails disintegrating and hijacks'.

Arguments from the industry itself that flying is no more dangerous than travelling by rail, and less risky than going by sea – and certainly by road – failed to impress. To be comparable with trains is scarcely a boast. And when crashes occur, their scale is commensurate with the jumbo age of aviation. Consequently, there are few more emotive issues today than airline safety.

An article in the *Observer* newspaper in September 1985 by Chris Birkett of *Flight International* magazine, Helen Gavaghan of the *New Scientist* and Jonathan Foster summed it up this way: 'What distresses the nervous passenger is the horror of the deaths and the numbers involved in each accident. It matters little that about 200,000 people are killed on the world's roads each year: these people die in ones and twos and they do not plummet out of the sky to burn alive or inhale toxic fumes.'

Even the figures for the good years do little to assuage public anxiety. In 1987, 950 million passengers worldwide travelled by air. The number of fatalities was 330, making odds of almost one in three million. More people were dying in air crashes at the end of the decade 1980–90 than at its inception. In 1985 the average number of annual fatal crashes was 20. By 1990 the number was 21.4. In the course of those ten years, the average number of deaths per year related to air accidents had climbed from 588 to 752, prompting *Flight International* scathingly to dub 1989 and the era to which it belonged 'The Complacent Year – The Arrogant Decade'.

The 1764 deaths in 1989 made that year the second worst in aviation history, just behind 1985, when there were 2000 fatalities. *Flight International* accused the airline industry of 'resting on its laurels', following what appeared to be a trend towards greater safety. However, although more people were dying in air crashes, the statistical odds were improving. On a strict mathematical calculation, as at the beginning of 1990 it was necessary to make 571,000 flights before encountering a fatal one.

The growing pains began long before Lockerbie. Deregulation in the United States had created anxiety: towards the end of 1983, Air Illinois, a small commuter airline, was grounded as a safety precaution; one month later, Air Vermont, another commuter outfit, voluntarily curtailed its services due to financial strictures; Freedom Airlines, Cleveland, took out of commission four of its aircraft, while Global International, a charter operation based in Kansas City, was grounded by the Federal Aviation Administration because of its record of poor maintenance, training and operation.

Suddenly the whole structure of the industry in the United States seemed unsound, with repercussions worldwide.

Lockerbie proved to be the apocalypse. In the early eighties sabotage would not have been considered a significant factor in air safety. Today, it is at the very heart. Even so, this book is far from being just the story of Pan Am Flight 103 and other disasters. I have tried to explore every feature of the overall safety issue by referring to airlines in Britain, the United States, Europe and many other regions of the world, such as the Far East, Africa and the South Pacific.

For their discreet and generous co-operation, which provided me with so much detailed inside information, I must thank pilots, airline officials, maintenance engineers, manufacturers, air-traffic controllers, investigating officers, regulation board officials, and the agents of numerous intelligence agencies worldwide.

Special appreciation for their invaluable assistance must go to Laurie

Taylor, a pilot for 30 years – five of them as chairman of the British Air Line Pilots' Association – and Jim Cozens, an air-traffic controller at West Drayton, London. Both invited me to their homes to talk in detail about their experiences, and I quote them extensively. On the few occasions when I refer to Taylor's own book, *Air Travel: How Safe Is It?* (published by BSP Professional Books), I draw the distinction.

Despite the proliferation of phobics, the airline industry has persisted in arguing that the public were over-reacting and that their fear was irrational. 'Study the statistics,' it recommended. 'Research the facts. Get the whole story.'

I took the advice and embarked on the crash course; hence this book.

But does it kill or cure?

You decide.

1 COUNTDOWN TO LOCKERBIE

There is a generation which will never forget where it was and what it was doing the moment news broke of President Kennedy's assassination in Dallas on 22 November 1963. The crash at Lockerbie of Pan Am Flight 103, a Boeing 747 called *Maid of the Seas*, blown out of the early night sky by a terrorist bomb on 21 December 1988, had a similar impact on the Western world as it prepared to celebrate Christmas.

The flight originated in Frankfurt, Germany, continued north-westwards from Heathrow, London, and ended prematurely 54 minutes later in Scotland, still 3000 miles short of its New York destination. The number 103 has become synonymous with 13 as a symbol of ill-fortune, and Lockerbie will for ever have its haunting place in history.

On that Wednesday evening, I was staying at a Heathrow hotel in preparation for a flight the next morning to Miami with Pan Am, and heard of the crash from the first television newsflash. Next morning, it was business as usual at Heathrow, with no overt evidence of extra security, though, to be fair, investigators were emphasizing that it was far too early for any speculation as to the cause of the disaster. However, it soon became evident that, from the moment it happened there were people in high places who knew exactly how the Pan Am 747 had been brought down and why.

As we checked-in our baggage at the airport, a woman security officer enquired persistently: 'Have the cases been left unattended since you packed? . . . Would you know if they had been tampered with? . . . Have you been given anything to carry for anyone else? . . . Are you prepared to be held responsible for everything in your luggage?' Only after the security officer was satisfied with all the answers were we allowed to proceed. Everyone flying Pan Am faced a similar inquisition, but this had become routine at Heathrow and pre-dated Lockerbie. Such was the effect of the disaster, however, that, once we were airborne, some of the passengers illogically counted off the first 54 minutes before they could relax.

The countdown to Lockerbie began five and a half months earlier on Sunday, 3 July 1988, when an Iranian commercial jet airliner was shot down in the Arabian Gulf by two Standard missiles fired from the United States Navy cruiser USS *Vincennes*, killing all 290 civilians on board, mostly Iranians on a shopping trip to Dubai in the neighbouring United Arab Emirates. The Iran Air Airbus A300, Flight 655, left Bandar Abbas at 10.45 a.m., after Captain Mohsen Rezaian had read a page of the Koran over the public address system to the passengers, who included 66 children.

Before take-off, Rezaian, an experienced pilot who regularly flew the Bandar Abbas–Dubai shuttle, had activated the aircraft's transponder, a device in the nose section which would identify the plane on all radar screens in the region as a scheduled civilian flight.

Although the Bandar Abbas–Dubai shuttle was a simple hop across the Strait of Hormuz, it could never be dismissed as routine. The Iran–Iraq war was still a month from a ceasefire and the southern Gulf was policed by American warships, while acts of piracy and unprovoked aggression by the Iranians were all too commonplace. Indeed, as Flight 655 had been boarding, the crew of the USS *Vincennes* were monitoring in the control-room the movements of a fleet of merchant ships and at least a dozen Iranian gunboats.

Captain Will Rogers III, the skipper of the American cruiser, dispatched a helicopter to appraise the situation from the air. Almost immediately, at 10.10 a.m., a Norwegian tanker was sunk; and the helicopter was shelled by three of the Iranian rogue ships before retreating to its floating base, where the pilot reported that 'things' were 'getting ugly'.

Rogers was in constant contact with the captain of another American warship nearby, the USS *Sides*. At 10.42 a.m., three minutes before the Airbus had taken off, the *Vincennes* and the *Sides* attacked the Iranian aggressors with their five-inch guns, sinking two of the gunboats, while the others scuttled for the cover of port.

Not to be forgotten is the importance of that weekend in the United States calendar: the Independence Day celebrations. Naval Intelligence had been tipped off that Iran was planning a major military offensive against the United States to demonstrate its contempt for everything

American. All the signs pointed to the accuracy of that information: the previous day there had been an alert when a squadron of Iranian fighter planes, ironically American-made F-14s, were spotted on the horizon.

This was the background to the tragedy that was about to occur.

Between Bandar Abbas and Dubai was a 20-mile-wide commercial flight corridor, known as Amber 59, which Captain Rezaian followed immediately after take-off that very hot and dusty Sunday morning: the sky was cloudless and the temperature had soared above 100°F.

By this time, tension was mounting on the USS *Vincennes*. Captain Rogers had taken charge in the control-room, known on United States ships as the CIC (Combat Information Centre), where four huge over-head screens displayed all air and sea activity in the area, these data being fed from the ship's Aegis radar system. The only light came from the illuminated screens and the glow of the control panels.

Rogers was trying to interpret what was happening in overall military terms at that precise moment in the southern Gulf, when a radar operator noticed that an aircraft had taken off from Bandar Abbas and appeared to be heading directly for them. This new development was relayed to Rogers, who was aware that the airport at Bandar Abbas was used by military as well as civilian aircraft, further complicating the issue. The radar operators on the USS *Vincennes* had equipment which enabled them to plug into conversations between civilian aircraft pilots and air-traffic controllers. If that facility had been exploited, Rogers would have known instantly that the approaching plane was the Airbus shuttle en route to Dubai. Instead, the radar operator projected the green blip on to one of the giant screens in the control-room as a possible bandit.

Quick calculations showed that the plane would be over the US warship in seven minutes. At that stage, two factors were causing alarm on the cruiser: firstly, the aircraft appeared to be outside the Amber 59 corridor; secondly, the speed of the plane seemed much too fast for anything other than a military fighter.

Unfortunately the radar was incapable of identifying the type of plane, but the automated identification system should have established whether it was friend or foe from the coded signal of the Airbus's transponder.

There was no cowboy reaction from Will Rogers at this point, despite the propaganda that was later to gush from Iranian sources. He gave the order for the pilot to be told to change course. This was done at 10.49 a.m. on an emergency frequency.

The USS *Sides* was briefed and both ships were placed on standby, during which time eleven more warnings, via military and civilian air distress networks, were sent out from the USS *Vincennes* and the USS *Sides*. According to the records of both ships, not one reply or acknowledgement was received.

We shall never know for certain whether Captain Rezaian and his flight-deck crew were ever aware of the warnings from the Americans. Established fact is that Rezaian was speaking with a Bandar Abbas traffic controller, requesting permission to climb from 7000 to 14,000 feet. This element of the jigsaw puzzle is crucial because Rogers was later to insist that the plane had been descending towards his ship.

Possibly, at the back of Rogers's mind was the fate of the USS *Stark*, hit by two Exocet missiles from a fighter which had been mistaken for a friendly Iraqi jet, resulting in the death of 37 American seamen. Rogers could be forgiven by all neutrals for being determined to avoid at all costs a repeat massacre. He could not possibly have known how high the cost would ultimately be: a bill that was not finally settled until that winter's night over Scotland.

There were about 25 radar and sonar operators, communications officers and technicians on board the USS *Vincennes*, all frantically trying to make sense of what was happening. All of them were responsible to the CIC officer and his deputy. In the centre of the darkened room was the 'throne', the captain's seat, and a special set of displays. Three separate units were simultaneously watching for aggressive signals from the air, from surface ships and from submarines.

But the whole detection and interpretation network relied almost entirely on the $525 million Aegis defence system, which had been developed to forewarn of any Soviet saturation strike. The course, radar signal and speed of 200 suspect targets could be tracked by Aegis for a distance of 250 miles, the chief source of information coming from the SPY-1 multi-function array radar, comprising two pairs of monitoring devices mounted on the forward and aft deck-houses. Each pair had 4100 radiating elements controlled by a digital computer, producing and steering multiple beams for target search, detection and tracking.

The coded signal from the Airbus should have put all minds at rest on the USS *Vincennes*, but it did not do so because it was misinterpreted as an Iranian F-14 Tomcat fighter. As a further check, a timetable of all civilian airlines was scrutinized, apparently confirming that no flight was due. However, if the USS *Vincennes'* wireless operators had tuned into the wavelength of ground control at Bandar Abbas, it would have been apparent that the worrying blip on the screens was a commercial flight which had been delayed and was running late.

For Rogers, time was running out. A decision had to be made. Accordingly, at 10.51 a.m. he declared the aircraft 'hostile' and contacted Rear-Admiral Anthony Less, the United States joint Task Force commander, seeking his advice. Less, who was on the flagship in the Gulf, made it clear that the buck must stop with Rogers; the final decision would have to be his, based on all the data and intelligence, plus the previous hostile events of that morning and the day before.

Three minutes after branding the aircraft 'hostile', Rogers gave the order for it to be shot down. Flight 655 was then just nine miles and thirty seconds' flying time from the USS *Vincennes*.

Aegis evaluates its target, coping with as many as twenty at the same time, sometimes as far away as eighty miles, relying on 'classified' criteria. The self-motivated system lines up its targets in order of priority and then requests permission to fire. As soon as engagement has been 'command approved' by the captain, it independently selects the most appropriate weapon.

That Sunday morning, after Rogers had handed over the fate of everyone on board the Airbus to the robots, two Standard missiles were directed at the target. Radar beamed the missiles along illuminated tracks.

The atmosphere in the CIC was taut and frenzied, though there had been no panic. By tradition, there is no cathedral reverence in a CIC, which contrasts dramatically, for example, with the austere quiet of a British Navy control-room. Nevertheless, despite all the noisy animation around him, Rogers, a master of computerized weaponry and the latest in modern technology, was totally in charge and completely self-possessed. He was the last man in the world to be stampeded into over-reacting.

One of the missiles scored a direct hit and Flight 655 was committed to the ocean near the Iranian island of Hangem. There were no survivors.

News of the blunder was revealed at lunchtime to the American people by President Reagan from his Camp David retreat, outside Washington, just as the nation prepared for firework parties to celebrate Independence Day.

The first press conference was chaired by Admiral William J. Crow Jr, head of the Joint Chiefs of Staff. Information was sketchy and Crow's line was that the Iranians appeared to have been deliberately courting disaster, an argument which soon had to be abandoned.

After further consultations with his political and military advisers, Reagan went on television, saying, 'I am saddened to report that it appears that in a proper defensive action by the USS *Vincennes* this morning in the Persian Gulf, an Iranian airliner was shot down over the Strait of Hormuz. This is a terrible human tragedy. Our sympathy and condolences go out to the passengers, crew and their families. The course of the Iranian civilian airliner was such that it was headed directly for the USS *Vincennes*, which was at the time engaged with five Iranian Boghammer boats that had attacked our forces. When the aircraft failed to heed repeated warnings, the *Vincennes* followed standing orders and widely publicized procedures, firing to protect itself against possible attack. The only US interest in the Persian Gulf is peace, and this reinforces the need to achieve that goal with all possible speed.'

Meanwhile in Britain, Prime Minister Margaret Thatcher was hastily announcing from 10 Downing Street: 'We understand that in the course of an engagement following an Iranian attack on the US Force, warnings were given to an unidentified aircraft, apparently closing with a US warship. We fully accept the right of forces engaged in such hostilities to defend themselves. This tragic incident underlines the urgent need for an early end to the Iran–Iraq conflict, including an end to all attacks on shipping.'

Perhaps it would have been more prudent of Mrs Thatcher to have reserved judgement until she was in possession of more facts.

Equally predictable was the Iranian response. Tehran Radio said, 'We will not leave the crimes of America unanswered. We will resist the plots of the Great Satan and avenge the blood of our martyrs from criminal mercenaries.' Iranian Foreign Minister Velayati accused the United States of being 'responsible for a barbaric massacre'.

Lockerbie was cold-blooded retribution. At no time did any Iranian authority try to allay fears about their intentions. It should have been transparent to anyone that the target would be American and civilian – a soft target.

Within a few weeks, intelligence sources in the Middle East were aware of a plot, then only in embryo, to bring down an American airliner. The conspiracy originated in Iran, but was to be executed by loyal 'lieutenants' and 'soldiers' outside the Gulf region. The first people to hear of the retaliation plan were underground agents in the Israeli Secret Service, Mossad, probably the most efficient in the world. The CIA was privy to this information almost simultaneously.

Since its inception, the CIA, like MI5 and MI6 in Britain, has exploited journalists as 'stringers', often without their knowledge. Free-lances were always favoured because they tended to be more hungry and intrepid than staffers.

It was from a freelance American journalist in Beirut, who was moonlighting for the CIA, that the United States intelligence agencies first heard that an unparalleled 'contract' had gone out from the Ayatollah Khomeini. The blood money reputed to have been offered by the Ayatollah to any person or organization – Muslim or otherwise – for the downing of an American airliner was $5 million. Bearing in mind the content of the statements emanating from Tehran, no one should have been surprised by the allegations in relation to the Ayatollah and planned reprisals, but, from all accounts, the prevailing wind from the West was one of complacency, ranging from amused scepticism to intransigent disbelief.

In diplomatic circles, credibility was given to the notion that the Iranians had finally accepted the unhappy episode as a tragic accident, devoid of any malice by the Americans. 'Time will heal', was the great cliché circulating in Washington and Westminster. Historically there was no justification for such confidence and all intelligence from agents in the field told a very different story, but few people were listening.

Lockerbie was rapidly becoming inevitable, even though alarm bells were ringing throughout Europe. However, it would be wrong to imply that nothing could have prevented retaliatory sabotage. The bomb, admittedly highly advanced in design, *was* detectable. Intelligence agents knew it was on its way. It was the system that allowed vengeance to have its day.

Safety did not come first.

2 DEADLY COCKTAIL

Whatever else, the Iranian Airbus incident clearly demonstrated that civilian and military air traffic do not mix. For instance, civilian aircraft from Miami en route to islands in the Caribbean have frequently been buzzed by Cuban fighter planes. What would happen if a civilian plane accidentally strayed off course into Cuban airspace? Would it be shot down?

When we buy an airline ticket we naturally assume that space is safe, but on the contrary it can be unfriendly – even hostile. For example, air-traffic controllers in the Gulf complained bitterly throughout 1988, even before the shooting down of the Airbus, that US warships 'rode roughshod' over the rights of civilian operators. In June a 747 was forced to change direction and was locked into a head-on collision course with another airliner which had just taken off. Controllers in the United Arab Emirates filed a complaint accusing navy ships in the Gulf of 'endangering lives' by the 'cavalier manner in which they challenged and abused' civilian carriers.

In another incident, a British Airways 747, bound for India and about to descend for a scheduled stop at Dubai in the Gulf, had a lucky escape when, by pure luck, it picked up a radio warning from a US warship. Flight BA 147 was 30 miles west of Dubai and the crew were fully occupied with pre-landing instrument checks. As the first officer flicked through the radio frequencies, he chanced upon a transmission on the international distress band, 121.5 MHz, and paused to listen only because he feared someone else might be in trouble. What he heard was a US warship challenging an aircraft, which was identified only by its height and heading. Only then did the first officer realize that it was his own aircraft which was being given a final opportunity to make a 180-degree diversion or be fired on. That was on 8 June 1988, a month before the Iranian Airbus was the target of two surface-to-air missiles from the USS *Vincennes*.

The warning to the British Airways 747 was identical to that given to the Airbus: 'This is a United States naval warship operating in international waters. Change course immediately. If you maintain your current course, you are steering into danger and subject to United States naval defensive measures. Over.'

The captain of the 747 was about to take emergency avoiding action, but this would have put the plane into a head-on collision course with a Bulgarian Antonov 12, Flight LZ 2101, flying from Bahrain to Sharjah. The International Civil Aviation Organization (ICAO) observed in an unpublished report, 'Prompt action by Dubai approach prevented BA 147 from changing its course and thus avoided a potential mid-air collision.'

There were at least six direct challenges and threats to civilian aircraft by US warships during the Gulf War, mostly on the military distress frequency, which is not normally received by civilian aircraft. The attitude of US warships did not mellow even after the shooting down of the Iranian Airbus: these assertions were also incorporated in the ICAO report.

There is a rule of the ICAO which states: 'Intercepting aircraft should refrain from the use of weapons in all cases of interception of civil aircraft.' Although that rule applies specifically to military air strategy, the principle is equally valid for navy policy. Also relevant is a code of practice laid down by the International Federation of Air Line Pilots' Association (IFALPA), which says that a civilian aircraft inadvertently straying from its correct flight path and infringing prohibited airspace, or threatening to, should 'be dealt with on the basis that the civil aircraft requires assistance, as distinct from police action'. IFALPA goes on, 'Invariably, the aircraft concerned will be in some form of distress, ranging from being lost to being in an emergency condition.'

On 1 September 1983 a Korean Air Lines 747 was intercepted and shot down by Russian fighter jets over the island of Sakhalin in the Sea of Okhotsk. Flight KAL 007, from Anchorage, Alaska, to Seoul, South Korea, had inadvertently strayed many miles north off course into Soviet airspace. None of the 269 people on board survived.

However, the Iran Airbus was not even off course when the USS *Vincennes* fired its missiles, despite assertions to the contrary at the time by the cruiser's crew. Captain Rogers was led to believe that the Airbus was four miles outside the commercial corridor and descending rapidly, when in fact it was four miles off the centre of the 20-mile-wide protected passage, well within the accepted route, and was *climbing*. Despite the sophistication of the Aegis radar, it was unable to differentiate between civilian and military aircraft. The *Vincennes'* crew somehow received two signals, one military and the other civilian, from the Airbus's transponder: a fatal and inexplicable mistake, especially as the USS *Sides* identified the plane for what it really was.

Unlike in most areas of the world, aircraft flying in the Middle East at below 15,000 feet were not required to operate a transponder. Therefore, Captain Rezaian would have been perfectly within his rights if he had not activated the transponder on the Airbus as he departed from Bandar Abbas at the outset of the scheduled 55-minute flight. Nevertheless, there is a strong possibility that the Airbus was fitted with two transponders, because it had been used as a troop plane during the Iran–Iraq war.

Most air crashes are the result of a combination of circumstances, rather than one single mechanical or human failure, and the Iranian Airbus incident was no exception. Defence officials at the Pentagon in Washington intimated that the Airbus might still have been attacked even if it had been correctly identified by the USS *Vincennes*, because US Navy commanders had been briefed to expect kamikaze raids from the Iranians. The Airbus could have been loaded with explosives and the pilot on a suicide mission, it was ventured. It was also suggested that enemy aircraft could 'hide' in a civilian air corridor, and the failure of the Airbus crew to respond to attempts at communication from the USS *Vincennes* would have planted that seed in Rogers's mind, thus proving that nothing could be guaranteed sacred in war zones. Normal codes and conventions do not apply there.

An ICAO study, authorized in 1983 by the Air Navigation Commission, produced a list of 'sensitive areas' where civilian planes could be targets. Into that category came virtually the entire Middle East and any region where military exercises were prevalent, either on land or sea. The problem for the average paying passenger is how to discover, in advance, the flight-path from A to B and what trouble spots have to be circumnavigated, especially as many routes are changed even after take-off.

It is a sad reflection on our times that the missile attack on the Iranian Airbus was not without precedent. Two Air Rhodesia Viscounts were blown up in 1978 and 1979 by terrorists using surface-to-air missiles (SAM). Seven years later, the mujahedin of Afghanistan, firing SAMs supplied by sources in Britain and the United States and with the knowledge of the British and American governments, brought down a number of passenger aircraft flying in the colours of Afghanistan's Ariana Airlines.

In the Gulf, Iran Air was the only airline to take the calculated risk of operating between Bandar Abbas and Dubai during the crisis of 1988. Their two main competitors, Gulf Air and Emirates, left the route well alone. All Western airlines kept clear of the region directly north of Dubai. Working practice for pilots on the Gulf shuttles was to call Dubai at the Mobar reporting point, about forty miles from Bandar Abbas and virtually directly above the spot from which the USS *Vincennes* opened fire, when a four-figure code would be allocated for entering into the transponder.

Early speculation that the Airbus had been shot down before its transponder was activated was ruled out by the two conflicting signals picked up by the USS *Vincennes* and the one recorded by the USS *Sides*. It was not unknown, however, for military pilots to use a civilian transponder as a ruse to confuse the enemy.

More than anything else, an out-of-date timetable was probably the main contributory factor to the accident. When a senior officer of the USS *Vincennes*, working under intense pressure and against the clock, thumbed through the civilian airlines' schedule, the only flights listed between Bandar Abbas and Dubai were for Mondays, Wednesdays and Saturdays, when IR 665, quoted as a Boeing 727, took off at 5.15 p.m., returning at 7.25 p.m. as IR 664. There was nothing listed for Sunday morning. But if he had been in possession of the new summer timetable, he would have seen that Iran Air – due to loss of revenue on the route – had reduced the Bandar Abbas–Dubai shuttle to twice weekly, on Tuesdays and Sundays, departing at 9.50 a.m. as IR 655, an Airbus, and heading back at 12.15 p.m. as IR 654. This new timetable had been in operation since the end of April.

Even so, British Air Commodore G. S. Cooper wrote in the *Daily Telegraph* at the time, 'For the military air-traffic control authorities to allow a civilian airliner, with 290 passengers on board, to fly into a battle zone, shows little regard for the safety of the passengers. The crew must have been either brave, foolish or dangerously ill-advised to have undertaken the flight under the circumstances.'

And so we come to the build-up to Lockerbie . . .

The identity of the individual and organization responsible for the planting of the bomb on Pan Am Flight 103 is irrelevant to this narrative. Germane, however, is the ease with which the crime of mass murder was committed.

By 1988 the exploitation by terrorists of an unsuspecting 'innocent' to carry a bomb on board a plane had become almost standard procedure, typified by a sabotage plot at Heathrow, two years earlier, against an Israeli El Al airliner.

A pregnant young Irishwoman passed successfully through the Heathrow security checks and threaded her way through the bustling departure lounge to the appropriate boarding gate. El Al have a reputation second to none when it comes to security. They employ their own security experts to search every piece of luggage destined for the hold. When passengers reach the gate, just before boarding, all their cabin baggage is examined. No one, not the Prime Minister of Israel or the chairman of El Al, is excluded.

The Irishwoman was carrying a holdall, which was opened by an El Al security officer. He almost immediately noticed that the bag and its harmless contents were inconsistent with the overall weight. Something was wrong. Responding to a gut reaction, the officer alerted his superior: the holdall was examined more closely and cut open at the bottom, leading to the discovery of ten pounds of plastic explosive, primed with a detonator. If that passenger had been allowed on board, the El Al flight would have presaged Lockerbie.

No one was more distressed than the Irishwoman. The subsequent investigation, over many days, confirmed beyond all doubt that she was an 'innocent', used by others without her knowledge. The bomb had been planted by her Arab lover, Nezar Hindawi, who was happily sending her to her death with all the other unsuspecting passengers. He was the man she thought she would soon be marrying and to this day she has still not completely recovered from the shock. Hindawi fled to the Syrian Embassy in London, where he unsuccessfully sought refuge. At the Old Bailey in October 1986, Nezar Hindawi was sentenced to forty-five years in prison for attempting to blow up an El Al airliner the previous April, using his Irish girlfriend, Ann Murphy, as an unsuspecting innocent.

El Al demonstrated that rigorous security in the hands of dedicated, intelligent and well-rewarded staff can beat the terrorists. Equally, the terrorists proved that no depth was too low for them.

By early 1988 the West German Secret Service had uncovered in and around Frankfurt a terrorist cell of the Popular Front for the Liberation of Palestine-General Command, whose leader was Ahmed Jibril. Later that year, on 26 October, the Frankfurt police simultaneously raided a number of flats and intercepted a car heading for the industrial town of Neuss. Fourteen Palestinians were arrested and from the apartments and car the police unearthed a terrorist arsenal. Among the weapons was a bomb containing half a pound of Semtex plastic explosive hidden in a small Toshiba Bombeat Model 453 radio-cassette player. A barometric device and a clock inside the radio were evidence enough that the bomb was intended for a plane. Most of the weapons were found in a flat at 28 Sandweg, Frankfurt, but the bomb had been concealed in the car.

Ten of the fourteen suspects were not detained for long. The reason given for their release was that direct evidence against them was flimsy. This was nonsense, although many journalists faithfully reported what they were told: most of the suspects were released so that they could be watched and followed.

Quite rightly, the West German police were delighted with their catch and were eager to broadcast their success. Accordingly, six days after the arrests, the alleged new-style bomb and other items from the cache went on public display in Wiesbaden and photographers were invited to take pictures.

The West German authorities believed that, by going public, they were acting in the best interests of air safety. On 11 November, written invitations were sent to the security experts of 'all friendly countries which co-operate in the fight against terrorism' by the Anti-Terrorist Unit of the Federal Office for Criminal Investigation (BKA) to a conference on 15 November at its Wiesbaden headquarters. This conference was attended by top officials from many embassies in Bonn, including those of the United States and Britain. Photographs of the bomb and full details were presented at the conference.

On 17 November the Federal Aviation Authority in Washington was briefed by the US State Department, while the Department of Transport in London received a similar report from the British Foreign Office. The following day, all United States airlines were made aware that Jibril's terrorists had been on the prowl in Europe looking for suitable targets. The airlines were also told about the 'new bomb' for which their security personnel should be on the alert. This information also went to the Department of Transport in London, and on 22 November all United Kingdom airports and airlines were warned by telex of the radio-cassette device.

Heathrow officials acted positively, simulating a radio bomb and having colour photographs taken of it and circulated to all security staff as part of their update training.

Message sent on November 22 from the British Department of Transport:

To all British airport security managers from Jack, Principal Aviation Security Adviser, Department of Transport, Room S8/18, 2 Marsham Street, London.

Discovery of improvised explosive device in FRG (Federal Republic of Germany). The Department has received information about an improvised explosive device contained in a radio cassette player which was discovered recently in the FRG following the arrest of a number of Palestinians in that country.

The following details of the device are for the information of British airport authorities and British airlines: it is recommended that security staff (particularly those employed on passenger and baggage screening and aircraft searches) should be informed about it in order that they may be aware for the discovery of similar devices, particularly when dealing with high risk operations or passengers who attract suspicion for other reasons.

The Department will distribute further details, and hopefully a picture of the device, and an assessment of the threat posed by the discovery under a separate and classified cover in due course.

Details of the device are: (A) Contained in a Toshiba Bombeat RTFA53D radio cassette player measuring 10" x 7" x 2". No outward sign that the radio was abnormal.

(B) The radio contained two sources of power. The standard radio batteries and additional 4" by 1.5 volt pencil batteries, to power the explosive device.

(C) The explosive comprised 300 grammes of sheet explosive wrapped in a paper marked 'Toshiba'. There was one standard electrically activated detonator. The elements of the device were linked with wires.

(D) There were two activating devices, one barometric concealed under the motor of the cassette player, and a timing device.

(E) It is understood that the radio would not work.

(F) The device could be armed by plugging in an antenna 'jack' plug.

Message ends.

Semtex plastic, which was used to make the Pan Am bomb, has no smell and can easily be mistaken for brown Plasticine. It was invented at an explosives factory in Semtin, Czechoslovakia, where it was still exclusively made late in 1988. The railway lines which led to the factory did not appear on any maps of the region. Armed guards looked down from bleak watchtowers alongside tracks which branched from the main Pardubice–Hradec Králové line.

The attraction of Semtex to terrorists is its stability in all temperatures and, most importantly, its immunity to detection by airport X-ray machines. Further, it can be stored for years perfectly safely without losing any of its strength or reliability.

The Czechoslovak government would neither deny nor confirm that it had been selling Semtex to anti-West terrorists, but under international pressure it did agree to 'consider' adding a smell to the plastic which would enable it to be traced by sniffer dogs. This was after the scientists at Semtin had devoted eleven years to removing the odour.

After Lockerbie, Miroslav Pavel, a spokesman for the Czechoslovak government, made a statement to the effect that the struggle against terrorism 'should involve all countries' and that the commitment had to be 'joint and international'.

Meanwhile, considerable research had been conducted in the United States into possible ways of detecting Semtex in luggage and a break-through was made in 1989, though it proved a very costly process. Baggage was assailed with neutrons, which released discernible Semtex gamma rays. One prototype machine alone cost the United States more than £500,000. There were plans to manufacture a mere six of these Semtex-trackers by 1990.

In the months prior to Lockerbie, all the feedback to Western agents pointed to a revenge attack via a bomb on board a US plane, rather than a hijacking or a hail of bullets sprayed into an airport concourse. In fact, it was Ygan Camone, the anti-terrorist adviser to the Israeli government, who warned the BKA that Mossad agents had evidence of a planned bomb attack on an American airliner flying out of Frankfurt.

One man not in the least surprised by the crash at Lockerbie was

Isaac Yeffet, who ran his own security consultancy in New Jersey. Between 1978 and 1984, Yeffet was El Al's director of security. In 1986, two years after setting up in business in the United States, Yeffet was included in a ten-man Israeli team of air safety specialists to investigate twenty-five of Pan Am's operations worldwide, six of them in the United States. On completion of the survey, a 200-page report was presented to the airline's management, concluding that Pan Am was 'almost totally vulnerable to a mid-air explosion through explosive charges concealed in the cargo'. There was a claim in the report that a passenger could check-in luggage and then not board the flight, yet the baggage would still be carried on the plane. The inference was obvious.*

On 5 December 1988, a bomb warning against Pan Am was given in an anonymous telephone call to the United States embassy in Helsinki, Finland. The male caller, described as having a Middle Eastern accent, specified the Frankfurt–America route, saying that the sabotage would occur within two weeks, and that the bomb would be planted by a supporter of the international terrorist Abu Nidal. Two people were named who, the caller said, belonged to Abu Nidal's group; one of them was in Helsinki and the other in Frankfurt. According to his story, one of those two men would be using a Finnish woman as an 'innocent' to take the bomb on board the Pan Am plane. The woman's name was either not known to the caller or simply not given.

Details of the call to the United States embassy in Helsinki were swiftly communicated to the US State Department. This information was relayed, in turn, to the Federal Aviation Administration (FAA), which issued a special bulletin on 9 December to all American international airlines, US diplomats throughout Europe and aviation security. Staff of the US embassy in Moscow received a circular on 13

*My own experience with Pan Am was at variance with that particular criticism. Several years ago, I boarded Pan Am Flight 103 at London. Just before the airliner was due to leave the gate, I complained of feeling unwell and was advised by a flight attendant to delay my departure until the next day. After I had left the 747, the captain came to me, said how sorry he was that I was 'under the weather', then asked to see my passport. He flicked through the pages, questioned me about my numerous foreign trips and enquired what 'freelance journalist' *really* meant. Turning to several members of the Pan Am ground staff gathered around, he said, 'I'm sorry, but I don't go until all his baggage is off my aircraft.' And to me, he commented, 'I'm sure you understand?' I did. I should have been critical of him if he had chosen any other course of action. That evening, PA 103 took off for New York twenty minutes late – a small price to pay for peace of mind.

December advising them of the warning so that they would be able to revise their travel arrangements accordingly if they planned to return to the United States for Christmas. The Department of Transport in London was also alerted by the FAA. There is no disputing that the tip-off in Helsinki was being given the respect it warranted.

Extracts from 9 December bulletin:

On December 5 1988 an unidentified individual telephoned a US diplomatic facility in Europe and stated that sometime within the next two weeks there would be a bombing attempt against a Pan American aircraft flying from Frankfurt, FRG, to the US.

The reliability of the information cannot be assessed at this point.

This bulletin, with full FAA comments, must be passed immediately to the principal security inspectors for dissemination to all US carriers with service to Europe. The bulletin should also be provided to other US carriers with international routes. The carriers must be specifically told that the information in this bulletin is solely for the use of US carriers and airport aviation security personnel.

The investigation into the Helsinki call was led by Sepo Tiitenen, Director of Supo, the Finnish Security Police. Three similar calls had been made to Israel's Helsinki embassy in 1987 and 1988, it was revealed. Contrary to most press reports and political statements, Tiitenen said that the police were 'not absolutely certain' that all four calls were made by the same man, though this conclusion, like many others on this score, was nothing more than educated guesswork. However, he did feel that the caller was trying to implicate a Finnish woman because of a personal grudge, a love affair turned sour. The Ministry of Defence in London, however, was of the opinion that the call to the US embassy in Helsinki could not be 'discounted entirely', while basically accepting an assessment that the odds favoured a hoax.

In the weeks after Lockerbie there was a well orchestrated campaign, through intelligence and political channels, to discredit the call to the US embassy in Helsinki, to such an extent that the *Observer*, one of Britain's most responsible national newspapers, was using the dismissive phrase 'utterly bogus'; the public brainwashing process was excessive, to a degree that made one very suspicious.

Time magazine quoted William Sessions, the FBI Director, as saying, post-Lockerbie, 'The Bureau believes that it was a hoax and not connected to Flight 103.'

The British Department of Transport was not divulging from which US agency it learned that the call was a hoax. Meanwhile, the US State Department denied categorically that there was any final assessment of the call before Lockerbie, and the FAA insisted that no 'all clear' was ever given by them as a follow-up to their warning bulletin of 9 December. The US embassy in Moscow took the matter so seriously that the FAA bulletin was pinned to every noticeboard on the premises. Sources within Mossad, the Israeli Secret Service, indicate that the call on 5 December was genuine and that ever since there has been an official cover-up.

During this same pre-Lockerbie period, TWA staff in Frankfurt were questioned by German-speaking 'detectives' about their airline's policy regarding the transportation of explosives, guns and detonators. On one occasion, the questions were asked at the TWA ticket counter. Yet at no point were these swarthy men challenged or detained while their credentials and status were checked. Only afterwards, when they had the data they needed and were out of the airport, did it dawn on TWA staff that they had been duped by bogus policemen, who were never traced.

Reacting spontaneously on 7 December to TWA's embarrassment, the FAA circulated an 'alert' bulletin to governments, airports and airlines. These incidents and procedures were not revealed until March 1989, some three months after Lockerbie, by the US House of Representatives' Transportation sub-committee in Washington. The FAA bulletin recorded, 'The incidents occurred within a few days of each other. There is a possibility that they are related.' And the sub-committee had this to say: 'Despite the Helsinki warning of a Frankfurt bombing, the discovery of a radio-cassette player bomb, and two attempts to test Frankfurt airport security, the FAA failed to order US airlines to take any security measures beyond those already in place.' Although no *order* was given, it is only fair to stress that the FAA had given a general alert.

On 19 December, exactly two weeks after the caller in Helsinki prophesied that a Pan Am airliner from Frankfurt to the United States would be sabotaged, the principal aviation security adviser for the British Department of Transport, Jim Jack, prepared for distribution to airlines colour photographs of a radio-cassette bomb, plus additional and relevant information which had not been included in the telexed message of 22 November. Among the points contained in this final briefing, which were not part of the earlier communication, were: many more wires than would be normal in a legitimate radio-cassette player would show up on the X-ray screen; the Semtex explosive plastic and the extra batteries would not be secured inside the device and would move around when it was tilted or turned; taped to the outside of the radio would be an aerial jack plug, which, when inserted, would arm the bomb; and the jack plug would not be attached to any wiring. The photograph of the bomb depicted a Toshiba Bombeat Model 453, whereas the 22 November communiqué had referred to a Bombeat RTFA53D. An illustration of the interior of the radio showed 300 grams of Semtex plastic packaged within the inside wrapping of a Tobler chocolate packet. An outer layer of Toshiba wrapping-paper around the explosive was intended to make it appear a genuine part of the radio mechanism.

Although dated 19 December, the photographs and additional information were not posted until the New Year, being delivered on 17 January at Pan Am's London offices. When challenged in March 1989 about the delay in sending this material and why it had been sent by post, the then British Transport Secretary, Paul Channon, denied all suggestions of negligence in an extraordinary statement: 'It was of such little importance that we put it in the post. The important information about the radio-cassette bomb had already been sent out. It was not a great new warning we had to send out by telex. It was a bit of supporting information containing some colour photographs.'

In one respect, however, it was exceedingly fortunate for the hapless Channon and his Department that the 19 December guidance was held back, in view of the following recommendation within it to all airport and airline security personnel: 'Any item about which a searcher is unable to satisfy himself/herself must, if it is to be carried in the aircraft, be consigned to the aircraft hold.' If that instruction had been received before 21 December, it is reasonable to assume that Channon's position would have been untenable and the British government would have been deluged with writs from lawyers acting on behalf of the bereaved. Pan Am would have been able to argue, quite reasonably, that its staff at Frankfurt and London had followed the latest security guidelines to the letter.

On the evening of 21 December nothing of a suspicious nature was permitted into the cabin of Flight 103: the bomb went into the hold. The delayed instructions were Channon's lucky break.

Interesting is the fact that the FAA, although privy to the same documents which the British Department of Transport sent out dated 19 December, did not themselves circulate the papers to their own airlines: after Lockerbie, this was projected in the media as just one of the myriad mysteries about the case. My information from the FAA is that they knew of the substance of Jim Jack's advice about the hold in the British circular and it troubled them, casting doubt on the rest of the information. It made sense, they felt, to distance themselves from something they rightly suspected would be discredited. Of course, the FAA could have omitted the dictate that potentially dangerous articles should be stowed in the plane's luggage hold. But still the dispatch would have looked too similar to the British counterpart for comfort, so Channon was left alone to carry the can.

The British Department of Transport delayed message.

ANNEX C

RESTRICTED
Department of Transport
Room S8/18
All UK airports
All UK airlines (and El Al, Air India, US airlines, South African Airways)
19 December 1988

1 I refer to my telex (not to non-British airlines) dated 22 November 1988 about the discovery of an improvised explosive device contained in a Toshiba Bom Beat Model 453 radio/cassette player.
2 I attach illustrations of:
   (a) The radio/cassette player.
   (b) The radio/cassette player with the back removed, with the additional batteries, timing and barometric triggers in place.
   (c) The block of Semtex explosive (in black and white). The wrapping was white, and the word 'Toshiba' was printed in red.

3 The explosive device will be very difficult to discover. The following considerations are appropriate:

(a) The radio/cassette player would not work.

(b) The aerial jack plug was taped to the side of the radio: it was the insertion of this plug that would arm the device. There was no wire attached to the jack plug.

(c) When X-rayed, it appeared to have more wiring than is normal in most modern equipment (it is acknowledged that this is not a significant indicator).

(d) The additional batteries and the explosive material were not secured inside the case, and when the item was rotated it was apparent that there were loose pieces inside.

4 It is assessed that devices similar to the one which is illustrated may have been constructed. The sophistication of the device and the effort taken to conceal it, suggest it could have been intended for use against an aviation target and designed to avoid discovery during relatively stringent security checks: possibly in support of a 'high-risk' operation.

RESTRICTED

5 It is recommended that:

(a) All staff employed on security duties in support of flights by Israeli aircraft, or British airlines operating to Israel, should be informed about the device and advised to look out for similar items.

(c) Any item about which a searcher is unable to satisfy himself/herself must, if it is to be carried in the aircraft, be consigned to the aircraft hold.

(d) Security staff employed in duties not associated with high-risk flights should be informed about the device, in the course of keeping them up to date.

6 Any further information about this device, or information which enables us to be more precise about the threat its discovery poses, will be distributed to you.

J. Jack, Principal Aviation Security Adviser.

On hearing early in 1989 of the instruction to store suspect baggage in the hold, Fred Dorey, a former head of security for the British Airports Authority, reacted: 'It's like Monty Python. You're telling me, "This is what the bomb looks like. If you see it, put it in the hold. Then put your fingers in your ears." It's utterly ridiculous.'

Scotsman Jim Jack was renowned for being economical with words but never with endeavour. By 1989 he had been a chief aviation security adviser for ten years and his peers throughout the industry spoke of 'a superman professional, with a long and honourable record'. There were very few people in commercial aviation with Jack's comprehensive network of contacts in intelligence. One of his colleagues branded the advice of 19 December 'a clear error of judgement', but added: 'We all make mistakes, Jim less frequently than most people. Any other time, nobody would have picked it up. Lockerbie has put everyone in the spotlight. We are all on our toes and we have to stay that way. Routine and complacency are the foes of air safety and the friends of terrorists.'

Despite all the intelligence, all the warnings, all the speculation, all the brilliant detective work, including the uncovering of the twin of the bomb which was destined to be used, nothing was going to save Pan Am Flight 103 on Wednesday 21 December.

3 RUNNING SCARED

Pan Am Flight 103 originated in Frankfurt at 4.50 p.m. local time as a Boeing 727 and continued from London to New York as a Boeing 747. It had always been one of the most popular flights of the day between Britain and the United States, particularly among the business fraternity. The 6 p.m. departure from Heathrow allowed for a full working day in London before heading for the airport to fly westwards home or to commence an overseas business trip in the United States. Thanks to the five-hour time difference, passengers could be at New York's JFK airport before 9 p.m. the same day. During the Christmas rush, however, there is no such thing as a preferred or less favoured transatlantic flight: they are all fully booked weeks in advance.

On 21 December 1988 the feeder plane from Frankfurt landed at Heathrow at 5.20 p.m., just forty minutes before the 747, continuing as 103, was due to depart. Only seventeen passengers made the transfer and just one container of luggage was taken from the 727 and loaded on to the 747.

The ongoing passengers from Frankfurt were joined by a meagre 211 travellers at Heathrow, leaving a remarkable 159 seats empty on the 747 at the peak of the Christmas exodus.

The luggage of one passenger who checked-in at London but failed to board the plane was nevertheless carried on the flight, a remarkable lapse for Pan Am. But the investigators were later satisfied that the missing passenger was not the bomber. Subsequently, Pan Am were fined more than $600,000 by the FAA for security breaches in London and Frankfurt relating to the flight. Proper procedures to identify thirty-one passengers at Heathrow before allowing them to board had not been followed, said the FAA. Five passengers at Frankfurt had been pinpointed for more thorough screening, but had been allowed on to the flight without further investigation. Passengers' carry-on luggage had not been checked by Pan Am, nor had the cargo area of the aircraft before loading.

A lot of people on 21 December 1988 seemed to be running scared of Flight 103, which brings us to one of the major controversies surrounding Lockerbie: why were American diplomats in Europe warned about the bomb threats to Pan Am, giving them the option of making alternative travel arrangements, while other people, the paying public, plus the airline's own operational staff and flight crews, were denied such a life-saving opportunity?

The general mood in the United States during the immediate post-Lockerbie period, as reflected through television and the press, was one of outrage. The State Department denied any accountability, which led to conflict with the FAA, whose Director of Civil Aviation Security, Ray Salazar, believed, 'The responsibility for publishing general threat advisories belongs with the Department of State. They would co-ordinate that with us, but it's their responsibility.'

Phyllis Oakley, a spokeswoman for the State Department, retaliated, 'We receive dozens of threats each day. We have to evaluate them.' Department of State policy, she said, was to notify the FAA, any airline specified and US embassies in the region of the danger. 'Our focus is to alert those responsible for doing something about security. It's up to the airlines to take precautions they deem necessary for the safety of their flights.'

White House spokesman Marvin Fitzwater was not satisfied. 'The public should be aware of the general threat level. There are very legitimate questions that have to be addressed.'

Chris Witkowski, Director of Ralph Nader's Aviation Consumer Action Project, was also unhappy about the selective and arbitrary approach to intelligence dissemination. 'We think the public is owed an explanation by the State Department. Why wasn't the public informed of this threat, so people could make the choice of whether or not to fly on those particular flights? It doesn't seem fair to tell a selected few. What's the worst that can happen? Some people would probably avoid taking those flights.'

Between 1 September and 22 December, the State Department issued 106 similar alerts to US embassies and diplomatic offices throughout the world. During that same cycle, 87 bomb threats of various kinds were received by US 'diplomatic facilities'. Several of those threats were still 'active' at the time of Lockerbie and after, Ms Oakley confirmed.

A revealing comment was made by State Department spokesman Ronald Spiers. 'You get a lot of these threats. People tend to get bored with it.'

Lois Schneider of the US Independent Union of Flight Attendants, said that cabin crews were briefed if any threat was 'considered serious enough', adding, 'Americans abroad are targets and Pan American is considered to be the flagship carrier.' My information from the FBI is that the crew of Flight 103, on 21 December, were not given an explicit notification of the risk they were running.

President Reagan was at variance with White House spokesman Fitzwater, supporting the view that it was 'impossible' to make public all sabotage threats against civilian airlines. 'All the precautions that could be taken were taken with regard to warning the airline and all.' And of a general public warning he argued, 'I think that would have been a virtually impossible thing to do on the basis of that telephone call. If you stop to think about it, such a public statement, with nothing but a telephone call to go on, would literally have closed down all the air-traffic in the world.'

Following the Reagan line, Vernon Walters, the US Ambassador to the United Nations, feared that 'disclosure could wreak havoc in air travel.' The Observer commented acidly, 'In other words, if they tell us everything they know, we might get frightened. Or we might insist that airlines and airports improve their security arrangements to stop terrorists smuggling bombs on to airplanes.' Both Walters and the Observer had valid points, which were not in practice incompatible. Walters's only guilt was one of brevity. Probably he felt that to spell out exactly what he meant would be counter-productive, encouraging a proliferation of anonymous calls as an economic weapon against Western airlines or to be exploited by over-zealous and unscrupulous employees of rival companies. Keep grounding one airline on a lucrative route because of continually publicized bomb scares and all the business goes to its competitors, encouraging retaliation. Walters did not mean that silence should be used as a substitute for safety, or as a shroud, but it did smack of condescension: *We know what is best for you and we should decide what you should be told.*

The experts maintain that security can be effective only in a climate of secrecy, a theory which is open to question. An overt display of strength is usually interpreted as a deterrent. If there are flaws in a security system, it would be naïve to imagine that the terrorists do not know about them. There is an argument that security, like justice, must be seen to be done if there is to be public support and confidence. The world has become too sophisticated to be content with assurances that all is well, and that we are being silly to sit there with white knuckles and a hand too shaky to hold steady our drink.

High street stores are evacuated whenever there is a bomb scare: the police arrive with sniffer dogs and the premises are meticulously searched. Seldom is there any panic when shoppers are informed precisely of the reason for the evacuation and most people have no reservations about returning to the shop after the 'all clear', probably because they have witnessed security being imposed and have made their own evaluation after being given the facts.

Public outrage at Pan Am's failure just before Lockerbie to warn passengers that there was strong intelligence to suggest that one of their aircraft was being targeted by terrorists certainly made an impact. Scandinavian Airlines System began warning passengers about credible threats shortly after the Pan Am sabotage and in March 1989, Pan Am itself told intending travellers, just before they boarded the plane on a flight from Boston to Paris, of a bomb warning.

On Thursday 28 December 1989, America's Northwest Airlines took the unusual step of announcing two days in advance that its Saturday Flight 51 from Paris to Detroit had been threatened. This information was passed to passengers on the telephone and at the airport by the company's reservations staff in Paris. Douglas Miller, a spokesman for Northwest, said it was his company's policy to keep the public informed of bomb threats whenever possible. He added, 'If the threat is specific enough and we feel it is warranted to make the passengers aware of it, we will.' However, Steve Hayes, the United States Air Transport Association spokesman, had this to say: 'It's almost always the case that air-carriers do not go public with security threats. Each carrier has to make that decision on its own.'

When Northwest's Flight 51 eventually took off two hours late on Saturday 30 December 1989, it carried only seventeen passengers, three of them journalists, and was running at a loss of £150,000, plus the cost of extra security at Charles de Gaulle airport in Paris, which had to be borne by the airline. Of those who had booked seats, 113 people had decided to switch to TWA or Air France, and Northwest estimated that at least another 100 were deterred from booking. The seventeen who flew were ushered on to the DC10 by ten airline security personnel, a dozen Paris policemen, six detectives and an assortment of American government officials, FBI agents and Northwest staff, specially flown in from Detroit. On board, passengers were welcomed with champagne, while the captain, Gary Ferguson, thanked them for travelling on this 'rather special flight'.

American security experts immediately predicted a new wave of terrorist threats aimed at disrupting the airline industry. On 10 January 1990, Cecil Parkinson, the Transport Secretary, told Parliament that in 1989 more than 460 warnings were given against British airlines. 'It is a sad reflection on some sick minds that the number has increased substantially since Lockerbie,' he said during a debate in the Commons on the Aviation and Maritime Security Bill.

Security at Frankfurt's international airport has been rated highly since 1985, when a bomb blast in the departure lounge killed three people and seriously wounded thirty-nine. Suitcases about which security staff are uncertain go into a steel decompression chamber in which flight conditions are simulated for twenty-two minutes; the theory being that, within that time, bombs armed by a timing device will be detonated. Police officers patrol the concourse and lounge continuously, looking for abandoned luggage.

There is no disputing that on 21 December the security agents at Frankfurt airport were on full alert, as they had been for several weeks – even though the two-week deadline had expired on the 19th, assuming the anonymous caller of the 5th had any credibility.

Most of the luggage stowed in the hold of Pan Am 103, the 727, was X-rayed at Frankfurt, but only a black and white screen was available and in any event X-ray machines are incapable of pinpointing Semtex explosives. Since 26 October, everyone in airport security had known that the terrorists' most deadly weapon was the cassette/radio barometric Semtex bomb. Into the equation must also go the factor that Mossad agents had the hard evidence that an American civilian airliner, almost certainly flying the Pan Am livery, would be a target before Christmas as a reprisal for the Iranian Airbus incident, the bombing of

Tripoli in April 1986 and the shooting down early in January 1989 of Libyan fighter jets.

Frankfurt had been the airport named to more than one Mossad agent by different sources. Everything from 26 October had pointed inexorably to Frankfurt, Pan Am, Christmas, Semtex, and a Toshiba radio/cassette player. One could argue that the bomb was being handed on a plate to the security authorities. However, even a colour X-ray screen would not have detected Semtex, but there would have been more chance of the radio/cassette's showing up.

Pan Am Flight 103 also took off from Frankfurt with four sacks of US military mail, weighing 22lb, and a bag from the American bank Manufacturers Hanover Trust, none of which had gone through any airport security check. The bank bag contained cheques and Christmas cards. Herbert Harth, a spokesman for the Frankfurt Prosecutor's Office, said the army sacks had not been inspected because they were guarded by military personnel at all times. He had no comment to make about the bank's documents.

All evidence pointed to the Semtex bomb's having gone into the hold at Frankfurt. A second and final chance to spot the device was missed at Heathrow, because all the ongoing luggage from Frankfurt was transferred from the incoming 727 to the outgoing 747 without further screening.

A 'Restricted' report of 6 January 1989 by the British Government's National Aviation Security Committee stated: 'Hold baggage belonging to passengers transferring from the Boeing 727 aircraft was transferred directly, without being screened: pieces were moved separately from the Boeing 727 baggage container to the Boeing 747 baggage container.' Too late, this loophole at Heathrow was closed.

On 28 December 1988, a week after Lockerbie, American airlines received the following directive from the Department of Transport: 'The operator shall not cause or permit any baggage which is being transferred directly from another flight to be placed in the hold of his aircraft unless that baggage has been searched by hand or screened by X-ray, and when there is doubt as to the contents, searched by hand to a sufficient standard to ensure that it does not contain any weapon or components thereof, explosives, or any components of an explosives device.'

It soon became apparent that probably no more than a kilo of Semtex had been sufficient to end the flight of Pan Am 103. This information came from Commander George Churchill-Coleman, head of Scotland Yard's Anti-Terrorism Squad. The quantity of explosive involved was smaller than a 3lb bag of sugar.

For months after the crash, forensic scientists and air accident investigators examined a million pieces of wreckage. Gradually, from broken bodies and twisted metal, there emerged a sharply-defined picture. Everything recovered was taken to a warehouse twice the size of a football stadium, at the British Army's Central Ammunition Depot in Longtown, Cumbria, some fifteen miles south of Lockerbie. 'By the time the experts had completed the operation, they had viewed almost every inch of the plane's fuselage on a flat base,' said Detective Chief Inspector Jack Baird, who co-ordinated the forensic exercise. 'It's as if the plane had been flattened and you were to look down on it from above.'

It was in the military warehouse at Longtown that the detective scientists came across the minute clues which verified that a cassette/ radio bomb had been used. The largest fragments of the device were the size of a thumbnail and had been scattered across vast remote areas of the Scottish countryside. Within a month of the crash, Detective Chief Superintendent John Orr knew exactly in which luggage container the bomb had been loaded. The explosion had blown the container to smithereens and fragments had been recovered from 33 locations, stretching 40 miles from the Kielder Dam, Northumbria, to the outskirts of Lockerbie. Piecing together this jigsaw puzzle was an achievement without parallel in airline history. Orr was technically in overall charge of the investigation, although many law enforcement agencies participated, including the FBI, Interpol, the West German police and Scotland Yard.

Pinned to the walls of the warehouse were colour photographs of the reconstructed container, still bearing the Pan Am logo, though scarred by rents in the sides. The container was capable of carrying 700 kilos of luggage and had stored the suitcases transferred from the Frankfurt flight, plus the baggage of a number of passengers who joined at Heathrow. Some 10,000 items of personal property had been collected from an area covering almost 100 miles. Everything had been X-rayed in the warehouse as a precautionary measure, in case a secondary explosive device had been on board.

In the United States, aircraft accident investigators are known in the trade as 'tin kickers' and a number of them, representing the US National Transportation Safety Board (NTSB), joined the British team at Lockerbie. Following proven techniques, they made use of a surveyor's laser transit and cameras to chart and photograph the descent path of the debris. By plotting where the splinters of wreckage had landed, they were able to determine quite quickly the probable cause of the crash. The history of the aircraft and its crew, prevailing weather conditions, load factors and reports from air-traffic controllers were all studied.

When the size and type of the bomb were established, the forensic scientists concluded that the aircraft was 'snapped in two' by a sheer chance stroke of ill-fortune. The container carrying the bomb had been placed by baggage-handlers alongside a stressed, riveted seam. The explosion blew out approximately 24 rivets, puncturing the aircraft's skin. Air in the hold and cabin, pressurized at 5500 feet, rushed out, causing instant decompression and disintegrating the plane before the captain, 55-year-old James MacQuarrie, or his co-pilot, Ray Wagner, aged 52, of Pennington, New Jersey, were able to make even the briefest Mayday call.

One of the senior crash investigators commented: 'If the bomb had been almost anywhere else, it might have killed half a dozen people or maybe even just shredded some bags. It was amazing bad luck.' And from the bomb's position in the container there was little doubt that it originated in Frankfurt and not London.

There was also evidence that the security authorities at Frankfurt had been bracing themselves for a hijacking rather than a bombing. In terms of airport security, there was heavy emphasis on Pan Am's direct, non-stop flights between Frankfurt and the United States: Flight 171 to Miami, Flight 67 to New York, Flight 73 to New York and Flight 61 to Washington. More attention to intelligence, however, would have shown that Pan Am's non-stop traffic was the least at risk. The Iranians and Libyans were gearing themselves for revenge not only on the Americans but also on Mrs Thatcher for her backing of Reagan's interventions in the Middle East. All the direct flights from Frankfurt to the United States would have carried a mix of Germans and Americans. Only one flight would have guaranteed the desired ingredients: the one that went via London – Pan Am 103.

In that case, why did the terrorists not load the bomb at Heathrow? Why double the jeopardy? The answer is probably twofold. Firstly, if one of the terrorists had tried to escort the bomb to London, there was always the chance that it could have been uncovered by customs officers at Heathrow. Secondly, the innocent person selected unwittingly to put the bomb on board was joining the flight at Frankfurt.

Now we come to the question which has dominated so many minds since Lockerbie: who was responsible for this international act of sabotage? Indeed, is it of any relevance to this book?

So long as there are fanatics who believe that political points can be scored through civilian airline targets, sabotage and hijacking will continue to pose a threat to air safety. Prevention and detection, therefore, are integral factors in the arithmetic. If the perpetrators are identified, tracked down, arrested and punished, terrorist cells are shredded and demoralized. Capture and conviction are persuasive deterrents, to which El Al testifies. Terrorism will never be conquered, but it can be contained. Of course, groups re-form, new cells are spawned, and the impulse for vengeance is intensified, thus perpetuating and sustaining the cycle. Prevention, therefore, has to be the priority, which can be achieved only by the security network keeping, in the words of Isaac Yeffet, 'ahead of the game', though unfortunately that does not always appear to be enough: it is impossible to avoid the conclusion that there was such a surfeit of intelligence about the bomb destined for a Pan Am Frankfurt to the United States plane that the crime was certainly avoidable.

The hunt for the mass murderers of Lockerbie will have a direct impact not only on air safety, but also on the economics of the industry as a whole. During the first half of 1989, all operators in Europe and the United States were complaining of a slump in trade on their prestigious international routes, due to a growing fear of terrorism. Lost revenue was an incentive to find solutions which nobody could ignore.

Most people think of bombs on civilian aircraft as yet another modern disease; which, in fact, is yet another modern misconception. On 13 April 1950 a bomb exploded in the rear toilet of a British European Airways (BEA) Viking, flying from Gatwick to Paris Le Bourget. Captain Ian Harvey was awarded the George Medal for making a safe emergency landing at Northolt airport, where two huge holes were found in opposite sides of the cabin. Only one person was injured, a stewardess. No one ever claimed responsibility for the crime and to this day the motive remains obscure.

Seventeen years later, another BEA aircraft, this time a Comet, the world's first jet airliner, was less fortunate when a bomb blew up the plane over the Mediterranean, near the island of Rhodes. The Comet sank in 11,000 feet of water and the accident might very easily have been dismissed as another aviation mystery if a number of bodies and seat-cushions had not floated to the surface. Tests showed that the bomb had been placed under a seat. This time there was no shortage of motive. Cyprus was one of the world's worst trouble-spots and Archbishop Makarios had planned to be on the flight, only to cancel at the last moment owing to a change of itinerary.

A JAT Yugoslav airliner, cruising at 33,000 feet between Copenhagen and Belgrade in 1972, disappeared without a word from the captain, circumstances similar to the events of Lockerbie, except that on this occasion, miraculously, there was a survivor, who was able to give a graphic account of what happened. Cabin attendant Vesna Vulovic fell with all the other passengers and wreckage, landing in the soft, deep snow on the slopes of a mountain. When she was found, her rescuers could not believe that a damaged right leg was her only injury. Seventeen years later, Vesna was still wearing the JAT uniform.

On Sunday, 23 June 1985, Air India's Flight 182 from Toronto, Canada, to London Heathrow was carrying 307 passengers and 22 crew. The captain on that long overnight haul was Hanse Narendra. At 8 a.m. he had the Boeing 747 cruising on autopilot at 31,000 feet. Weather conditions could not have been better. A gentle tail breeze was helping to push them along at 600 miles per hour. Five minutes later, at 8.05, Narendra made radio contact with ground control at Shannon in the west of Ireland, correctly giving his position as 120 miles south-west of Cork. The Shannon air-traffic controller punched the flight's ID code into a computer and then called on Narendra to signal a squawk, jargon for a transmission, from the transponder, which would then reply automatically to electronic questions from the ground.

Flight 182 appeared on the radar screen in the vivid green image of a diamond, plus a tail of four dots. Flight number and altitude were attached like a flag to the diamond. From that point, the crew of the

747 would not have to speak with Shannon again until the aircraft was leaving Irish airspace and moving into the Heathrow jurisdiction.

But at 8.13 the diamond on the Shannon radar screen began to fade. The computer signalled its questions at the aircraft, but the responder failed to answer. Twice the computer estimated Flight 182's height and speed, then refused to guess any further. At that moment, the diamond and flight details disappeared completely from the radar screen, leaving only the dots, which also vanished, one by one, as the 747's responder continued to ignore the computer's repeated questions. The controllers knew that, theoretically, the responder could have developed a fault, but they were also aware that the 747 has a back-up for every conceivable defect.

Air India Flight 182 had been blown up at 31,000 feet, with no survivors.

All the forensic clues from Lockerbie substantiated the supposition that the bombers of Flight 103 had calculated that the Pan Am 747 would also be lost over the Atlantic, thus drowning all incriminating evidence. The timing device would have been set for some time after 6 p.m., the scheduled hour of departure. The doomed Pan Am 103 was 25 minutes late taking off, which was nothing unusual for a transatlantic flight and was of no importance that evening. The clock timer was not, in itself, capable of detonating the bomb; it would activate only the barometric pressure gadget, which would have the final say on when the explosion would take place. We have to assume that 31,000 feet was the nominated altitude for destruction. Terrorists conceived the barometric timer in order to avoid premature detonations. A conventional clock timer cannot make allowances for a delayed flight and will explode a bomb at the prescribed hour, even if the plane is still on the ground and without a passenger on board. Normally, Pan Am 103 would have been over the sea by the time it reached 31,000 feet, but on 21 December it had been sent the long way round from Heathrow, owing to high-altitude winds, heading up-country to Scotland, where it was to make a left turn to embark on a belated due westward setting.

There are other disturbing similarities between Air India 182 and Pan Am 103. On 17 May 1985, five weeks before the Air India crash, the Indian High Commission in Ottawa issued a warning of a possible terrorist attack against Indian aircraft or diplomats, as a result of Grade One intelligence. Consequently, the security at Toronto airport was stepped up to full-scale emergency proportions, including the recruit-ment of the Royal Canadian Mounted Police, who were deployed as armed guards on duty at the Air India check-in counters, departure gates, ramps and maintenance hangars. It was made impossible for any unauthorized person to get near an Air India aircraft. In addition, a private security company was engaged to provide guards, who rode the planes and backed up the Mounties on the ramps and throughout the entire boarding procedures, all of which should have been more than enough to deter any potential assassins.

The tension between the different Hindu castes in Canada, which had absorbed a high intake of Sikhs, had been simmering for several months, especially since the storming of the Golden Temple at Amritsar and the assassination the previous year of the Indian Prime Minister, Indira Gandhi.

The subsequent post-crash inquiry revealed that the bomb had been locked inside a suitcase, which had been carried on a feeder plane from Vancouver and transferred at Toronto to the Air India 747, an identical pattern to Pan Am 103. As this story unfolds, it becomes apparent that Lockerbie had *already happened* more than three years before the 270 lives were lost there, and all the lessons had gone unheeded.

The Canadian Aviation Safety Board traced the suitcase to a Sikh who checked-in his luggage, but failed to board the flight. Air India and its handling agent, Air Canada, were criticized for a breach in security, despite the show of strength at Toronto airport, where it was all too late.

During the investigation into Air India Flight 182, Arthur Laflamme, the Canadian Aviation Safety Board's chief investigator, discovered that the X-ray machine at Toronto had broken down on the day the lethal suitcase was transferred from the incoming plane out of Vancouver to the Air India 747. Security officers had therefore used a hand-held explosives detector, which also failed. The inquiry report stated, 'There are indications that it would have been ineffective in detecting explos-ives, especially plastics.' Experts were amazed that the bomb, small enough to be hidden among clothes in a suitcase, could have brought down a sturdy, elephantine 747, and speculated that, by sheer chance, it must have been loaded next to the plane's nerve centre in the forward cargo hold: a replica *sheer chance* had sealed the fate of Pan Am 103. The correlation does not end there.

On the same day, a Mr L. Singh – or someone using that name – checked-in baggage, also at Vancouver, for a Canadian Pacific flight to Tokyo. Mr Singh did not board the plane. The Canadian Pacific 747 landed fifteen minutes early at Tokyo's Narita airport and the 390 passengers had just disembarked when a container being unloaded from the forward hold blew up, killing two baggage-handlers and injuring four others.

The explosion at Tokyo was caused by a plastic bomb, possibly Semtex, concealed in a *radio* or *tape recorder*. The world's security organizations knew all about the radio/cassette bomb as long ago as 1985. Yet three years later, they were pretending, in the immediate aftermath of Lockerbie, that it was something new.

On 26 November 1987, the Japanese Secret Service heard of the possibility of a joint offensive by two extreme left-wing terrorist groups, the Japanese Red Army and the North Korean Yodo. This confirmed what was already suspected by South Korean intelligence agencies. A few days earlier, Osamu Maruoka, one of the Red Army's top brass, had been arrested in Tokyo on arrival from Hong Kong. He had been in Libya on a training course with Colonel Gadaffi's assassins. North Korean extremists were known to be plotting something substantial to try to wreck the forthcoming Olympic Games, planned for Seoul in South Korea. The Red Army, with its headquarters in Syria and a hideous track-record of massacre in Europe and Asia, was seeking simultaneous world revolution, and saw its counterparts in North Korea as ideal partners.

During November that year, an odd couple were beginning an air tour through Eastern Europe and the Middle East. They were Kim Sung Il, aged 69, and 27-year-old Kim Hyon-Hui, posing as father and daughter. In Baghdad, they picked up plastic explosives, supplied by contacts in the Red Army, as Japanese and South Korean Intelligence had foreseen. Travelling on false Japanese passports, on 29 November they boarded Korean Air Lines (KAL) Flight 858 from Baghdad to Seoul, via Abu Dhabi. Into an overhead locker, they placed a *radio*, which, yet again, was nothing of the sort. The couple left the flight at Abu Dhabi, leaving the radio-bomb in the locker, wrapped in cabin rugs.

The last contact the Boeing 707 had with ground control was when it was 130 miles south of Rangoon and cruising at 37,000 feet. It crashed into the jungle 150 miles north-west of Bangkok in Kanchanaburi Province, near the Thailand–Burma border. All 115 people on the airliner died.

Meanwhile, the couple had doubled back in the Middle East, only to be arrested in Bahrain by immigration officers as they attempted to board a flight to Rome, whereupon they swallowed cyanide capsules. The man died immediately, but the woman survived. During months of interrogation by South Korea's Agency for National Security Planning, she confessed that they had both been agents for North Korea and had allegedly been carrying out the orders of Kim Jong-Il, the son of President Kim Il-Sung of North Korea, in a bid to sabotage the Olympics: a story she repeated at her trial in Seoul in April 1989, when she was sentenced to death, though her life was later spared. She had eventually co-operated fully with South Korea's national security agency, providing prime information on the working arrangements of all the international terrorist groups, their immediate and long-term objectives, plus the names and locations of many agents and spies.

Despite so much quality intelligence, bombs and hijackers still get on civilian aircraft with alarming frequency. As one MI6 agent said, 'What's the point finding out what's going to happen, how it's going to happen, where it's going to happen, why and when, if those in Security at the sharp end aren't smart enough to catch them? To be honest, we're wasting our time, while others waste lives. It's very disheartening. The public needs to be made aware. There has to be a public outcry, internationally. Only then will something be done. Only if the public stop flying in protest will the airline industry not only listen, but act and put its house in order: really act. Money has to be invested. Not millions, but billions. But it will never happen. You see. We'll totter from one disaster to another. Always the fire brigade response; chasing fires instead of preventing them from starting.'

Predictably, and with a certain amount of justification, a senior security officer at London's Heathrow reacted, 'Give us the resources in manpower and hardware and we'll finish the job.'

Also in November 1987, a South African Airways 747 crashed into the Indian Ocean ten minutes before it was due to make a re-fuelling stop at Mauritius, after a non-stop flight of 5330 miles from Taipei, the capital of Taiwan, to Johannesburg, South Africa. All 160 people on board were killed. A bomb was suspected and intelligence once again implicated the Red Army.

Laurie Taylor, for five years chairman of the British Air Line Pilots' Association (BALPA), gave a vivid insight into the workings of an airline captain's mind when faced with a potential bomb incident. 'I was involved in a number of bomb scares and none of them came to anything,' he said at his home in Camberley, Surrey. 'I often flew the Detroit–Boston–London run because it suited me for personal reasons. One night, I was just leaving the terminal building at Boston's Logan airport and preparing for take-off when I received a message from ground control requesting me to change radio frequency. Immediately I knew what that meant; there was trouble. I switched to a private frequency so that my conversation would not be overheard. It transpired that since leaving the gate and making towards the runway, there had been an anonymous call to British Airways indicating that there was a bomb on my plane. The caller had been male with an Irish accent. Of course, I had to take into consideration that Boston had a large American/Irish population and there was considerable anti-English feeling in the city. But these threats were a regular occurrence. It had happened to me a number of times. That particular night, I talked with BA Operations who said the decision had to be mine. The question I wanted answered was whether we were carrying any baggage without its owner. Ground staff double-checked, then put my mind at rest on that score.

'I was asked, "What are you going to do?" I answered, "I'll go." Operations said, "You're sure?" I said, "Yes, I'm sure." We were late off, but not grounded, and we made up lost time in the air. You can't give in to these people or they're winning and it merely spurs them on.

'I had a newish crew member with me that day and he looked at me as much to say, "You've gone mad!" when I made the decision to go, but today I should still have done the same thing.'

Even after Lockerbie?

'Certainly.'

This was a frightening response. Not because he had been careless, negligent or reckless; charges that would be utterly unfounded. You could not meet a more responsible professional. His record speaks for itself: thirty years a pilot with an unblemished career, firstly with the RAF during World War II, then with British Overseas Airways Corporation and finally a senior 747 captain with British Airways. For two years he was principal vice president of the International Federation of Air Line Pilots' Association and ten years its executive secretary. He was a member of the Council of the United Kingdom Air Registration Board and sat on the Airworthiness Committee of the International Civil Aviation Organization and the Flight Time Limitations Committee of the Civil Aviation Authority. For his public service he was awarded the OBE. In addition, he is a Fellow of the Royal Aeronautical Society and a member of the Association of British Aviation Consultants. In 1988, he wrote his own book, *Air Travel: How Safe Is It?*

Nevertheless, millions of people must resent being patronized. There is something arrogant about the imparting of information on a *need to know* principle, rather than a *right to know*. Passengers are the real shareholders of airlines. Remember what Spiers said: 'You get a lot of these threats. People tend to get bored with it.'

Might not intending travellers also become bored if public announcements were made every time there was a threat, if there are, indeed, as many as claimed? Would not that in itself be a safeguard against chaos and loss of revenue in the industry? Would not most passengers yawn and board because the warning would be as familiar as the last call over the public address system for a departing flight? But at least they would have been treated like adults and the final decision would be theirs and not left to self-appointed guardians of public welfare.

When you buy a ticket, you have bought more than a seat on an aeroplane; you have paid for a stake in safety. Hospitals are at last beginning to realize who owns the bodies they treat. Some politicians have even come to terms with democracy and acknowledge they are servants rather than masters. Is it not time the airline industry, too, accepted that its patrons have come of age?

One paragraph alone in Laurie Taylor's book is enough evidence to demonstrate that he has never been cavalier about bomb threats. 'From the large number of incidents and different methods employed in the bombing cases on record, it is clear that the authorities responsible for security in civil aviation face a formidable task in seeking effective measures to end the threat of sabotage by bombings. On flights where a known threat exists, it may be necessary to inspect every item of baggage, cargo and supplies on board the aircraft, and the increased costs that will arise and the delays that are incurred, must be accepted as the price to be paid for safety.'

It is possible to extend *too much* democracy to the public. American Airlines Flight 492 was heading at 30,000 feet for New York from Chicago on 22 November 1989, when the radar warned the crew of an impending severe storm. The captain advised the sixty-two passengers that, because of strong winds ahead, there was a possibility they would be diverted from New York's La Guardia airport. He then said, 'Hands up all those passengers who would like the flight to continue,' adding that it was still not too late to return to Chicago. The hand vote was counted by the stewardesses and the result announced by the captain: a majority favoured continuing. The captain's suspicion that they might be diverted proved well-founded. They had to land at Newburgh, some sixty miles from New York, and were taken by bus to their destination.

An FAA spokesman commented, 'I have never heard of passengers being asked to vote on whether a flight continues. Any decision regarding the aircraft is the captain's; it isn't a democratic process.'

Two hours after the plane landed at Newburgh, the area was hit by a tornado, which killed seven children.

4 CATALOGUE OF CHAOS

The Federal Aviation Administration keeps a list of foreign airports it deems most liable to be targeted by terrorists. In 1986 and 1987, American inspectors, who scrutinized 54 of those high-risk airports outside the United States, found that 33 of them had inadequate security arrangements. Examples of more than 100 lapses in safe security practice were included in a study by the Congressional watchdog agency General Accounting Office (GAO), published in Washington, by coincidence, the day after Lockerbie. While the GAO praised the FAA for monitoring anti-terrorist measures overseas, there was criticism too. 'The FAA does not test or validate the operational effectiveness of security measures at foreign airports. FAA recognizes the importance of testing, but believes it is inappropriate for FAA inspectors to make tests in foreign countries because of sovereignty concerns and possible danger to inspectors.'

Victor Rezendes, a GAO official, says that neither London nor Frankfurt was looked at by his agency when they accompanied FAA inspectors to five foreign airports early in 1988. 'We found that they [the five unspecified airports] were in compliance with most of the security standards, except that FAA doesn't test the foreign governments' system, or even witness their tests. We still think this is something worth pursuing and that the FAA can make a bigger effort in this area. But our basic message applies to all airports, including Heathrow and Frankfurt.'

In the United States, FAA officers regularly try to smuggle mock weapons through airport security and on to planes. In 1987, for example, 20 per cent of the attempts to spirit make-believe bombs and guns on to aircraft succeeded. A 1985 law required the US Secretary of Transportation to draw the attention of any foreign airport to slack security. In the years 1986 and 1987, the FAA carried out 600 inspections at 200 airports. On only two occasions in that period did the FAA consider it necessary to make an official complaint to a country about security deficiencies.

In the wake of Lockerbie and the GAO study, *Life* magazine commissioned Isaac Yeffet, the former director of security for El Al, to inspect and appraise seven of the United States' biggest and busiest airports. They were: John F. Kennedy (JFK), New York; La Guardia, New York; O'Hare, Chicago; Stapleton, Denver; Miami International; Los Angeles International; and San Francisco International. This is what Yeffet had to say in March 1989.

JFK: 'The Port Authority's parking-lot on the roof of the Pan Am terminal is the most dangerous spot at the airport. From here you are within a stone's throw of several jumbo jets, separated only by a cyclone fence. A terrorist could inflict the largest multiple-target attack ever. You could do what you wanted. Bomb, bazooka, grenades; they all would work. It wouldn't take much to fix this problem spot: a better fence, an electronic signal to alert guards when the fence has been penetrated, a second fence on the outside to delay an attack, a regular security patrol.'

La Guardia: 'Perhaps the worst security breach at most US airports is curbside check-in. It allows luggage to go directly to the belly of the plane without being X-rayed, without opening the bag, without making sure the passenger will be on the plane too. A passenger wearing a T-shirt that says "Abu Nidal, the 15th of May Organization", as long as he has a ticket, can even have his luggage loaded beneath the cockpit uninspected . . . I was able to place my suitcase on United Airlines Flight 67 to O'Hare without ever showing a ticket or getting on the plane. I took American Airlines to Chicago instead and picked up the bag. If Lockerbie tells us anything, it is that airlines must match luggage to passengers.'

O'Hare, Chicago: 'They [passengers] can leave baggage anywhere, for any amount of time, and nothing happens. In United Airlines' glistening, new $500-million terminal, I saw luggage unattended in at least seven different locations. We placed a bag near a departure gate. Security people walked by, two planes arrived and left the gate, a custodian swept around the bag three times and mopped around it once, three travellers tripped over it and an electric cart-driver nearly ran over it twice. After three hours, we gave up hope that it would be picked up – or even stolen.

'At El Al, no piece of luggage can be left for more than a few seconds without attracting the attention of security agents. The planted suitcase bomb is one of the easiest and commonest types of terrorist attacks, and dealing with it should be part of basic security. At London's Heathrow, speakers on the public address system warn passengers in public areas at ten minute intervals not to leave baggage unattended. In America, there doesn't seem to be an awareness among security people that seemingly abandoned luggage could pose a threat.'

Stapleton, Denver: 'Most security agents at US airports are employees of an outside firm that won a contract because its bid was the lowest, not because the outfit provides the best security. At Stapleton, we talked with a guard who said he was responsible for X-raying all baggage at international departures on his 5.30 a.m. to 1.30 p.m. shift. But no human being can watch a screen for that many hours and still do an adequate job. No one should watch for more than twenty minutes at a time. The Denver guard, who earned $3.60 an hour, said that one of the incentives to stay alert was the $25 reward for each gun found. The man said his training consisted of one eight-hour session on how to operate the X-ray machine. From this instruction, all he remembered was that he was supposed to look for the colour green on the monitor, indicating metal. Dark spots, he said, are usually books but could be bombs. If he saw something suspicious, he said his instructions were to ask the passenger what it was, and if the passenger told him what the object was, he was to trust the passenger and allow the luggage to go through. This clearly contradicts FAA rules. I asked him what would happen if he made a mistake and then a plane blew up. He said he would have to go back for re-training. If it happened twice, he could be fired.

'This is another major weakness in American security. The airlines put their trust in gadgets – metal detectors and X-ray machines – spending millions on equipment and little on the people who operate it. The machines can help, but they cannot make a judgment . . . Americans place the decision on whether or not a plane is secure in the hands of poorly trained, underpaid, unmotivated, overworked contract employees. The secret of El Al's success is that it focuses on the passenger and not on the luggage. Security agents ask these questions at the counter: "To whom does the luggage belong? Who packed the bags? What presents or gifts are you carrying? Who gave them to you?

Where has the baggage been since you packed it? What are you carrying that does not belong to you – or that you do not know the contents of?" The agents ask questions that cannot be answered yes or no. It gives them a chance to scrutinize the traveller for telltale signs of lying.'

In 1986 an ex-convict was questioned by an El Al security officer as he was about to board a flight from Zurich to Tel Aviv, Israel. The passenger's baggage had not been X-rayed, but as a result of his answers to the questions, he was judged a security risk and subjected to a thorough search. Four kilos of explosives were found in a package. He thought he was carrying drugs for a smuggling syndicate who had paid him $5000. As soon as he realized that his accomplices had been sending him to his death, he co-operated fully with the police.

Miami: 'Miami serves Latin America, a region that accounts for 20 per cent of the world's terrorist incidents, and functions as a major drug importation centre. Yet security is sadly lacking. All international luggage that enters Miami to connect with flights out of the country is X-rayed . . . Yet bags loaded in Miami and bound for foreign destinations are not checked. It doesn't make sense. The incoming suitcases have already been on an airline for some time. It is the ones being loaded for the first time that present the greater threat . . . '

Los Angeles: 'From the moment we entered Los Angeles International Airport, appropriately known as LAX, it was clear that traffic-flow had priority over security . . . We stopped outside Gate 30, where TWA's Flight 760/790 non-stop to London Heathrow was boarding. It was impressive. At last we were seeing something done right! But the feeling soon faded. An elderly woman entered the gate and her bags were searched. She was cleared; in security jargon, she was sterile, no longer a threat. But, to my surprise, after having gone through security, she was then allowed to go back out to kiss her companions goodbye. The entire screening process was undermined. As departure time approached, tardy passengers began arriving. None was searched. A late passenger is always a security threat. You have to assume that he is relying on the last-minute rush to help him smuggle something on board. To do the job right, attendants would have to hold the plane, but their preoccupation at that point is to get away from the gate on time.'

San Francisco: 'To its credit, this airport has probably invested more in security than most. Yet San Francisco is not secure. Perhaps the worst thing we saw was the loading of a Pan Am flight to Guatemala and El Salvador. Just a few weeks after Lockerbie, agents were boarding passengers to these high-risk areas without asking any security questions.'

A full three months after Lockerbie, Yeffet had this to say about American airports and operators: 'There is no airline security in the United States. What little is being done to protect passengers, is not done well. The US carriers are spending enough money, but they are not spending it on the right things. But as international security tightens, the US, with its lack of safeguards at airports, becomes more inviting to terrorists. It would be wrong to single out Pan Am: its security is not better nor worse than the industry norm. It was the victim of bad luck. The problem lies with the system. The carriers follow FAA regulations, but these aren't tough enough . . . Airline executives have made security a low priority. There is no reason to believe this will change until there is a major disaster at an American airport.'

Not surprisingly, Ray Salazaar, head of security operations for the FAA, did not agree. 'Terrorists are not very common in the US. We do not have Abu Nidal running around the streets of New York or Detroit. If we were to have any indication from Intelligence agencies that there is a domestic threat, we would make changes overnight.' Not very convincing: reliable intelligence was not sufficient to bring about changes to avert Lockerbie.

So, what *is* being done on a global basis to combat the menace of terrorism in the skies?

In the United States, the FAA has been investing $12 million annually in technical research, leading to the breakthrough with the thermal neutron analyser (TNA), which can highlight plastic in luggage, however ingeniously camouflaged. In an exercise to boost public confidence, armed FBI and CIA agents flew some American aircraft between continental USA and Europe. Selected airline staff were also being trained to shoot and were issued with automatic handguns. The air marshals worked in teams of three, two men and a woman, posing as passengers. Only the flight-deck crew knew they were aboard. When the flight originated from East Coast airports, such as New York or Washington, the armed riders completed the round trip without leaving the plane, thereby avoiding a clash with gun regulations in the country where the aircraft landed. If the flight was out of the West Coast, from Los Angeles or San Francisco, say, then the air marshals had a stop-over at their destination. They left their weapons on board to be picked up by their colleagues who were making the return journey.

In the spring of 1989, Marvin Fitzwater, a White House spokesman, said, 'Travellers on US carriers should be confident that all reasonable precautions are being taken to assure that the highest level of security exists.' Hijackers they might catch. Bombers they would not.

Closer co-operation between the United States and British authorities was also seen as a constructive initiative. FAA agents were allowed access to British airports from May 1989 in order to gather intelligence and to monitor security. A joint agreement between American and British immigration departments allowed for new 'look-out' posts at airports in both the United States and Britain. 'Hot' names making up a sort of international 'wanted list' are circulated among all immigration agencies in the West and the concept of the 'look-out' posts was to provide special areas on the check-in concourse where suspect passengers' passports could be scrutinized by skilled officials. Congress also passed a new law forbidding airline staff from leaking information connected with terrorist activity received from the government.

The tightening-up was not limited to airports; far from it: for example, all doors to flight-decks are now locked from the moment the crew board and every aircraft is fitted with a 'squawk button', which alerts air-traffic controllers, should a hijack be under way.

As the Lockerbie investigation rolled through the seasons, from winter and spring into summer, so airport security personnel in Europe continued to be obsessed with radio/cassette players, perpetuating one of the greatest mistakes of the past, that of stereotyped thinking. For too long the terrorists had been allowed to call the tune, with the airline industry seemingly unable to catch up. Radio/cassette bombs had been found in the Frankfurt raids and put on public display for the entire world to observe and copy. If there was such an animal as a terrorist who did not know how to construct a barometric explosive device, all he had to do was read the newspapers. A radio/cassette bomb subsequently brought down Pan Am Flight 103. Is it not probable that the terrorists by now already have something more ingenious? Are they not more likely to use a radio/cassette player as a decoy, hoping to distract security officers from the real weapon? Semtex is so pliable that it can be moulded into a camera, the lining of a suitcase, or an electric shaver; literally anything. It just happened that radio/cassettes were the favoured equipment for airline bombers in the run-up to Lockerbie, but equally it could have been a shaving-stick, hollowed out and filled with plastic, which would have produced the same result. A bullet from an MI6 rifle leaves the barrel at 3000 feet per second, but when plastic blows up, it throws debris at a rate of 26,400 feet per second.

On a conventional airport X-ray machine, a piece of Semtex in a suitcase can easily be mistaken for a book or soap. In May 1989, a plot was uncovered in the Middle East to use a child as an 'innocent'. Semtex was to be packed into a tub of Halawi sweets, which are popular in the Middle East. The belief was that a child would be able to carry the barometric sweets bomb into the passenger-cabin of an aircraft without arousing suspicion. Some imaginative lateral thinking by airport security is long overdue.

However, Salazaar did not believe it either necessary or practical for all luggage on US domestic flights to be X-rayed. He thought that making a comparison with the El Al operation was unfair, pointing out that United Airlines, Pan Am, TWA and American Airlines were all 200 times bigger. If there was X-raying of domestic luggage, he believed the boarding process would be slowed to a level which would be unacceptable both to the industry and the American public, who have become accustomed to a step on/step off flying bus service.

One of the first thermal neutron analysers into production entered regular service at JFK in June 1989, prompting Salazaar to insist: 'We're not sitting on our hands. We're constantly trying to figure better ways of doing the job.' On the subject of security personnel, he said: 'They don't work for the FAA. They are the responsibility of airlines.'

In April 1989, Swissair became one of the first airlines to match bags electronically to checked-in passengers. At Zurich airport, all the fences were replaced and made secure. Copying the Americans, Swissair also put their faith in travelling armed guards. The women sometimes travelled disguised as nuns or pregnant mothers, while their male partners usually adopted the role of jaded, seen-it-all-before businessmen. The Swissair planes on transatlantic routes were adapted so that agents in the cabin could use ordinary passengers' headphones to keep in touch with the captain.

The accolades which have been heaped on Swissair in recent years have made airline spokesman Jean-Claude Donzel very uneasy. 'It could happen to any of us, anywhere, anytime. Total security doesn't exist.' Similar sentiments were echoed by Australian aviation security expert M. H. Mackenzie: 'We are in a front-line against terrorism, fighting a war we cannot win, but dare not lose.'

Since 1985, when a bomb detonated in the departure lounge, police patrols at Frankfurt were constantly searching for abandoned suitcases. The decompression chamber, described earlier, was brought into use: it should activate any barometric apparatus, but not if there was a twin timer, the first triggered by a standard type battery-operated clock. Neither was all hold luggage being opened and the contents examined.

Within hours of the Lockerbie disaster, an anti-terrorist squad was permanently on duty all day and night in Greece at Hellenikon airport, Athens. Armoured cars, two police patrol vehicles and secret service agents surrounded all planes which were classified as high-risk, including every US carrier and El Al. Passengers had to pass two metal detectors, when checking-in baggage and again at boarding. Marksmen, working around the clock in eight shifts, manned the perimeter fence, while labrador dogs were employed in the detection of explosives.

Security had been tightened at Rome's Fiumicino airport long before Lockerbie. Police and soldiers, armed with submachine guns and protected by Alsatian dogs, stood guard twenty-four hours a day at every entrance, and continued to do so a year after Lockerbie. Helicopters and sharpshooters were poised for action around the airport's outskirts. A bomb squad was equipped with remote-controlled water guns, which were designed to shoot through a locked suitcase to disrupt electronic circuits, while more soldiers patrolled the tarmac and taxiing areas in armoured, bullet-proof vehicles.

In London in April 1989, Paul Channon, the Transport Secretary, announced that Britain would be spending more money on high-tech bomb detectors, and security inspectors were to be deployed within six months among the nation's airports. More radical changes were also on the horizon. The Transport Department's aviation security section was to be reorganized and renamed the Aviation Security Inspectorate. The number of inspectors was to be doubled from eight to sixteen. Their brief would be to conduct unannounced checks at Britain's twenty largest airports and, whenever necessary, propose new or amended measures. Part of their job specification would be to review the security operation of British overseas carriers. Also doubled was the money earmarked in 1989, rising to £1 million, for the research and development of machinery to detect explosives. A new security code, introduced by Channon, included: stricter control of cargo, mail and courier consignments; the screening of all luggage on high-risk flights, though he refused to define *high-risk* (this was taken by politicians and the airline industry to mean everything operated by El Al, South African Airways, all American companies and British Airways planes bound for the United States, the Middle East and Asia, especially India); a closer examination of all electrical equipment which could have been converted into a bomb; the separating of arriving passengers from those departing (which is a feature of US airports); and design changes to the interior of aircraft, making it more difficult for weapons to be hidden on board. The streamlining and refining of airport security would be an 'ongoing, progressive programme', Channon assured.

While Lord Brabazon of Tara, the Minister for Aviation and Shipping, deplored the 1982 Aviation Act for its 'inadequacy', Channon did not see a need for elaborate changes through Parliament, only tinkering with the existing regulations to enable him to impose fines on subcontractors at airports who allowed security to be breached. Channon was prepared to redecorate but not rebuild.

Labour MP John Prescott, the Shadow Transport Secretary, commented: 'If these measures improve security at airports, we will very much welcome them, because our security is characterized by mistakes and confusion which alarm the Americans and other authorities.' Americans should be more alarmed by Yeffet's investigation into their own airports than by any shortcomings in Europe.

The first TNA screener to operate in Britain was introduced at Gatwick in the summer of 1989. The machine was on loan from San Francisco airport, where it had been on trial. Sam Skinner, the US Transportation Secretary, reported that the TNA had caused 'only minimal delays' at San Francisco and its rate of protection was 'better than expected'. Other European countries were expected to follow Britain's initiative. Skinner commented: 'We hope the airlines will meet the cost, relatively small compared with the cost of a transatlantic flight, and put these in airports, although only after the governments of those countries have found them acceptable and safe.'

One proposal at a meeting in Montreal, Canada, in June 1988 on air security was that terrorists should be jailed in Spandau-like international detention centres, though the concept had not been thought through to the extent of who should run them. The idea came from the International Air Transport Association (IATA) and coincided with a plan outlined by the British Foreign Secretary, Sir Geoffrey Howe, while attending the World Economic Summit in neighbouring Toronto. IATA held up the example of Spandau in Berlin, where the Nazi Rudolf Hess was imprisoned, as part of a five-point policy to 'internationalize' the response to hijacking and bombing. Hess was watched over by American, British, French and Russian guards. IATA called for an international court to be established specifically to hear cases against air terrorists. The association also advocated an international advisory group which would be available to support governments during a hijack crisis. Such a team would comprise experts on aviation, police and military strategy, in addition to psychiatrists, trained negotiators and specialists in regional politics and language. An international trouble-shooting force was envisaged which could work alongside the advisory unit, providing an instant military response anywhere in the world, to terrorist aggression against any air industry target, whether an airliner or an airport terminal building. By creating an international emergency force, pressure on individual countries would be relieved with the burden spread across a global theatre of war.

Broadly supporting this concept, Dr Gunter Eser, IATA's German director general, had this to say: 'When terrorists are jailed, there is nearly always an attempt to free them through a hijacking. It might be possible to avoid this if there is an international court and an international jail. Then, no one country is a target.' Only the 'top-trained' and 'best military people in the world' would be recruited to the international 'Flying Squad'. Although there was overwhelming support for the plan in the industry, there was not much international political will in the West, mainly because it was felt that a workable agreement was beyond any reasonable expectation.

There is much to be said for an international Air Crime Squad, even though the practical problems of organization are likely to be prohibitive, because the best friend of the murderers has always been the absence of co-ordination between the diverse agencies making up the complex security command structure. The left and right arms were for too long disconnected from a central body. Arteries of communication were blocked by petty autonomy and jealously guarded secrets, as if the various bodies were in competition instead of being allies. At the time of Lockerbie, for instance, responsibility for air safety in Britain was diffused among the Department of Transport, the British Airports' Authority, the Home Office, the Ministry of Defence, the Foreign Office, the Metropolitan Police, the country's airlines and regional police forces. True, they would all be represented on the Aviation Security Committee of the Department of Transport, but this was more of a talking shop than a council of war. Here is how their duties were divided: it was the obligation of airlines to search aircraft; baggage checking came under the auspices of the BAA or local airport authority; the Ministry of Defence would deploy troops and military equipment; control over the flow of people into the United Kingdom was the sole domain of the Home Office; the police were in charge of dealing with terrorism inside airports; and it was the task of the Foreign Office to draw up a list of imperilled airlines. Daily the various ministries, departments and agencies would be making decisions in isolation, inevitably conceding the initiative to the terrorist.

During the winter of 1989–90 three newspapers and a television company, in quick succession, spotlighted serious shortcomings in security at Heathrow. Three reporters, using bogus references, had little difficulty getting themselves hired by aircraft cleaning firms, while an unemployed butcher, who had never even mended a fuse in his life before, got himself a job as an electrician with a company specializing in servicing airliners at Heathrow. They all had access to aircraft and were in a position to plant bombs or weapons. One of them was even photographed at the controls of a Pan Am 747, prompting a beleaguered Paul Channon immediately to announce that new rules would make it illegal for any aircraft cleaner to work alone until he had been employed at the airport for a minimum of six months, and the company which had recruited one of the reporters, Skyliner Services, lost its airport franchise. There were verified stories of some security guards having 'substantial' criminal records and others falling asleep while on duty, allowing people to come and go without restriction.

A routine police check on Andre Reich, for example, would have shown that he had seventeen criminal convictions, including one for possession of a gun and ammunition. He was convicted at the Old Bailey, London, in November 1983 of illegally being in possession of a shotgun and ammunition and given a six-month prison sentence, suspended for two years. Other convictions included causing grievous bodily harm and burglary. Yet Reich was employed at Gatwick for ten months in 1986 by external contractors as a carpenter, which gave him freedom of movement around the airport without once being challenged. 'The only identification I ever provided was a medical card,' he admitted to the *Daily Express*. 'At no time was I ever asked about my background or whether I had a criminal record. Within twenty minutes of arriving at the airport to start work, I was issued with a security pass which gave me unlimited access to anywhere in the airport, including airside. I couldn't believe or understand how anyone with a record like mine could be allowed to wander freely anywhere I chose. I have turned my back on crime now, but I have to admit that during the time I worked at Gatwick I could have been tempted for money to carry a bomb on to a plane. The point is that there are many, many people working at Gatwick who are on the breadline, who could be persuaded by terrorists to do their dirty work for them, and who have the access to do it.'

After Reich completed his assignment at Gatwick, it was a full year before he was asked to return his security pass. If so inclined, he could have sold that pass to any terrorist. 'While I was there, security was virtually non-existent. Apart from the fact that they made no real effort to vet employees, anyone with a security pass could go anywhere they wanted, unchallenged. There were never any routine searches made on staff, either. When I applied for the job, I imagined I would only be working in non-restricted areas. I was flabbergasted when I was issued with a security tag allowing me access to anywhere in the airport, without any checks at all being made on my past. I know other people who are still working at Gatwick who would never have been taken on and given security clearance had basic, routine checks been made.'

Professor Paul Wilkinson, who lectures on international relations at Aberdeen University, Scotland, and is also an authority on terrorism and a security adviser to the Geneva-based International Foundation of Airline Passengers' Association (an organization which campaigns for the consumer), referred to 'scandalous weaknesses' in security at Heathrow. 'It is time that the Government promise of a radical overhaul in airport security was implemented,' he wrote in the *Daily Express* on 14 January 1989. 'It should be carried out by an independent expert inquiry and not by the Department of Transport and the British Airports' Authority, where complacency has contributed to the present sloppy security.' And hinting at the findings of Yeffet in the United States, he stressed: 'We should be aware that there are even worse gaps in security at international airports in many other countries.' He believed there should be sanctions against countries whose security standards were judged inadequate.

In a direct response to this kind of pressure, Mrs Thatcher's government warned on 15 March 1989 that airlines whose safety precautions persistently fell short of acceptable guidelines would be banned from all British airports. This was to be a provision of the Aviation Security Bill, which was then in the process of being assembled. Another duty of the inspectors would be to ensure that all airport staff with access to aircraft were properly screened. Sloppy workmanship by private security firms employed to search baggage would result in their contracts being withdrawn.

Lord Brabazon, however, was unconvinced that there could be a workable system of vetting workers with access to restricted areas of airports. Writing in a letter to Donald Anderson, the Labour MP for Swansea East, he said: 'It would be extremely difficult to devise and operate an effective system, given the vast numbers involved and the high staff turnover in some areas. In addition, there would also be problems over defining suitable criteria for acceptability. For example, should a conviction for a minor offence, perhaps many years ago, automatically debar an applicant from such employment?'

Anderson was not impressed. 'Any Civil Servant will give 101 reasons why things cannot be done. Surely when ease of access to aeroplanes by non-vetted cleaners has been exposed on many occasions, even Transport ministers should be alert to public concern and decide that much tighter vetting of cleaning, catering and baggage-handling personnel must be brought about.'

One of the most astonishing lapses in security on record occurred in March 1989, when a British Airways 747 flew worldwide for many days with mock explosives in the passenger-cabin; these had been placed by SAS troops and police, and subsequently forgotten, during an exercise, remaining there until being discovered by a cleaner. Scotland Yard launched a full-scale inquiry into the embarrassing incident and the Department of Transport demanded an explanation from the British

Airports' Authority, Heathrow's ruling body. John Prescott said: 'This incident underlines the absolute necessity of having one security authority at Heathrow, an airport police force, to avoid the sort of Mickey Mouse approach that we seem to have towards security. What happened in this case was unbelievable.'

The Lockerbie crash came at the end of the worst year for terrorist attacks on airliners, and the number of deaths in air disasters worldwide in 1988 was also higher than average. There were 54 fatal accidents in which 1585 people were killed. Of those, 1007 died in 'unprovoked incidents' and 578 were the victims of terrorist or military action. These figures are exclusive of the eleven inhabitants of Lockerbie who were fatally injured by the falling wreckage of Pan Am Flight 103. Scheduled passenger services suffered 15 'unprovoked incidents', in which 633 people died. Sabotage, hijacks and military strikes against civilian targets claimed nearly as many victims in 1988 as weather-related accidents, which ranked second as a major cause of airline deaths. 'Aircrew error' remained the single most common factor in airline accidents. In 1987, more than a quarter of the 1167 deaths were the result of terrorism; a third of those in eight terrorist incidents. The previous year, the percentage was roughly the same, but on a much lower overall count: accidental deaths, at 607, were the second lowest of the decade, making it a *safe* year, if one could exclude the 219 fatalities due to deliberate acts, but to make such an exclusion would be to delude. The blackest year for fatalities in air transport history was 1985, when the figure was 2129. Although more passengers died because of terrorism in 1985 – 329 in the Air India crash alone – there were actually more terrorist crimes in 1986, demonstrating an alarming upwards spiral.

Almost a year after Lockerbie, I returned to Heathrow's Terminal 3 to witness the alleged stricter security. I paid most attention to the security staff questioning passengers for the 6 p.m. Pan Am flight to New York, which a year previously would have been 103 but has since been given a new number. One could not help but be impressed by the heavy presence of security personnel – nearly all women – but I was left questioning the quality. One of them was only too eager to talk about procedures, without knowing who I was or the purpose of my interest.

'Things are very different now since Lockerbie,' she said, implying that security had been slipshod before the crash of Flight 103. 'We've all been trained by El Al, the best in the business for security.

'But it's still chaos here in the mornings, when most of the Atlantic flights leave. It's almost impossible to keep on top of it, but we manage. Most people are patient; they know it's for their benefit. No one checks-in now without being thoroughly interrogated. All the questions we ask come from El Al. We know exactly what we're looking for. If anyone's hiding anything, I'm confident I'd spot something guilty in their manner.'

. A couple of people approached with their suitcases. The black-and-white X-ray machine was to their left, at the side of the security officer. A few feet from the X-ray machine was a long table, where suspicious baggage was being opened and searched by yet more security officers. All this took place several yards from the actual check-in counters. A rope barrier prevented passengers from crowding the security and check-in concourse.

This is a reconstruction of the dialogue between the woman security officer, who had spoken to me, and the couple who were booked on the flight to New York, now Pan Am Flight 11.

Q: 'May I see your passports and tickets?'

A: 'Sure.' The documents were handed over by the husband.

Q: 'You're returning home?' She asked the question with her eyes down, while examining the tickets and passports.

A: 'That's right.'

Q: 'How long have you been in England?'

A: 'A week. Just over a week.'

Q: 'Who packed your luggage?' Now she looked up, at the same time passing back the documents.

A: 'I did.' This answer came from the wife; the husband had done all the previous talking.

Q: 'Since you packed, nothing has been left unattended?'

A: The couple looked at each other and shook their heads. It was then the husband who said, 'No.'

Q: 'You're fully responsible for everything you're carrying?'

A (husband): 'Absolutely.'

Q: 'Are you taking anything which has been given to you by someone else and you're not sure what it is? Are you acting as a sort of unofficial courier for anyone?'

A (husband): 'Absolutely not.'

Q: 'Are you taking back any electrical equipment; a radio . . . portable cassette/radio; something like that?'

A (husband): 'No . . . well, I've got some electrical shaving stuff . . . and headset equipment, for listening to music: I brought it with me. It wasn't bought over here.'

Q: 'And you can vouch for that?'

A (husband): 'Oh, sure.'

These answers seemed readily accepted and no physical search was made of the suitcases to inspect the electrical items.

Q: 'You understand I have to ask these questions?'

A (husband): 'That's OK; you go right ahead; you make me feel safe.' All three laughed.

Q: 'Not everyone feels that way.'

A: 'Then they're stupid.'

Q: 'Enjoy your flight.'

A: 'Thank you.'

The baggage was then fed through the black-and-white X-ray machine. Nothing in that conversation, during which a friendly rapport was encouraged, could possibly have alerted the security officer to a bomb. Most of the questions could have been answered with a simple yes or no.

Even worse was to follow a week later, on 19 December, when I flew with Pan Am from Heathrow to Miami. At the check-in, a Pan Am female security officer, with sleep-walker eyes, asked if I was carrying any electrical equipment, such as a cassette/radio player. When I replied, 'Yes, I am,' she then wanted to know, 'Is it yours?' And when I answered, 'Yes,' she said, 'That's fine, then.' She did not even demand to inspect the equipment, contrary to the latest airport security code, backed and endorsed by Pan Am. Once again this great airline was being let down in the war against terrorism by its front-line staff.

A few minutes later, in the departure lounge, a male airport security officer decided he wanted to see inside my briefcase, the combination lock of which had jammed. A supervisor was summoned and my briefcase was taken to another X-ray machine and fed through the system. For almost two minutes he froze the frame, then tried to force open the briefcase, but failed. After half a dozen attempts, he shrugged and said resignedly, 'All right, go on. I trust you.' Did he really expect a terrorist to look like one? I was handed back my briefcase, still unopened and containing electrical gadgets, even though the images on the X-ray had clearly given him cause for concern.

Full marks, though, to my Pan Am pilot who announced over the plane's public address system, 'I must apologize for our delay: a baggage problem has now developed into a security alert. We shall not be departing until it is sorted.' A passenger had checked-in his luggage but had not boarded the aircraft. All the missing passenger's belongings were unloaded from the hold before we departed; just the way it should be done.

A look at the trend of air crimes over a longer period helps to put in perspective the impact terrorism has had on air safety. In the sixteen years between 1970 and 1986, there were 25,000 acts of terrorism relating to the air industry, 6000 of those crimes committed in the two-year period 1985–6. In 1969 there were 82 hijackings compared with 22 in 1986. Since 1968 the favourite final destination for hijackers has been Cuba and the carriers hardest hit have been North American airlines.

Not all hijackings are politically motivated. Occasionally old-fashioned greed is the motive, as in the case of the 'Great Plane Robbery' of 1971. On 24 November, Thanksgiving Day, a passenger using the alias 'D. B. Cooper' on board a Northwest Airlines Boeing 727 in the United States handed a stewardess a note for the pilot, warning that his brief-case was filled with dynamite, which he would explode if his demands for $200,000 in $20 notes and five parachutes were not met. A deal was negotiated whereby the hijacker would receive his ransom and parachutes at Seattle airport in exchange for the passengers. This done, the captain was made to take off for Mexico and fly at 10,000 feet and 200mph over the mountainous region of the north-west in the states of Washington and Oregon. Originally, the plane had taken off from Portland, Oregon. But somewhere in the vicinity of Mount St Helens, to the south of Seattle, 'Cooper' strapped on a parachute, attached another to the suitcase with the cash and gave the pilot two orders: an altitude of 10,000 ft was to be maintained and the rear door opened. Then he parachuted into the mountain forests near the Columbia River, carrying the money in a laundry-bag. He was never caught and was presumed to have either drowned or been eaten by wild animals. The police file remained active and in the summer of 1989 FBI spokesman John Eyre announced that they had a live suspect. Because of this case and a spate of attempted copycats, design changes were made to the 727 and similar aircraft so that the rear doors could not be opened in flight. No one, of course, would be foolish enough to jump from a forward door because of the danger of being sucked into an engine.

It is debatable whether armed sky marshals on civilian aircraft comfort or frighten the flying public. There are many well-documented instances of their contributing to loss of life rather than its preservation. A classic example occurred on Christmas Day 1986: an Iraqi Airways Boeing 737 was two-thirds of its way through an hour-and-a-half flight from Baghdad to Amman, in Jordan, when one of four hijackers headed for the flight-deck, only to be pounced upon by one of six undercover Iraqi armed guards covertly riding the plane. In the ensuing gun battle, 107 passengers, who were in the middle of their lunch, were caught in the crossfire, realizing the recurring nightmare of all those who had been uneasy about the prospect of violent encounters in the skies. Hijackers are fanatical enough, without provocation. When trapped at altitude in the environment of a sardine-can, their madness may be exacerbated, as on that Christmas Day. Two handgrenades were thrown, one at the captain in the cockpit and the other at passengers and a security agent towards the back of the cabin. The aircraft was severely damaged and the crew seriously injured. Even so, the captain managed to maintain control and commenced a steep descent towards nearby Arar airport, in Saudi Arabia, for an emergency landing. Unfortunately, the plane crashed and burst into flames just before reaching the runway. Sixty-two people perished, including the hijackers and a further twenty were badly hurt. The shoot-out had lasted seventeen minutes.

Pan Am and its Frankfurt–New York route seems to have held a fatal attraction for Middle Eastern political bandits. On 5 September 1986 a Pan American 747 was being prepared at Karachi for a flight to Frankfurt and then non-stop to New York, when it was approached by a truck which appeared to be transporting a group of airport workers. The truck stopped beside the 747, whereupon four men jumped off, drew guns from inside their overalls, and raced up the aircraft's steps, firing into the air as they ran. However, by the time they reached the cockpit, the cupboard was bare: hearing the shots, the flight-deck crew of two pilots and an engineer had escaped through their emergency exit, a move which fuelled controversy later. The action of the crew earned the approbation of the doyens of counter-terrorism. Vacating the aircraft was not comparable with a ship's captain jumping overboard and leaving the passengers at the mercy of pirates. It was a tactical manoeuvre which confounded the hijackers: they had a plane, but it might as well have had no engines. The negotiators were able to argue that a fresh crew would have to be flown from the United States, which would take a minimum of twelve hours, probably much longer. The balance of psychological power was pitched in the negotiators' favour from the outset, because they were making the rules and the hijackers had no choice but to abide by them.

Flight attendants were made to collect passports from the passengers and the hijackers selected a male American as a sacrifice in an attempt to change their fortunes. He was summoned to the front of the aircraft, where he was shot dead and pushed from the plane through a forward door. From then, the situation disintegrated and in the eighteenth hour of the hijack, when the auxiliary power unexpectedly failed and all the lights went out, the terrorists became convinced that the aircraft was about to be stormed by troops. In panic, they started shooting and throwing handgrenades. Eighteen passengers were murdered, and three of the hijackers were killed when the Pakistani security forces did finally rush the plane on hearing the explosions. Afterwards there were recriminations about slow reactions: every move should be a reflex from a well-drilled anti-terrorist airport force. This hijacking once again illustrated the inherent dangers of incoherent security.

On 7 December 1981 three planes were hijacked at a South American airport in the space of 49 minutes. The airport in question was Simon Bolivar in Caracas, Venezuela, and this story of bungling incompetence underlines the fact that air safety is subject to dramatic regional fluctuations. During the period 1973–84 these statistics for fatal events per one million flights were recorded for the airlines of the countries named: Colombia 27.464; Turkey 17.369; Egypt 13.423; United Kingdom 1.279; United States 1.179; Japan 0.642; Scandinavia 0.455; Australia 0.328. Fatalities per one million flights were: Turkey 1717.121; Colombia 509.693; Netherlands 383.515; Egypt 362.416; India 333.858; United Kingdom 56.763; United States 36.593; France 2.156; Australia 0.656. In other words, you were 775 times more likely to die in an air crash flying with a Colombian airline than with an Australian carrier. Travelling with a British or French company involved a risk three times greater of being in a fatal air crash than if you had used a Scandinavian carrier. In a league table for safety, Australia came top, followed by Scandinavia and Japan, with the United States in fourth place. The United Kingdom headed the fourth group, which included France, West Germany and Italy. At the bottom were Turkey and Colombia. Outstanding over a shorter recorded period was Singapore with a zero score for both categories. (Figures for the Soviet Union and China are usually a closely guarded secret. However, there were reports from China of more than 2000 people killed in 70 plane crashes in 1989, apparently making it the country's worst year for aviation deaths.)

On 21 December 1989 two diametrically opposed views on air safety appeared in the American newspaper USA Today, which has an international circulation. Guest columnists for the day were Samuel K. Skinner, the United States Secretary of Transportation, and Emmanuel Winston, an international trustee for the Jaffee Center of Strategic Studies, Tel Aviv University. Skinner wrote: 'Since the advent of the first "take-me-to-Cuba" hijackings in the early 1960s, the US Government has been faced with a continuing challenge to maintain both safety and security of US air travellers. I believe the Government has responded appropriately and well. US flag-carriers are safe to fly, and airline travel is one of the safest forms of transportation.'

Skinner's comments were in direct contrast with Winston's assessment. '"The skies are safe," say the governments and the airlines. If those who plunged to Earth a year ago from Pan Am Flight 103 over Lockerbie, Scotland, could speak, they would give testimony to the fact that governments lie and airlines lie.

'The technology of terrorism has bypassed the ability and willingness of the airlines to defeat the terrorists. Regretfully, we treat only the symptom and not the cause. Syria, Iran and Libya are exporters of these terrorist squads. The airline pilots could refuse to fly into those countries, but they won't.

'Terrorists choose aircraft because there is something about a plane falling out of the sky in flames, the passengers experiencing the sheer terror of their last seconds as it plunges to Earth. We, the observers, share some of the horror, and it is that shared experience of the last word in terror that makes the terrorists choose aircraft.

'It's a great story. It sells newspapers. Politicians can bleat on public

TV how all this must stop. The President expresses, what is it? Oh, yes, "shock and rage", promising retribution – which, of course, never comes. Airline spokesmen follow suit, promising more protection.

'Instead, they hire staff who seem not to be very smart and would not really know a terrorist bomb hardware unless it were sticks of dynamite wired to an old-fashioned alarm clock. It is a Laurel and Hardy act followed by Chicken Little saying, "The sky is falling".

'The fact is travel is not safe and it won't get better. The terrorists are not merely a symptom of the right to free expression, but are the problem. The nations that sponsor and train them are the root cause.

'Until the President is ready to deal a direct blow to those nations, aircraft will continue to rain down their victims. We talk of war against drugs, we talk of fighting terror – we talk, talk, talk – and never do.'

The US President's Commission on Aviation Security and Terrorism, which investigated Lockerbie, severely censured the FAA and Pan Am for complacency before and after the event. However, the Commission's most controversial conclusion was that the US government should initiate pre-emptive military strikes against known terrorist targets.

Seventeen months after Lockerbie, some luggage was still being loaded unchecked on to aircraft at London Heathrow, admitted by the Aviation Security Inspectorate. Jim Jack, the chief inspector at the Transport Department's aviation security branch, established after Lockerbie, told an anti-terrorist seminar: 'It is ironic that we are embarking on such a major programme (total baggage searching) when – and I hesitate to say this in public – we really do not yet have the machinery to do it.'

One day in November 1988, the vice-president of a North American airline was talking shop with Laurie Taylor, the former Principal Vice President of the International Federation of Air Line Pilots' Associations. The conversation turned to metal fatigue, whereupon the American executive shocked Taylor with the revelation that 'the whole industry in America' was 'just waiting for a 747 to come apart in the air because of a structure failure.' Taylor says: 'When I first heard the news of Lockerbie, I said to myself: "That's the one they've been waiting for. My God, it's happened!" I was aware of the age of *Maid of the Seas*. That night, like so many other people in aviation, I believed Pan Am 103 had died of old age. It would have come as no surprise if she had.'

5 ROULETTE IN THE AIR

Although Pan Am's *Maid of the Seas* had not, after all, died from old age, there was no escaping the fact that she had been past her prime. In the months leading up to Lockerbie she had suffered numerous age-related conditions, including cracks and severe corrosion. There had even been a fire and twenty-four mechanical faults deemed serious enough to be filed with the FAA. Even though she had been in service for eighteen-and-a-half years, she had many older sisters still working as hard as in their infancy: *Maid of the Seas* was the fifteenth 747 to be built at Seattle by Boeing Commercial Airplanes and, although she came through her regular check-ups, there was no denying that she was one of the old girls of the fleet. But there were people who believed that modern maintenance was the elixir of aircraft life. One such devotee was Frank Shrontz, Boeing's chairman.

'We believe fundamentally that with proper maintenance and proper inspection an airplane can, in fact, last for ever,' Shrontz said in Washington at a meeting of aviation experts on 24 February 1989. The industry held its breath. Not everyone shared Shrontz's optimism.

Shrontz no doubt felt justified in delivering his upbeat message. Understandably, since Lockerbie, morale in the industry had been ebbing. However, by February 1989 there was no longer a question-mark hanging over the cause of the crash of Pan Am 103: it was a terrorist bomb, not metal fatigue; not shoddy workmanship by the manufacturer or a maintenance error. The time must have seemed ripe to Shrontz for bold rhetoric; time to reassure a jittery public; time to put back the buck in a business languishing in post-Lockerbie self-analysis and debilitating introspection; time to guillotine negative speculation and to bang the Boeing drum.

Two days after Shrontz's stirring speech his statement had boomer-anged.

At 1.30 in the morning of 26 February, United Airlines Flight 811 left Honolulu, Hawaii, for Auckland, New Zealand. On board the nine-teen-year-old 747 were 336 passengers and a crew of eighteen. Seven-teen minutes later, when the aircraft was climbing through 22,000 feet and just as the flight attendants were starting their rounds with the pre-meal drinks, there was a shuddering bang, followed by an equally loud roar of rushing cold night air, as a hole forty feet by ten appeared in the fuselage on the starboard side, directly behind the first-class section and below the upper deck. Nine passengers, occupying three rows in business class, were sucked out to their death. The vortex inside the aircraft was so violent that the wind wrenched off the earrings a passenger was wearing and Roger White, who was sitting in Row 18, recalled: 'The walls seemed to be popping in on everybody. I kind of got resigned to the fact that I was going to die. I put my head down and told my wife I loved her. She said she loved me.' Another passenger, David Birrell, remembered the events like this: 'You're watching the clouds and the moon and the stars, and you're waiting for the sea.'

But the sea never came, even though the two starboard engines were dead, one of them fouled by the intake of a body. Flight 811, skilfully handled by Captain David Cronin, returned shakily to Honolulu, where it landed safely at 2.33 a.m. 'The longest hour of my life,' was passenger Bruce Lampbert's description of the 100-mile journey back to Hawaii.

The aircraft had been bought from Pan Am, and since coming off the Seattle assembly-line in 1970 it had spent 57,000 hours in the air, making approximately 14,000 take-offs and landings, putting it towards the end of its originally intended natural lifespan of twenty years.

First thoughts, naturally, were of a bomb. After all, the position of the rent in the aircraft's belly was uncannily close to the eye of the explosion on Pan Am 103. However, the FBI bomb specialists and air accident investigators, who flew into Honolulu that same morning from the US mainland, quickly ruled out sabotage. 'There was a big noise, but it didn't sound like an explosion,' they were told by Rochelle Perel, of Beverly Hills, California. 'It sounded more like the plane coming apart. There was a kind of hissing sound, like air, and then a tearing away of the plane.'

An examination of the hole conclusively ended any bomb speculation: the rectangular tear was without frayed edges, there was no damage to the floor between the passenger and cargo compartments, nor were there any scorch marks. The on-the-spot verdict was that 'the break' was 'too clean for an explosion.' Metal fatigue, that old demon from the fifties and sixties, had returned to haunt the industry, and those, like Laurie Taylor, who had feared such an eventuality, unfortunately were vindicated. Whatever the veracity of Shrontz's claim that airliners could be made immortal, he was not believed by the people who mattered – the public. During early 1989 the research firm Yankelovich Clancy Shulman carried out a public survey in the United States on the issue of air safety, and their findings were a revelation. Of those questioned, 43 per cent did not think that air travel was 'very safe'. Some 64 per cent expressed an opinion that flying had become more dangerous during the past five years, regardless of official statistics.

Ageing aircraft and slipshod maintenance were cited as the major anxieties, with terrorism in third place. Despite the continuing saga of mid-air near-collisions, a shortage of air-traffic controllers fell a long way short of the top of the Worries League. Significantly, the American public was less concerned about crew performance and pilot stress, although human error remained the predominant factor in the majority of mishaps. Rightly or wrongly, there was a trend towards more trust in the man than the machine.

In Britain and the rest of Europe, safety and security dominated the minds of the hardened flyer. A survey was commissioned by *Executive Travel*, a London magazine for the frequent business traveller. Questionnaires were sent to 7300 readers, randomly selected, and the results were sent for analysis to the Marketing Centre, a research organization with a special commitment to the travel industry.

The editorial comment from *Executive Travel*'s November 1989 issue, in which the findings of the study were published, stated:

'For the general peace of mind of our frequent business travellers, 1989 has been a bad year. Disaster has been piled on catastrophe – adding a nastier dimension to the habitual rigours of the already tricky and demanding job of quartering the globe in the interests of the company.

'This month's important survey on the theme of travel safety and security – steadily becoming a central concern of both firms and the individual executives – does not turn out to be reassuring. A mass of fascinating anecdotal evidence gathered in the process of analysing the response, argues strongly that airports and airlines are falling down badly on the job of ensuring that their customers can fly with few concerns, apart from the commercial task in hand.

'The shortfall in security, so evident in our report, is clearly not a result of a lack of sophisticated technology – more of which, cheeringly, pops up all the time – but of simple human inadequacies. No matter how elegant the detection machinery and control systems, they take people to run them. And people are notoriously fallible.

'One of the major problems highlighted by our sample is that the level of the available detection technology far outruns the performance of the personnel in charge of it. It is not by chance that conference interpreters work in 15-minute bursts – any longer than that and the performance graph goes into a sharp decline. Airport security staff, working under equal pressure, habitually spend much longer looking at their control screens. This is not good enough.

'The problem is that the small groups of terrorists who constitute an international plague are as difficult to spot as a needle in a haystack. And this is where individual initiative can extend the official range of security services. Each of us is responsible for the safety of the flight we are on.

'Keep a sharp eye out for anomalies and oddities – the strange abandoned parcel, the strikingly odd behaviour of a fellow passenger, the small group of travellers taking an undue interest in the pattern of plane seating and passenger disposition – and report it as quickly as possible. This is one of the few excellent reasons for abandoning one's traditional British reserve. After all, it might be your life on the line.'

During the six months prior to the survey, 45.7 per cent of all people who took part in it admitted to choosing airlines for reasons of safety rather than comfort, punctuality, efficiency and speed, as in the past, demonstrating a significant shift in attitude by the hard core of regular flyers, though hardly surprising in view of the terrorist strongholds and activity in Europe, from which the American domestic traveller must have felt far removed.

The most popular carrier for both safety and security was British Airways. In the safety category, BA was followed, in order of popularity, by Swissair, Singapore, Cathay Pacific, Lufthansa, KLM and Qantas. The airlines nominated after BA for their tight security were Swissair, El Al, Singapore, Lufthansa, KLM and Cathay Pacific. All American airlines were well down the lists. It must be remembered that these are not official statistics, merely the public's perception, which is important enough.

On the question of safety, the magazine reported that 'an overwhelming number of respondents looked first at the record of the airline in question; the second most important element turned out to be age of aircraft . . . ' The most avoided aircraft was the DC10, followed by all Eastern bloc planes. Sixty per cent believed that governments and regulatory bodies, such as the CAA and the FAA, could be doing much more towards security and safety; only one-fifth of those people surveyed had the slightest confidence in the legislators.

Some 57.1 per cent said that they would keep away from Athens airport, if at all possible, followed by Rome, Heathrow and New York's JFK. A high number also called for all cabin and hold baggage to be searched.

One-third of the random sample had experienced 'serious lapses' of security at airports during the previous twelve months, reporting no checking of hand-luggage, X-ray machines unattended, free access to outlawed areas, baggage loaded on flights without being matched to a travelling passenger and the failure to inspect electrical goods being carried on board.

One reader of the magazine recalled that four Haitians were allowed on to his KLM flight thoroughly unchecked, whereupon they demanded that the plane should be flown to the Lebanon.

Someone else wrote, 'I carried a bronze head, which looked like a grenade, through security in Bangkok, Manila, Jakarta and Singapore. Only Manila queried it.'

According to another reader of *Executive Travel*, eight Arabs at a Middle East airport were waved through security with no check of hand-baggage and no body search.

Here is a selection of other complaints:

'On the day it became known that the Lockerbie disaster was caused by a cassette-player, I travelled through Heathrow with a Walkman in my briefcase. It was not checked.' . . . 'I have watched screening of hand-baggage at Athens airport with no operator at the video screen.' . . . 'I observed total disinterest of security staff at Athens, despite the metal detectors being activated by most passengers.' . . . 'I carried a telecom product – with curly wires, and so on – in my briefcase through three US X-ray detection screens. I was not once asked to open my briefcase.' . . . 'On one BA flight this June, the aircraft was delayed for 30 minutes after boarding. One rather suspicious-looking passenger was allowed to leave, while his bags stayed on board.' . . . 'Follow any attractive young woman through the security check at Madrid, Milan or Rome and all eyes are riveted on her – nobody pays any attention to the businessman behind her. I have witnessed this many times.'

Analysing the results of the research, Brian Hammond, one of the magazine's correspondents, had this to say: 'Travel is always disconcerting. The crews of Columbus set their historic course for the Western Ocean in the knowledge they would, in all probability, sail over the edge of the world. Today's business travellers are better informed and more rational – but almost as nervous about the prospect of arriving safe and sound at their destinations. The findings show – disturbingly – that a high proportion of frequent travellers are extremely unhappy about airline standards of safety and security, and have little confidence in the performance of carriers, airports and governments.'

In Alexandria, Virginia, in the spring of 1989, the consumer protection organization Airline Passengers of America was inundated with calls from people who wanted to know if it was possible to discover the age of an aircraft they would be flying in: of course there was no way of finding out. Looks and cleanliness could be as much a camouflage as a giveaway: the object of make-up is to cover the years.

Airlines became so sensitive to the issue of aircraft longevity that staff were briefed on how to cope with the most frequently asked question: *Excuse me, but how old is the equipment on this flight?* The staff of United Airlines were instructed to reply: 'I'm unaware of the age of this particular aircraft. However, the average age of a United aircraft is 13.5 years.' If 13.5 was the average, then some planes were much younger and others were considerably older, but the passenger was no wiser in respect of the aircraft he or she was about to board: in that context, flying remained a lottery.

Of all non-Communist countries, the United States was operating the oldest commercial jets in the world. By the summer of 1988, the American airline with the oldest average equipment was Northwest (15.5 years), closely followed by TWA (15.3) and Eastern (15.1). Only slightly better were United (14.9) and Pan Am (14.6). The middle order included Continental (12.1), while American (10.8), US Air/Piedmont (10.2) and Delta (9.5) fared considerably better.

Despite repeated assurances that there could be safety in old age, the operators with money in the bank to spare reacted to the mood of the people and invested in new stock. Even so, America's 3300 commercial jet airliners maintained an average age of around 13, which compared badly with many European and Far Eastern companies: Singapore Airlines (4.5), Lufthansa (7.7), KLM (8.4), Swissair (8.5) and British Airways (10.02). The airlines with the healthiest trading figures began updating their fleets, responding to the growing anxiety in the marketplace. Before the end of 1988, United had acquired 23 new Boeing 737-300s, bringing its fleet total to 400 and reducing its overall average age from 14.9 to 13.5. By March 1989, American Airlines had clipped the average age of its planes from 10.8 to 9.4, a figure which was planned to come down still further within three years.

Regulated air fares in Europe generated much envy in the United States. European price-fixing had produced profits for re-investment in new aircraft, placing the American carriers at a disadvantage on the prestigious international routes. Deregulation in the United States was proving to be more of a noose than an unshackling.

The first jumbo jet into service – in February 1969 – was named Clipper *Juan T. Trippe*, in memory of the founder of Pan Am. Twenty years later, the oldest wide-bodied aircraft in the world had still not qualified for retirement, despite having clocked 66,000 flying hours, 6000 in excess of what was envisaged by Boeing when Clipper *Juan T. Trippe* was towed from the gigantic Seattle production hangars on 28 February 1969. No one was celebrating this particular anniversary. If anything, the *Juan T. Trippe*'s twentieth birthday was something of an embarrassment, coinciding with more gloomy news to alarm further an already apprehensive public.

Boeing, conscious of the fermenting fears about geriatric aircraft, had co-operated in an investigation throughout the world into its commercial jets. A task force of eminent engineers and airline technicians had been established in 1988 by the US Air Transport Association. During a period of many months, they put Boeing planes through the equivalent of a rigorous health check, wherever they were based; throughout Europe and Britain, the Middle East, the Far East, Australia and New Zealand, and at home, of course. The results were announced on Clipper

Juan T. Trippe's historic birthday, but there was no party spirit. Some $800 million needed spending on 1200 ailing Boeing jetliners, if they were to be able to continue flying safely. Of course, it was the responsibility of individual airlines to fund the cost for the upkeep of their planes: some co-operated readily, others were less committed.

All new planes are sold with an economic design life (EDL) prescribed by the manufacturer. The EDL of the 747, for example, was 20,000 flights, 60,000 flying hours or 20 years. By the beginning of the summer of 1989, there were 68 Boeing 747s which had notched up 60,000 flying hours or more, and five of these had made more than 20,000 flights. Clipper *Juan T. Trippe* was the first to fly into the unknown 20-year-plus territory, and was still in commercial service long after that anniversary. The 'voluntary retirement' of aircraft had been reduced to a record low: most airlines could not afford to pension off aged equipment. 'Involuntary retirement' – trade parlance for the plane crashing – had become more common.

It would be wrong to give the impression that only 747s were being pushed beyond their projected lifespan. The EDL of the Boeing 727 was 60,000 flights, 50,000 hours and 20 years. Yet 435 of these planes were more than 20 years old and 358 had flown over 50,000 hours. Among the newer 737s, used extensively in Europe for package holidays and in Hawaii and the Caribbean for island-hopping, 38 had already surpassed the 51,000 recommended hours. Of the older generation long-range workhorses, there were 123 Boeing 707s over the age of 20. The sky had become the meeting-place for the world's largest Darby and Joan club.

There was even a case of a Boeing 727, which was an insurance write-off following a belly-flop landing in Mexico, being sold, restored and returned to flying, this time in Europe. When the plane was damaged in August 1982 in Acapulco, it was owned by Mexico Airlines. The pilot, at the end of a training flight, had forgotten to put down the gear, so it landed without wheels, slithering along the runway for more than a mile. A huge rent was forged in the under-fuselage and the plane burst into flames. Later, after the insurers had paid out, the wrecked aircraft underwent basic repairs and was shipped to Springfield, Virginia, in the United States. After major surgery during a two-year period, in 1984 the FAA re-issued the plane with an airworthiness certificate. During the next two years, it changed hands five times, before being bought by Dan Air, a British charter company. Before the CAA would pass it fit for flying, Dan Air's maintenance engineers spent 24,375 hours on the plane.

Captain Steve Last, chairman of the Airworthiness Committee of the International Federation of Airline Pilots, had this to say about rebuilding crashed planes and putting them back into service: 'I would look on purchasing a severely damaged plane, which has been re-assembled and rebuilt, rather the same way as I would look upon a severely damaged car which has been re-assembled and passed on. I don't think I would be particularly enthusiastic about assuming that a rebuilt aircraft is going to have quite the same integrity as an aircraft which is new.'

Ronald Ashford, who was head of safety at the CAA, was worried that checks on older aircraft had 'been found to be flawed'. Referring to the pressure to keep old aircraft flying, British MP Barry Sheerman, vice-chairman of the Parliamentary Advisory Council for Transport Safety, said: 'It's a sort of conspiracy between everyone to keep those jets in the air. I don't want to frighten people, but we are on the margin.'

Naturally enough, Dan Air defended its decision to buy the once written-off Boeing 727, re-registered G-BMLP, stressing that it had been given the most searching of examinations by the CAA. 'We are not cowboys,' a spokesman for the firm emphasized. 'It is not a clapped-out crashed aircraft, which it was until brought into this country. Don't make it out as a rogue type of aircraft. Age is irrelevant. It is just another plane we have bought in the long history of Dan Air. Our reputation in the industry is second to none.' Dan Air, who did no wrong, continued to fly this aircraft. If there is a quarrel, it is with the legislators. I suspect most passengers would feel uneasy about flying in a plane which insurers had written-off, despite the official seal of approval.

The reason for the operation of so many geriatric planes was blamed on the shortage of available new aircraft, but this was only half the story. In many cases, a shortage of cash on the part of the airlines was the root cause, prohibiting them from buying new stock from the manufacturers. Pan Am, the trailblazers for so long, pioneering new routes and concepts, and more than anybody helping to shrink the world, was a classic case in point. Pan Am could not afford new 747s, so instead had to opt for a programme of high profile maintenance, or cosmetic surgery, which, in itself, was no cheap compromise. Pan Am's maintenance overheads in 1988 came to $815 for every hour that one of its planes was in the air. The comparable hourly maintenance bill of other leading American airlines for each aircraft was: Eastern $694; TWA $692; United $565; Northwest $530; Continental $455; American $433; US Air/Piedmont $492; and Delta $377.

But in other parts of the world, particularly Britain, countries of northern Europe, the oil-rich nations of the Middle East, and Singapore, where the state-owned airlines were economically viable, fleets were being radically updated, putting the Americans at a disadvantage, much to their chagrin. Boeing's biggest orders for new 747s were all coming from outside the United States.

In its own glossy publicity brochure, *The Business Traveller Bulletin*, Pan Am made the dubious assertion that its rebuilt ancient 747s should be accepted as new aircraft, thus reducing the average age of its transatlantic fleet to a very respectable 7.48 years. Published in 1989 to cover the quarter August to October, the bulletin carried the story under the heading *Pan Am 747s Rebuilt in $359 Million Programme*: 'More than half of Pan Am's fleet of 747s have been rebuilt to virtually new condition under the Civil Reserve Aircraft Fleet programme (CRAF). Organized and paid for by the US Government, CRAF modifications are carried out by Boeing and take four months to complete.

'The $11-million-per-aircraft programme starts with stripping the plane back to the bare structure, and includes the reinforcement of all floor beams, and the installation of new wheels and axles. When completed, the aircraft is ready to be used, at 48 hours' notice, by the US Government in case of a national emergency – and is strong enough to transport tanks.

'Additionally, Pan Am is spending an average of $6-million per aircraft on extra structural and internal improvements. While the plane is stripped down, Boeing carry out indepth service checks, while the interiors that are refitted have improved galleys and lavatories, and larger overhead bins.

'The 18 747s that have been rebuilt through CRAF may now be regarded as new planes. This means that the average age of our entire transatlantic fleet currently stands at 7.48 years. Pan Am's investment in the additional work on the planes, plus our $300 million annual maintenance budget, verify our commitment to the very highest standards of safety and comfort expected of a world-class carrier.'

CRAF was a back-door form of government intervention, allowing Pan Am to remain viable against its state-owned competitors without losing its capitalist independence.

Shrontz's argument that eternal life for the contemporary airliner was a reality, and not a pious hope, was supported by many of the most reputable airlines. Boeing's EDL was not a safety threshold, they stressed, but purely a cost-effective barrier, beyond which it would be uneconomic to keep a plane airworthy because of the prohibitive expenditure on repairs.

Times had changed, though, since Boeing had introduced its EDLs (September 1958 for the 707, February 1964 for the 727, February 1968 for the 737, and February 1969 for the 747). Maintenance capability in the interim years had improved beyond all recognition. Proof of this, boasted Pan Am, was the success story of the *Juan T. Trippe.* In 1988 she was subjected to a $21 million refit, which, said Pan Am, restored her to pristine condition, as strong and robust as any other 747 in service, whatever its age. For Pan Am to have bought a new 747 from Boeing, the outlay would have been $150 million. These statistics alone were seen as justification enough for Pan Am's policy, a strategy thrust upon them by circumstance rather than choice. The public continued to be unimpressed. Passengers were convinced of the nexus between old and unsafe. Rejuvenation smacked of presenting mutton dressed as lamb. The Americans knew too much about powdering over age-lines and wrinkles, and the ghastly truth behind facelifts.

Of course, there was far more to the public unease than the one United Airlines mishap. Flight 811 was the culmination of a series of incidents all related to age or inadequate maintenance. A few days after Lockerbie, an Eastern Airlines 727, carrying 110 passengers from Rochester, New York, to Atlanta, Georgia, made an emergency landing late in December 1988 at Charleston, West Virginia, when metal fatigue caused a 14-inch hole in the fuselage of the 22-year-old jet. The FAA records showed that the same plane had been treated for cracks on four previous occasions and had made more than 51,000 flights, putting it within 9000 of Boeing's EDL. In 1985 the crack was six inches long and on a wing-flap: the damaged part was replaced. A year later, an eight-inch crack was detected on the centre engine: a new duct section was fitted. Two cracks were located in 1987, one of them a mere one-tenth of an inch on a horizontal stabilizer, but the other more serious and on a tail component.

A few hours after the lucky escape at Charleston, another Eastern 727 incurred a similar problem and had to be grounded, this time at Boston's Logan airport. An inspection revealed a three-inch crack in the 24-year-old plane, which had recorded 54,480 take-offs and landings on the hectic New York–Boston commuter shuttle. The cracks on the two jets were in similar areas of the fuselage. Eastern's spokeswoman Karen Ceremsak said that the airline would be 'voluntarily' checking all those 727s which had registered more than 30,000 take-offs and landings. Forty-six of Eastern's 727s were given a 'triple check' to demonstrate that there was nothing cavalier about the company's approach to safety.

Anthony Broderick, associate administrator of the FAA, was quick to announce that all US airlines which flew the 620 oldest 727s would be ordered to replace thousands of rivets. The 737 had already been targeted the previous autumn and the 747 was in line for a similar purge. 'We're going to go through this with every old airplane,' Broderick promised. The previous week, operators had been told to replace or repair 122 known weak points on 727s and 737s, rather than waiting for something to snap and having to be dealt with as an emergency.

Despite all the propaganda and the big sell that old was beautiful, public anxiety was not to be assuaged. In the first six months after Lockerbie, American airline ticket agents reported sales on transatlantic flights down 30 per cent compared with the same period the previous year. 'It's not just the terrorist threat,' explained one spokesman. 'It's a combination: bombs, hijackings, crew mistakes and old equipment; especially old equipment.' Unfortunately, though, there seemed to be no access to absolute truth, if indeed it existed. As the Americans say, everyone seemed to have 'an angle'; for those in the industry, it was survival. Politicians refer to this process as the positive manipulation of a negative. So, were the public on both sides of the Atlantic right to remain hostile to old planes or were they over-reacting to media hype?

Paul Turk, a leading aviation consultant and president in the United States of the Aviation Space Writers' Association, had this to say: 'Older aircraft are continuing in service beyond what their designers originally saw. The experience before this time had been that twenty years was a very long life for a transport aircraft. With the jets, however, we're finding they have economic lives that extend well beyond any arbitrary design life, and as an aircraft gets on in years it requires higher and higher levels of maintenance.

'As long as an airline can make money with [an aircraft], it's going to continue in service. Replacement aircraft are simply not available. Demand, partly as a consequence of deregulation and partly because airline travel is the only meaningful inter-city travel-method left to us, is always going to be there.

'The short-haul airplanes – the 737, 727, DC-9 and BAC 1-11 – that tend to fly short hops and take off and land every hour, or every hour and twenty minutes, work harder. They're pressurized and depressurized more often. That's going to wear the airplane out. It is metal. You bend metal often enough, and it cracks.

'The key is to inspect rigorously: to use the data you have that tells you where cracks are most likely to occur; repair them when you find them and control corrosion. Then the airplane has a virtually infinite physical life. With the older airplanes, there is some kind of incident that causes an unscheduled landing about every eleven days. For many airlines, the continued use of ageing airplanes is not a decision over which they have a great deal of control. The manufacturers are sold out of new planes through 1992. If you want to buy a new airplane, you're going to wait at least five years. You can't get airplanes to replace the ones that you ought to consider retiring.

'Without a big jump in fuel prices, new noise regulations, or some kind of arbitrary limit on aircraft life, those older airplanes are going to continue to fly until the replacements are available. And keep in mind that the United States is the biggest market for used transport aircraft that are no longer in the fleets of foreign carriers. Carriers in Europe and Asia buy new and sell their used airplanes here.'

Explaining the difference in economics between the air industries in the United States and those elsewhere, Turk said: 'They [Europe and Asia] have different tax and financing structures. In many cases, they're government-owned. Government-owned airlines are concerned with an image, with immediate re-sale for profit. They don't need depreciation and tax write-offs. So, they're able to order new. They're in a position to order new airplanes and have fleet replacement plans that are not as sensitive to the economics of the system as the US carriers.'

Turk believed that if potential passengers knew the age of the planes they were about to fly, the industry would be 'crippled'. If airlines had to issue government health warnings on tickets, the way cigarette companies do on their packets, the US transportation system would not survive, he feared, and the US economy would collapse. And it would favour extensively certain carriers that were financially strong and able to afford new airplanes. There would be even more of a monopoly situation, because those with older airplanes would be forced out of the market.

Here again we witness a conflict – between safety and self-interest. The industry and especially the legislators cannot afford the luxury of tunnel vision. Safety is viewed by them as one of many portions of a pie, none of which can be tackled in isolation. The overall economy dictates acceptable safety levels, which may differ dramatically from the public's expectations. In catering, there is an aphorism: let the consumers into the kitchen and you do not have any customers. The same maxim applies to aviation: ignorance is good for business. Despite some reservations, Turk remained in the optimistic camp. 'All airplanes, even new ones, develop cracks – for reasons of heat, cold, pressurization and depressurization. Wings flex up and down in gusts: the airplane is designed to do that; if it didn't, it would be so rigid it would crack apart immediately, so it will develop cracks over time.

'If the FAA oversees inspections, corrosion control and maintenance procedures with diligence and with some energy, and is able to make sure that the airlines do it that way, then the airplanes are safe for a good while yet.

'As a result of the deregulation, US carriers have smaller profit margins. They have to compete for money and equipment in the market-place, and they have to compete for passengers. This basically makes them search for lift where they can find it, and at prices they can afford and still provide a competitive product.

'There is no way to simply say, "Government, fix it!" It's too complex for that. There are too many factors, physical as well as mechanical and economic. Remember, the system is not seriously broken. The system needs the attention it is getting.'

In contrast, Laurie Taylor, talking from personal experience of years on the flight-deck, sympathized in full with public trepidation. 'Geriatric aircraft are an enormous problem,' he told me. 'It is only just beginning to be fully appreciated that a plane begins to crack and corrode the moment it leaves the hangar from the production-line: just like humans, they start dying at birth.

'All modern jets are supposed to be failsafe. In other words, if there is a structural failure, another part can accept the load. That's the theory, but not what always happens in practice. I agree that if inspections unearthed every crack and area of corrosion, planes could indeed fly for ever, but hairline fractures are very difficult to pinpoint: they can be under paint, in the belly, below a serving galley, inside the skin and in creases. Despite all the advanced technology, cracks still continue to defy detection in certain circumstances. Professional engineers have been aware for some considerable time of this developing crisis, which is likely to worsen before improving. There are so many factors contributing to the wear and tear of an aircraft.

'Well documented is the consequence of the daily cycles of ups and downs, changing pressures, turbulence, steep climbs, sharp descents, strong winds, heavy landings and rough runways. They all have an accumulative effect.

'Unappreciated until more recently was the part played in corrosion by the toilets and galleys. Urine acts as a rapid corrosive agent. So, too, does tea when it is poured away by flight attendants. You would never think that an airplane, like a 747, could be rotted by urine or tea, yet I've encountered such corrosion from those sources that I've been able to push my finger through the skin of an aircraft. Salt-laden atmospheres and high temperatures also speed up corrosion, which is why metal fatigue is a particular plague of islands, especially in the Pacific and Caribbean; something worth bearing in mind by the discerning air traveller. All these points add up when considering the overall world air safety pattern.

'After deregulation in the United States, the number of federal inspectors decreased, while the number of airlines increased. There were not enough inspectors to provide adequate supervision, but the FAA budget was beefed up to allow for the employment of more qualified inspectors, so important for the regulation of the industry and the attainment of superior safety standards. The Australians have set an example for everyone to follow. They have demonstrated, beyond all dispute, that definitive air safety is attainable. How have the Australians achieved such excellence so consistently? Credit must go to the Australian state regulating authority, which is very strict; in fact, to a degree unknown anywhere else in the world, and, as a consequence, the airlines excel: they thrive on the rigorism.

'The Australians buy good airplanes, they are scrupulously maintained, crews are superbly trained and there's a pride in everything they do. The aviation industry in Australia is seen as a partnership between government, airlines, crews and mechanical engineers; everyone playing a vital role. Inspectors ride the flight-decks, helping to keep everyone on their toes. That kind of approach to safety is long overdue elsewhere, especially in South America and Africa, where regulations are so poor. It is no coincidence that there's a direct relationship between the strictness of the regulating authority and air safety.

'Before deregulation, US airlines were spending much more money on maintenance than the required minimum, but during 1984–9 the amount spent was reduced by an average 10 per cent, at a crucial period, when airlines were flying more old aircraft. There is no doubt that the system was being abused in the US. At one point, Eastern's planes were flying with an average 52 defects per aircraft, a fact made public by a Congressman. Yet Lufthansa prides itself on never taking off with a single defect, if at all possible; not even a blown toilet light-bulb or a dripping tap. That sort of fierce professional pride is reflected in the company's safety record.

'Before the era of the jet, aircraft models were obsolete within about seven years. They had such a short lifespan and they were quickly out of fashion. But with the jetliner came a plateau: the DC-8 and 707 were very similar in performance and cost per passenger mile, and so the incentive had gone to scrap airplanes. Whereas planes used to be paid for within seven years, they can now be 15 years old and still not written-off.

'The time has come for a policing approach to maintenance. Maybe we shall have to consider going back to a safe-life concept. That means an authority stipulates, in advance, the age at which an aircraft shall be retired, as opposed to the decision being dictated by the economics of airlines. Of course, that would revolutionize the balance sheets and the money would have to come from the public in higher fares: you get nothing for nothing.

'Public opinion is paramount. If the public demands to know the age of aircraft and refuses to fly without that knowledge, then the airlines will not only listen but act. No one in business can ever afford to try swimming against the tide. To survive, you always have to be going with the flow. So the public should not only be concerned but angry and militant. The consumers can always win as long as they recognize their muscle and flex it.

'At the moment, most passengers are completely in the dark: many will book a flight through a travel agent and will not even know which airline they'll be flying. This usually occurs with a particularly long journey, say from the United Kingdom to one of the outer islands of Hawaii. He could be aware that he's booked on British Airways to Los Angeles, say, but he might never have heard of the carrier who would be taking him on to Honolulu, where he would be transferred to an island-hopping operator. In those circumstances, the consumer is buying blind, totally ignorant of the quality of service to expect. Would you spend so much on anything else without being certain what you were getting? Old airplanes can be a danger; make no mistake of that, whatever you hear to the contrary. That doesn't mean every old airplane is going to crash, but it does mean they need extra care and attention, which cost both time and money.

'When your car has clocked up a certain number of miles, you know that you can expect problems to develop and you consider trading-in, if you can afford a replacement. If you keep the car, it's usually because you haven't the money available for such a big financial commitment. Your policy decision is determined not by your needs, or desires, nor even common sense, but by your resources: so, too, the airlines. If your car breaks down on the motorway, at least you can pull on to the hard shoulder and phone for help. If something goes drastically awry at 30,000 feet, it's not so easy.

'There has to be a political will to face head-on the dilemma of ageing aircraft. There are few other businesses where company policy is so closely related to public safety. Strong government is the only answer. Too much is at stake for safety to be left to the natural law of the market-place. As airplanes become older, the authorities have to decide whether to ground them or fly them: there's no halfway house. Someone has to draw the line somewhere, and that must come from government. The airlines' case is always made forcibly, but it's about time the collective voice of the public was heard and taken into account.'

The investigation into the tearing of the United Airlines jumbo focused on a forward cargo door, which was not without significance. Seven months earlier, in July 1988, the FAA had directed US airlines to inspect the locks on all cargo doors of their 614 Boeing 747s and to make the relevant modifications. The rogue door of the United Airlines jumbo was one of those which should have been tested, but the FAA notice gave airlines until the end of 1989 to comply, a directive which was hastily amended to a 30-day deadline in the wake of the evidence from Honolulu.

Najeeb Halaby, Pan Am's chairman and a former FAA administrator, was encouraged by what he saw as a developing awareness of endemic dangerous conditions in old aircraft by so many people and different institutions and corporate bodies. 'It means that the industry is casting off the old standard that an aircraft could fly for ever. Sometimes we react to accidents rather than act positively to prevent them. But we should discuss how much safer we can make the system by being pro-active and believing that the system is never safe enough. We just don't know how safe is safe.'

Northwest Airlines has always been held in high esteem in the industry, as well as enjoying a faithful following among the public. Northwest is not only a domestic carrier, but also crosses the Pacific and runs a prestigious transatlantic service. Shock, therefore, is not too strong a word to describe the reaction in February 1989 to the disclosure that Northwest's 24 Boeing 747s had made more than 8000 flights without suspect engine mountings being checked, in breach of an official FAA ruling. This unexpected lapse, totally out of character for North-west, was discovered by the FAA during a routine examination of the airline's maintenance records. After the news leaked out there was speculation in the United States as to the possible extent of ignored safety instructions.

Maintenance records were not being examined as regularly as for-merly because of the shortage of inspectors to cope with the prolifer-ation of airlines after deregulation, substantiating the point made by Laurie Taylor.

Through the years, there has been an abundance of evidence to sustain the view that, for maintenance, the airlines of Europe, plus Qantas and Cathay Pacific, lead the world. British Airways, KLM, Lufthansa and SAS, to name but a few, had been doing much more than ever was required of them by law. If there was a mandatory deadline, you could rest assured that the required work would regularly be completed in advance of schedule. In Britain, the equivalent of the FAA is the Civil Aviation Authority (CAA), which considers itself ahead of the field in keeping on top of the ageing aircraft problem; and with some justification, having launched Structural Integrity Audits in 1978, a move designed to catch the onset of corrosion and metal fatigue in the earliest stages. If a plane was registered in the United Kingdom, it was usually regarded as a gilt-edged guarantee that it had been maintained to a standard of excellence, and therefore would command a top secondhand price if it went on the market.

Despite the CAA's reputation, it often simply followed the example of the FAA. An example of this occurred in 1986, when the FAA gave orders for adjustments, following twenty-nine engine failures. However, the FAA saw fit to allow American airlines three years in which to complete the work and the CAA imposed a similar timescale for British operators to undertake those modifications. This directive had no sooner been disseminated than a Pratt and Whitney engine exploded on a British Airways 747 just as it was landing at Heathrow. As the engine broke up, flying debris penetrated the fuselage and damaged a wing. The response from British Airways was exactly what one would expect from that particular company: all the work on the engines was brought forward, regardless of the three years at their disposal. Neither the CAA nor the FAA saw reason to compel other airlines to follow BA's initiative – until the eruption in December 1987 of another engine, yet again at Heathrow, this time involving an El Al 747. Even then, speed was not considered of the essence because, although the overhaul called for from all airlines using British or American airports was more detailed, the time-limit of 1989 was not lowered.

The exploding engines on the British Airways and El Al 747s could, in the opinion of the FAA, have resulted in carbon copy tragedies of the blaze at Manchester in August 1985, when 54 people died on the runway inside a Boeing 737, which turned into a fireball in a matter of seconds.

The recognition that regular maintenance checks, however stringent, did not always expose the onset of wear and tear in remote areas of airplanes, brought about a subtle change in the way old planes would be kept healthy in future. The authorities have learned from the medical profession that prevention is always preferable to cure. A crisis in the air is equivalent in emergency terms to a heart attack. The outcome can never be predicted: better, therefore, to avoid it altogether. Hence the conscious move by governing bodies towards the enforced replacement at an elected age of certain parts – those within an aircraft's anatomy known, from experience, to be at risk of dangerous deterioration towards the upper end of middle age. Waiting for something to become worn, before replacing it, has been shown to be courting disaster. This must be an improvement on the old way of doing things, but many critics feared that airlines would be even more inclined as a result to fly their fleets beyond safe limits. In 1989 there were 421 jet airliners registered in the United Kingdom, of which 38 were over the age of 20. British Airways reinforced the cargo doors on 37 of its 40 Boeing 747s within a few months of the bulletin from the CAA.

Money gives away more clues about safety than almost anything else, but the public have no access to the information which could help to steer them away from danger. An airliner owned by Lufthansa or British Airways can fetch 30 per cent more when sold secondhand than the average price for aircraft owned by other airlines.

Most people in the industry are reluctant to dwell on the subject of those airlines whose planes could not even command a value at the lower end of the normal secondhand scale. 'I wouldn't accept money to look over the airplanes of some airlines,' said an executive of one North American international carrier. 'I'd rather recommend we buy a hot-air balloon; it would be much cheaper and considerably safer. There are cowboys getting away with murder, literally, and they're not always the little fellas. The sort of negligence I'm talking about amounts to grandscale corporate crime.'

After an aircraft is sold, its livery is changed and its history painted over. The customers would never know whether it came from a reputable stable or one infamous for its dereliction.

Metal fatigue was the cause of several Comets – the first jet airliners and British-built – crashing in the early 1950s. The first real warning of a possible new outbreak of metal fatigue came in April 1988, when the top of an Aloha Airlines 737, operating between the Hawaiian island of Hilo and Honolulu, was ripped off in flight. One stewardess of the Hawaiian airline fell to her death from 24,000 feet as the plane, carrying 95 passengers, was transformed into an open-topped convertible. The American pilot, Captain Robert Schornstheimer, was universally praised for the skilful way he nursed the damaged plane for a further 25 miles, enabling a successful emergency landing to be made at the nearest airport, on Kuhului Island.

Of the pilot's handling of the plane, Maurice Myers, the airline's president, said it was 'an extraordinary performance'. George Harvey, area co-ordinator for the FAA in Honolulu, remarked: 'It was like somebody had peeled off a layer of skin. You could just see all the passengers sitting there.' Mark Eberly, a ramp superviser at Kahului, dropped to his knees as he watched the plane land, one of its engines smoking. 'I saw hair flying in the wind and arms dangling.' In tribute to the captain, passenger John Lopez, from Hilo, commented: 'He brought the plane in so smoothly it was like riding in a Cadillac.'

Also deserving credit was Mimi Tompkins, the second-in-command on the flight-deck and the airline's only woman pilot. After the cabin door was blown away, there was so much noise they had to use hand signals to communicate.

The Aloha 737 had made 89,192 flights: of all the 737s in the world, only one had notched up more, and that was a sister aircraft in the same Hawaiian fleet. This incident highlighted the potentially dangerous mixture of salty air, high temperatures and island-hopping operations. The average length of flight between the Hawaiian islands was less than 25 minutes. A shuttle service of that nature inevitably multiplies the number of take-offs and landings.

Boeing wasted no time in recommending that all 737s should be inspected if they had exceeded 55,000 flights. Most at risk were the first 291 off the assembly-line, built in the late sixties and early seventies and produced with a cold bonding lamination process which has since been abandoned. Evidence of cracking and delamination were discovered in 60 of the early 737s, all of which had been in the air more than 55,000 times.

A year earlier, Boeing had experimented with the fuselage of a 737 to demonstrate that it could tolerate 130,000 flights, through all sorts of atmospheric conditions, from clear air turbulence to gales and wind-shear, a violent downburst of air, undetectable on instruments, which can hurl a giant jet plane to the ground if the aircraft is at low altitude. All Boeing aircraft were supposed to be able to withstand stress 50 per cent greater than that envisaged during its normal lifetime: before the first 737 was released from its Seattle workshop, this resistance was proven with a prolonged structural test.

In 1970 commercial jet aircraft were being retired at the age of five. Now Boeing anticipated that thirty-year-old 747s would be commonplace very soon.

At the beginning of March 1989 a conference was held in London to discuss airframe corrosion and methods of control. Lord Brabazon explained to the gathering that equipment for inspecting airframes was all too often developed as a spin-off from other scientific engineering applications. 'This is a reversal of the normal situation with aerospace products,' he alleged. 'Air safety standards must not only be maintained, but, with the ever-increasing demand on services, must be steadily improved.'

Between September 1980 and June 1984, the number of mechanics employed at US line stations (maintenance depots) was reduced by some 4300, a direct consequence of American deregulation, though by late 1989 deregulation was also becoming an issue in Australia, where commercial pilots were earning 75 per cent more than their British counterparts. A British charter pilot could be flying 900 hours a year, whereas in Australia 500 hours was the limit.

American airlines did add to the maintenance staff at their depots towards the end of the decade 1980–90, but the overall decrease of repair engineers throughout the airlines in the United States was 3000. The number of FAA inspectors totalled 2012 in 1979, with 237 airlines to monitor. By 1984 that number had been pruned to 1332, brought about by budget cutbacks under the Reagan administration. Although there were many fewer FAA inspectors, there were considerably more airlines to supervise – 407 compared with 237 just five years earlier. Airline revenue was up, but expenditure on maintenance was down.

A dangerous and unacceptable trend was the pressure applied to pilots to try to force them to fly aircraft, even though they believed them to be unsafe. Evidence of this nature came to light in 1987 during the testimony of two pilots who were appearing before a US Senate committee, convened to investigate deregulation. One had been a loyal servant of his airline for seventeen years, yet he had to report that twelve of his colleagues had been suspended for refusing to take planes from the terminal because the lives of passengers might be endangered. He told the committee that he had received a warning from his chief pilot for refusing to fly a plane which needed several parts replaced, including a hydraulic pump. The other pilot before the committee reported that he was admonished and sent home for refusing to 'sign off' an aircraft after landing. During the flight, one of the aircraft's navigational systems had become inoperative.

One pilot (not called before the Senate committee) with another North American airline has also confided that he had been regularly flying dangerous aircraft since deregulation 'and before'. His reasons for doing so were exclusively pragmatic. 'You don't win any friends or do your career any good by grounding airplanes; I found that out the hard way. If you refuse to fly a plane after the passengers have boarded and the baggage and food have been loaded, you're costing the company money; lots of it. No one comes up to you and says, "Congratulations! You may well have just saved the lives of 400 people. Let me pin a medal on your chest." You don't get that. What you do get is the chief screaming at you, "What the hell are you at? Are you trying single-handed to bankrupt the company? Don't you realize half the opposition is flying with kaput compasses? Do you think you'll get thanks from all those passengers who are going to be too late for their board meetings or miss out on contracts or a day's sunshine? If you do, you're nuts. They're more likely to try to sue you. If you won't fly that airplane, there are a thousand out-of-work, hungry pilots who will. Have you given thought to your pension? If I have to bomb you, I'll see you're blackballed throughout the industry." I've had all of that at different times. Instead of a medal pinned to your chest, it's a knife in the back.

'"Be a company man," I was advised. "Oil the wheels. Don't make waves; that's the way to promotion." Even my wife is on the company side. I go home and pour out my frustration to her and she berates me for being a "perfectionist" and an "idealist". I'm in as much trouble as if I'd been with a whore. The truth is, we're both victims of a legal form of blackmail. I'm held hostage by all the material trappings that go with the job: a large house, swimming-pool, three cars, kids at college and cheap holidays virtually anywhere in the world. My wife says, "Think of me, think of the kids, think of what you could be sacrificing, think of our future. Don't throw it all away now. You haven't long to do."

'And I say, "But one day I may walk out of that door and never come back. All you'll get is a phone call from the chief, saying, 'I'm sorry.

He was a helluva guy. He died the way he would have wanted to go. Be proud.' " It would be grotesque movie cliché all the way. Then she accuses *me* of emotional blackmail, of dramatizing, of not living in the real world. And that's the way we go on.

'I'm sure many of my colleagues are going through all the similar soul-searching, and management know exactly what the domestic pressures are. My chief would hold his own against any poker player in the world. And what do I do? I go on flying unsafe airplanes. I make my reports and leave it to others to decide whether or not the airplane is fit to fly. I play the American national game of passing the buck.

'Passengers get solace from the myth that the airplane they're sitting in must be safe or the pilot wouldn't be prepared to take it off the ground. That really is living in a fool's paradise. I've flown fully loaded airplanes aware that there's something so seriously wrong with them that the consequences could be fatal; I've resigned myself to playing roulette for a living, but the passengers have not made that choice. They haven't paid to play the tables, yet that's exactly what they're doing. The passengers still believe that safety comes before everything, even the dollar. Well, they're being deluded, or deluding themselves. It hadn't used to be that way, not before deregulation, but now it is – sadly. Now it's a free-for-all, and to a large extent safety has become a fingers-crossed exercise.

'Whenever I fly an airplane that's flawed, I console myself with the thought that the odds are still stacked in my favour. After all, just reflect on the state of some of the shot-up bombers that staggered back to base in Vietnam, Korea and the Second World War. After each flight, as I vacate the cockpit, I say to myself, "OK, now it's down to the next man." My monthly pay cheque is supposed to convince me that I'm making the right decisions.

'When I retire, I shall write a book. Until then, I'm a slave to my domestic situation and the responsibility to my family. My wider responsibility, including to myself, will have to wait awhile, I'm afraid, until it can be afforded.'

It is easy, and tempting, to dismiss this kind of account as the malice of an employee with a grievance, someone, perhaps, who has been continually overlooked for promotion: indeed, it would be both soothing and convenient to be able to reach that conclusion. Unfortunately, the facts deny us that comfort. The pilot who confessed to bowing to commercial pressures was, at the time of writing, one of the highest paid captains in the world. His military record with the US Air Force was exemplary, and during his many years as a civilian pilot there was no noted attitude problem; not one blemish to his name. In any case, too much of what he said had the ring of truth when matched against other substantiated evidence. An instance documented by the FAA concerned a 727 which was allowed to make two flights while the fuselage was severely distorted as the result of a heavy landing. The damaged aircraft was only grounded when the maintenance engineers of another airline inspected it in Chicago and would not declare it airworthy. The mechanics found several snapped supports inside the hull and the outer skin was wrinkled in a number of places to a length of seven feet. The whole structure had been knocked out of shape, yet that plane would have gone into the air yet again if it had not been summarily grounded by the contract maintenance team at Chicago's O'Hare.

The International Air Transport Association's annual conference in 1987 was held in Caracas, where the chairman of the technical committee had this to say: 'Currently, many engineering and maintenance departments are confronted with older aircraft types with a very large number of airborne hours, including re-engined airframes extending their useful lives even further into the future. At the same time, new aircraft types with highly sophisticated technology are being introduced into airline fleets. Both of these trends will produce extra and sometimes new problems, which are often difficult to solve.

'At the same time, many airlines are reducing manpower. These reductions may seriously affect professional engineering staffing. There is no question that productivity of engineering and maintenance departments had to be increased and new technology has produced many benefits. However, we must recognize the trends and take positive action to preserve the levels of safety and reliability.' He feared that further staff cutbacks would 'reduce reliability and eventually erode safety margins too much'.

Whenever there is an accident, the investigators take into account every possibility; nothing is automatically excluded, however obvious the cause may appear. At Lockerbie, they looked not only for evidence of a bomb, metal fatigue and corrosion, but also probed the crew's background and flight-deck behaviour, not because there was any suggestion of human error, but due to the emergence of a relatively new menace: the drunk or drugged pilot.

6 JUST ONE FOR THE RUNWAY!

'Good evening. My name is John. I'm an airline pilot and I have a drink problem.'

Thus began the Thursday evening meeting of an Alcoholics Anonymous group in Surrey, two women and sixteen men, including session leader Andrew. No surnames or addresses are ever used, thus avoiding identification and possible blackmail.

'I wouldn't be taking this chance if I thought anyone might find out who I really am,' John was to say later that evening in 1989 over a drink of orange juice. His testimony was prosaic and free of histrionics.

'I've lost everything, except my job. My wife is living with another man. She took my children and wants a divorce. I can't afford to fight her because she's threatened to contact my company unless I make it easy for her. I've been to the bottom of the pit. I've felt sorry for myself. I squandered an amount of money that to many people would be a fortune.

'We had to sell our home to pay our debts . . . my debts. But I'm determined to survive, though I could not have done so without a couple of very special friends, who carried me for all of six months. Now I recognize what I am, which is nine-tenths of the battle won, so I'm assured. I never thought I'd wind up at a place like this. It wasn't until I hit rock bottom that I sought professional help, and then it was reluctantly. I still tried to fool myself that AA was for other people, not me. I hate myself. I'm ashamed of myself. Some days I wish I was dead. Some days I made a decision to end it all, but I'm too selfish for that. I feel very uncomfortable and self-conscious standing here, and it would be a lie if I said I felt it was doing me good.

'But I *am* here, even though I walked up and down outside for half an hour before coming in. I can't sink any lower. Life can only get better, but I have to do it mostly alone. Other people, like yourselves, can help me only so much.'

He spoke like someone treading carefully along a ragged route of stepping-stones, his speech maundering and distant, and his words agonizingly long in surfacing, his head hung low and his eyes continually darting for cover. Then he sat down. No one reacted. Andrew thanked him for his contribution and the spotlight focused elsewhere.

It is an alarming thought that the man in charge of your fate at 30,000 feet might be an inveterate alcoholic. But as Laurie Taylor pointed out, 'If drink and drugs, such as cocaine, have reached the industrial boardroom, it would be naïve to suppose there are not cases of pilots indulging. After all, a pilot is an ordinary member of society, just like anyone else and just as susceptible.'

Even if pilots are identified as alcoholics, they are not automatically fired. There are numerous case histories of alcoholic pilots being rehabilitated and returned to the flight-deck. Airlines are reluctant to write off the vast financial outlay that goes into training flight crews. Airline medical officers, rehabilitation centres, Alcoholics Anonymous and airline management work together to save, if at all possible, a pilot from being lost to his profession due to drink.

I first met John in the seventies when fate placed us next to one another on a transatlantic flight from New York, while he was returning 'dead-head' (as a passenger) to London: he had flown the plane on its outward journey the day before. One could not have wished for a more convivial and entertaining companion. Not unnoticed by me, however, were the six miniature bottles of whisky, plus the wine and brandy with the meal, which he consumed with gusto. Nevertheless, a friendship was forged and we kept in touch, though not during what he refers to as his 'lost years'.

What happened to John is only exceptional because he is a pilot.

'I telephoned my wife to let her know I'd reached Heathrow. It was something I always did; it was ritual. The most hazardous section of any trip is the drive from home to the airport. The flight to Miami that day would be the easy bit, or so I reckoned.

'An hour and a half earlier, I'd kissed my wife goodbye, told her to look after herself, and promised to bring her something back from Florida: whenever I flew abroad, I always brought back a present. I wasn't buying her off with gifts; it was just a gesture, acknowledging that it could be a rotten life being married to a pilot, but it paid the mortgage, school fees and private medical insurance. You get what you pay for and everything has a price. A succession of enforced separations was the price my family paid for a high standard of living.

'On that all-important morning, when my world was pulled from under me, my wife didn't sound herself on the phone, to such an extent that at first I thought I had a wrong number. Eventually I said, "Is there anything wrong?" "Nothing's wrong," she replied. "Everything's fine. It's been a long time since I felt this good." Something was going on in her head, but I hadn't time to try to find out what. "I'll call you from Miami," I said.

'Her retort pole-axed me; it really did. "Don't bother. I shan't be here." Her voice was cold and detached, with an unrecognizable quality, a bitchy hardness I'd never encountered before. I can remember thinking to myself that she must be going to visit her parents, but normally she would tell me in advance of those sort of arrangements because she had always been very orderly and disciplined. Then she spelt it out for me. "I'm leaving you. For good. It's over."

'I tried to say something; I don't know what, but she was no longer there. The line was dead.

'In all honesty, I can't remember a thing about that flight to Miami. I was mentally and physically numb; I felt nothing. A corpse at the control couldn't have been less efficient. I, just as much as the airplane, must have been on auto-pilot from start to finish: everything's a blank with me until I reached my hotel in Miami. I suspect that I delegated take-off and landing to my right-hand man, but that's only supposition.'

At the hotel, John went straight to his room and dialled direct to his home in England, where it was 11 p.m., but there was no reply, not even from the answerphone. Sleep had never come easily to him after crossing time zones, but that night he was kept awake for very different reasons.

'I was in a daze. My head was full of questions. I kept asking myself what I'd done wrong. I thought we were happy. We rarely fought and my wife had never intimated she was dissatisfied with her lot. I tried hard to laugh it off, telling myself something must have upset her and she was throwing a tantrum, though deep down I didn't believe any of my own kidology. She wasn't emotionally inclined; she didn't fluctuate between highs and lows.

'By midnight, I knew sleep was out of the question. I hadn't eaten since breakfast, but I wasn't hungry; not a bit, so I decided on a drink, something I'd never done before on a one-night stopover, however bad my insomnia. People never seem to appreciate that air-crew suffer jet-lag just as much as anybody else: at least the passengers usually have a few days to recover, but the pilot may well be flying back the next day, which in itself is a whole safety area to be explored. You can well do without a sleepy pilot at the controls in an emergency; at any time, for that matter.

'I put on casual civvy clothes and took a taxi ride into the city, where I loitered like a pimp on Flagler Street for almost half an hour, before going into a neon-lit bar, a seedy place, seething with Spanish.

'I ordered a Budweiser beer, the macho stuff, determined to make it last, hoping it would help me to relax and induce sleep. I was shocked by the speed with which it disappeared. "Another?" the barman – a Cuban, I suppose – asked. I nodded. After two beers on an empty stomach, I was feeling brighter. Much better. My feet were tapping to the beat of music I would never normally dream of listening to.

'After the third beer, I started talking to the woman next to me at the bar. Spanish was her first language, but her English was passable for that time of night and my condition. She was drinking tequila, something I'd never had, so I tried it as a chaser, then had another, and another, and another. I really got smashed and I have to confess I was tempted when my companion asked if I was "looking for business". Looking back, I think I said, "No thank you" only because I knew I'd never make it. I only just made it to the taxi before throwing up. I was a mess. I just prayed no one would recognize me as I crawled back into the hotel, the sun already climbing over the ocean.

'Although I collapsed on to my bed, I didn't sleep for more than a couple of hours, and even then it was fretful and feverish. I felt awful, wretched. I was still wearing the clothes of the night before and the acrid smell of dried vomit was everywhere. The room was spinning, my eyes wouldn't focus and raging toothache of the brain is the only way aptly to describe my headache. I flopped back on the bed, abandoned by my legs, and tried to phone home, but I kept punching the wrong numbers. I never travelled without a packet of paracetamols for head-ache and something else for upset stomachs, so I plied myself with a selection of both.'

It was midday before his physical co-ordination was sufficiently restored to enable him to walk, and his vision was improving, though still remaining blurred. He had no appetite but had the sense to know he must eat. The co-pilot called from the poolside, suggesting they lunch together. John declined, using the excuse that he was 'bogged down with paperwork' and also had to go shopping for a gift for his wife. 'I'll catch up with you later,' he said, angry with his voice for sounding just what it was; the voice of a man with a mega-hangover.

From room service he ordered an all-day breakfast, his liver craving fat and sugar. He kept down very little of the meal and began to think about reporting sick, pretending to have gone down with food-poisoning or some form of stomach virus, endemic in the sub-tropics. But when his wife was still not answering the telephone, he decided that nothing would stop him from flying home that evening.

By mid-afternoon, after a cold shower and a shave, his headache was tolerable and full vision had been restored, though he remained both physically and emotionally shattered, yet too overtired and overwrought for sleep.

During the afternoon he dozed on the balcony, before changing into his uniform. A look at himself in the bathroom mirror endorsed his worst fears: the black cushions under his bloodshot eyes and the jaundiced complexion of his puffy face were a giveaway, so he put on sunglasses before joining the crew in the hotel lobby, making a comment about jet-lag and the heat having kept him awake. 'Another damned kaput air-conditioner!' he lied, enlarging the cover story.

'During the pre-flight instrument checks that evening, I found it increasingly difficult to concentrate. Whenever I looked up to the overhead instrument panels, I went dizzy. And then, on the way to the runway for take-off, in the hurry to catch a tight slot, I made a wrong turn on to the taxiway and failed to make a radio frequency change, similar mistakes to those of Northwest pilot John Maus just before his airplane crashed at Detroit in August 1987. My co-pilot gave me an odd look, but said nothing, though I knew exactly what he must have been thinking. By the time we were starting our roll, I was overheating and in a sweaty lather from head to toe, but worst of all was the uncontrollable tremble afflicting both hands. I shouldn't have been there, but it was too late for the honourable course of action, so I just had to bluff it out.

'Quite early into the flight, long before commencing our Atlantic crossing from Newfoundland airspace, I went walk-about, handing over to my first officer. I went downstairs, spoke with every passenger in first class, and was kept talking for about five minutes by a film star, a very nervous flyer who wanted reassuring that every nut and bolt was secure, the wings weren't about to drop off, the four engines were running smoothly and there hadn't been a bomb threat. Thus assured, she went back to her free champagne, which gave her more confidence than I ever could. She did not think to ask about the condition of her captain, which she doubtlessly took for granted.

'It was neither a sensible nor convenient time for me to be doing my rounds. Usually a captain will wait until the meal is over and the trays have been cleared away before embarking on his public relations exercise, equivalent to a politician's baby-kissing drill. The gangways were blocked with flight attendants and their drinks trolleys, but I had to keep on the move and on my feet or I knew I'd crash out and it was too soon for that.

'I exchanged a few words with a number of passengers in coach class when I found my progress impeded by a trolley on which were stocked the bottles of wine and spirits. A young female flight attendant was stretching across a couple of seats to serve passengers in the central section. I looked at those bottles and not only wanted but needed. The flight attendant pushed the trolley another row towards the rear, turning to me and saying, "Do you want to squeeze by, Captain?" "Carry on," I replied. "I'm in no hurry. I'm just stretching my legs and saying hello to a few people."

'Everyone around was busy opening cans and bottles. As the flight attendant leaned forward to take another order, I bumped against the trolley, simultaneously slipping a bottle of whisky into my trouser pocket with almost Fagin-trained sleight-of-hand. I scanned the surrounding faces for a tell-tale reaction; no one had seen.

'Flushed with an equal mixture of success and shame, I beat a retreat to the front toilets, where I locked myself in and opened the bottle of whisky, my hands shaking more than ever now. As I put the open neck of the bottle to my lips, I caught sight of myself in the mirror, and it was as if I was witnessing a crime, but I was neither culprit nor victim, simply an innocent bystander who didn't want to get involved. After hesitating momentarily, I took a sip. Just one. It was warm, soothing, strong, masculine. Then I tossed back my head. Now it was burning, all the way down. Handsome! Straight down to my socks and straight up to my brain! I finished the entire contents in three neck-jerks, then dumped the empty bottle in a disposal unit, pushing some tissues down to make sure it was well and truly concealed.

'My mouth was on fire. I couldn't believe how quickly it was getting into my bloodstream. But now I had to be very careful. I guessed my breath was reeking of alcohol, so I returned to the cockpit, murmured something about having forgotten my washbag, and took my toilet kitbag from my case, saying I needed to freshen up. While I was gone, the other two might well have commented about my strange behaviour. That didn't matter. The world's full of eccentrics, even in aviation. I was the captain and I could command loyalty and obedience, just as long as my attitude was right for the part, but I was finished if anyone suspected I was drinking on the airplane.

'Back in the sanctuary of another toilet, I gargled with mouthwash, using more than normal to compensate for the special circumstances.

'By the time I took over the controls, the alcohol was really working wonders. My tiredness had gone, I was experiencing a high, because alcohol reacts much quicker at altitude. From being withdrawn and remote, I'd become voluble and animated. I hoped nobody noticed the sudden change in personality, but I didn't care too much. That's alcohol for you!'

John ate a full dinner that night on the plane, then put up his feet and managed about three hours' sleep, but when he woke he was feeling dreadful again; depressed, hung-over, head-throbbing and shaky. He asked for a sweet black coffee and took another two paracetamols. Twenty minutes later he was downstairs sneaking another bottle of whisky from a trolley, drinking it all neat in one go in a toilet and then using a mouthwash to mask the evidence.

'That gave me the pick-up I needed for landing at Heathrow. I talked to the passengers at greater length than was normal for me. My PA performance as we crossed the tip of Southern Ireland was something like a "Good morning campers, wakey, wakey!" announcement.

'I was crisp and punchy with air-traffic control, incisive and decisive in everything I did at the controls. If there had been an emergency on board, such as an explosion, I would have been a hero and saved everyone; that's how I was feeling; absolutely juiced-up, floating. And the landing was one of the softest and most delicate I'd ever made. But I was as pleased as hell to get away from Heathrow that morning. I collected my car and not until I filtered on to the M4 was I sure no one would tap me on the shoulder and say, "Excuse me, Captain, but would you mind coming this way to answer a few questions . . . ?"'

Before leaving Heathrow, he had tried telephoning home again, with no more success than when he was in Miami. The first thing he noticed on arriving home was the absence of his wife's car. He hurried indoors, calling his wife's name in every room and from the bottom of the stairs, but to no avail. On the dining-room table was an envelope addressed to him. It looked official and it was. The letter was from a firm of local solicitors, explaining that John's wife had gone to live with another man and she did not wish for any further contact with her husband. He would be hearing from them in 'the near future regarding arrangements for a fair division of the property and assets, including capital'. In the meantime, a third of his salary, before tax, would be expected as maintenance.

'To myself, I seethed, "Get stuffed!" I rang my wife's solicitor, demanding to know where she was and what was happening and why, but he hung up on me. Instead of immediately finding myself a solicitor, I went out and got drunk again; really smashed. I didn't sober up for a week; it was a marathon bender. Another solicitor's letter arrived, but I didn't want to face reality. Alcohol was my escape and I took it.

'I was all prepared for my next flight, which was to New York: I washed out a green Brut aftershave bottle and filled it with vodka. I'd never been a vodka drinker, but it is odourless, which was reason enough for my conversion.

'I drank very little the day before the flight to New York, resulting in my feeling very low and hardly sleeping at all that night. I was up at 5 a.m. For breakfast, I had sweet black coffee, toast and half a tumbler of vodka. I was drunk by six o'clock in the morning and brimful of confidence and bonhomie. Roll on, New York! Fun City, here I come! My God, when I think back!

'I'd never before flown with any of the crew on that fully-loaded 747, so they probably thought I was a mouthy extrovert by nature. Twice during that uneventful flight, I went to a toilet with my wash-bag and gulped from my vodka-loaded aftershave bottle. Each time, I brushed my teeth and gargled before returning to the flight-deck, investing in double insurance.

'When I was drunk, I didn't care that my marriage was over. When

I was sober, I was devastated. Hence my commitment to the bottle. It was the magic brew that made life rosy, when without it everything was blue.

'I became very adroit at camouflaging my drunkenness. While I was flying, I was like the drunken car-driver who is stopped by the police and sobers up instantly. I had amazing control over my mind and body, or so I thought. I suppose it's what every white-collared, middle-management drunk deludes himself into believing.

'After a while, I was having to get drunk just to be as sober as other people. I had become dependent. My life was plummeting and I couldn't see any way of arresting my fall. Apart from anything else, the will wasn't there.

'It was not long before my whole existence revolved around drink, although I would never have admitted the fact. If pressed, I'd have called myself a regular and consistent social drinker. I did most of my drinking in pubs and hotels, but I drifted away from my friends because most of them were pilots or ex-pilots or airline executives, and I didn't want them to see me the way I was, not because I was ashamed but through the instincts of self-preservation. I didn't want to run the risk of losing my job, my career, the only means I had of making a living.

'My doctor was also a friend of mine and he was the last person I wanted to meet in my local pub: the sight of me knocking back two whiskies with every pint of beer would certainly have sounded warning bells for him, especially as he knew all about my domestic traumas. So, true to the cunning fox I'd become, I kept to the suburban undergrowth.

'It's so obvious to me now that I had become as potentially deadly as any time-bomb on an aircraft . . . and had been that way within a few hours of the break-up of my marriage. Detonation grew closer every day as I burned up the fuse with an ever-increasing rate of furious drinking, yet not once considering it necessary to duck out of flying. In fact, I thought I was having a great time. I would have said my social life had improved beyond all recognition. My wild oats were being sown in middle age and I didn't give a damn about the consequences and penalties I was likely to reap; I lived only for the transient rewards and ephemeral pleasures.

'I began making mistakes on the flight-deck, but I was bold and brash enough to cover them up with a panache that made me elated. I eyed up female flight attendants, but I was always wary of taking the next step, just in case the word started getting around. But on stop-overs in the United States, especially in Miami and Los Angeles, I did start going to parties, all-night flings, after having struck up a number of dubious friendships with women crew members of other airlines, mainly American domestics.

'I experimented with things that, even now, I have immense difficulty coming to terms with and talking about. I'm talking about sniffing cocaine; insane things like that. Mixing cocaine and alcohol! Can you begin to imagine what was happening inside my head? I didn't feel so guilty after I'd come across a Mexican air crew who were using cocaine openly at a party, still wearing their uniform! That night disintegrated into an orgy of narcotics, booze and sex. At the time, it was the apex of my life, which just goes to show that I was standing on my head because, in retrospect, I realize it was my nadir.

'I'd reached the point at which I'd try anything. When I was drunk and still couldn't sleep, I took Valium, which my GP prescribed. In that respect, I was far from alone or exceptional. Many airline medical officers do not hesitate to put pilots on mild tranquillizers and sleeping tablets to overcome the problem of sleeplessness brought about by jet-lag.

'Of course, no medical officer would expect any pilot to be daft and reckless enough to mix the drugs with alcohol.

'For months I continued drinking every time I was in charge of an airplane, using my secret cask. There came a time when I was scared to be sober. I was terrified that I wouldn't be able to cope with untinted life: I needed a world of soft surfaces, all the sharp edges smoothed away. I was even frightened of flying; heights began to make me dizzy and enclosed places symbolized the traps of life. I seldom ate, but I didn't lose weight; instead, I became grotesquely bloated.

'Every time I flew into Los Angeles or Miami, I got high on cocaine and sniffed it before the return trip. My doctor noticed a rise in my blood-pressure; so, too, did the airline medical officer during a routine check-up. Even so, it was still within the upper limit of normal. The medical officer wanted to know if my life had changed dramatically: did I have any domestic or financial pressures? I shook my head to all those kind of questions, but I have a feeling notes were made, reminding him to keep an eye on me. I don't think he liked the look of my eyes, which had become yellowish, nor my tongue, which, if anything, was worse. I should imagine my dilated pupils also gave him something to think about, but I had such an establishment background, including unblemished service with the Royal Air Force as an officer. Hard drugs and alcoholism must have been a million miles away from the medical officer's thoughts.

'My wife learned all about my activities from a private detective she hired for a week. That week must have been an eye-opener for the private investigator and I'm very fortunate he was one of the reputable ones and didn't go to a Sunday newspaper or try to get money out of me. My wife was less scrupulous for a while, making it plain that if I didn't agree to all of her demands she'd post a copy of the private eye's written report to my employers, though she later relented. She had me where it hurts, but I was past caring, or so I thought.'

The turning point came at the end of an overnight flight from New York. At 2000 feet on the final approach to Heathrow, he was throttling back when everyone on the flight-deck was alerted by the automated cockpit warning system that a stall was imminent because the wing-flaps had not been extended to provide extra lift at minimum flying speed for the 747. The co-pilot shot John a hard, reproving look which seemed to protest, *How come I drew the short straw and was paired with you? There are less selfish ways of committing suicide, you know!*

'We had little leeway; scarcely any time in which to manoeuvre. The mistake was corrected by me, before it became an emergency, but I had the reflexes of a corpse. "How come you allowed it to happen?" I retaliated, reminding my first officer that responsibility was collective and any critical report by him of me would be tantamount to self-indictment.'

The expression on the younger man's face assured John that the message was understood and the matter would go no further. 'But I was wounded. My professional pride had been scratched and I was sore. I knew that my luck wouldn't last for ever. I wanted to get off the treadmill, but I didn't know how it could be stopped. I'd heard about airline pilots getting *the cure* through their medical officer and self-help groups, sometimes being rehabilitated and returned to flying duties after being grounded.

'Usually the airlines were first alerted by the pilots' families, mostly the wives, who would be worried sick. I'd never heard of a pilot voluntarily putting up his hand, without being cornered, and declaring,

"I think there's something you should know: I'm an alcoholic. I've been flying your airplanes stoned out of my mind. Perhaps I shouldn't fly today!"

'I didn't feel I could trust anyone in my airline with my secret, but I'd developed a frame of mind in which I desperately wanted to pull myself together. There were several reasons for my change of heart. I'd always been a perfectionist and that is perhaps why I reacted so badly when my wife walked out: I couldn't accept that I had failed in marriage. And after hitting the bottle, I couldn't settle for failure in my job. The perfectionist within made me hungry for success again.

'My solicitor could see that I was cracking up and I was beginning to worry that he might feel duty bound to make a confidential report to somebody. When you're on the bottle, you become very paranoid. I began to believe I was being followed everywhere. I'd walk through the cabin during a flight and my eyes would lock on to one face and that would be the enemy, the person who was out to get me. I would really build up an antipathy towards him or her; it wasn't always a man.

'My solicitor was working towards a reconciliation in my marriage, and that was also an incentive for me to change my ways, so I did it myself. One morning, while my hangover was at its peak, I just picked up the phone and called AA. Though I hadn't taken action until I'd hit rock bottom, fortunately it was in time . . . but only just. It was also lucky that I had not yet become addicted to hard drugs, or the task would have been doubled.

'My medical check-ups have shown me to be perfectly fit, physically. Emotionally, I'm now stable once more. What I do have to accept is that I shall always be just one drink away from alcoholism again; every alcoholic knows that.

'I'm sure I'm competent to fly and have the lives of hundreds of people in my hands. If I thought otherwise, I'd walk away from it, I promise you. Why should you believe me when I flew for so many months stoned? All I can say to you is that I've learned a hard lesson. I'm rehabilitated and reformed.

'I suppose the public would like to be reassured that I was a one-off; that I was the first and last alcoholic airline pilot. I'm afraid I can't give that comfort. Despite the stress, I do not believe pilots are more prone to drugs and alcohol abuse than the captains of industry and the professions. Neither is there any reason why they should be less prone.'

He is right, of course, which gives just cause for considerable concern. Other impeccable sources give further corroboration.

On 19 January 1988 a Fairchild Metro aircraft, on a commuter run in the United States between Denver and Durango in Colorado state, crashed into a mountain. Nine people died, including the two pilots. One survivor clawed his way through snowdrifts five feet high to reach a telephone to summon rescuers to himself and seven other passengers who survived. The United States federal air-safety investigators concluded that the propeller aircraft had been making a too fast and too steep descent. Their other discoveries were more startling.

Captain Stephen Silver, aged 36, was a cocaine addict. Not only was he hooked on cocaine, but he also regularly mixed hard drugs with alcohol. Only the night before the fatal flight, the FBI revealed, Silver and his lover had been 'sharing a bag of cocaine'. When Silver took off in that airplane he was stoned, not just from cocaine but also from drink. Somehow, just like John, Silver managed to keep his secret from his airline. He even falsified a medical certificate and doctored records to hide three automobile accidents while under the influence of alcohol.

'This is the first tangible evidence of what can happen when drugs are introduced into the cockpit of commercial aircraft,' said James Kolstad, the acting chairman of the US National Transportation Safety Board.

Silver had not been flying the aircraft at the time of the crash, presumably because he was too impaired. The investigators were in no doubt that the captain was incapable of monitoring and assisting his first officer, 42-year-old Ralph Harvey, as a direct result of the drugs and drink.

Kolstad said he hoped that mandatory drug tests could be introduced for commercial airline pilots, despite the opposition of the pilots' unions.

'I'm all in favour of random breath and blood tests for pilots,' said John. 'I don't care what the unions say, I know they make sense. Whatever my troubles, I know I wouldn't have turned to drink and drugs if I knew I was likely to be chosen for testing. Even if it only makes the public feel safer, it would be worth while, merely as a public relations exercise. But I know that it would be much more beneficial than that. There are men at the controls in the sky every day who are physically and mentally incapable. That cannot be good news for anyone. In those circumstances, extreme measures are called for. This is no time for diffidence.'

Kolstad's statement that the crash of the Fairchild Metro was 'the first tangible evidence of what can happen when drugs are introduced into the cockpit' is open to question.

In 1983 the autopsies on two cockpit officers, who had died when a cargo plane crashed while landing at Newark airport, established that the pilot had been smoking marijuana, almost certainly on the flight-deck. Maybe Kolstad was only counting passenger airplanes, though the phrase he used was 'commercial aircraft'. Of course, drugged or drunk mechanics and air-traffic controllers are just as potentially lethal as legless pilots.

In March 1985, a private plane had to take emergency avoidance action over New York to avert a head-on collision with a fast-closing DC-10, filled with passengers. The conduct of the air-traffic controller responsible for locking these two airplanes on a crash course was such that a medical examination was ordered by federal investigators. Doctors and detectives discovered that every day in the toilets at the airport he had been injecting three grams of cocaine into his bloodstream. That man was responsible for some of the busiest air-corridors in the world. In that environment a controller's job was tantamount to a professional juggler having to keep dozens of balls in the air at the same time without dropping one. He had also been undergoing routine medical checks and had been working alongside a team of astute and observant technicians, disproving the often heard statement that it would be impossible for a pilot to be on the flight-deck under the influence of drugs or drink without his fellow crew members being aware.

Another US airline lost $19-million-worth of business due to a marijuana-smoking employee, though there is the consolation that no lives were at risk. The employee worked the reservations computers and one day he was so fuzzy that he failed to load a tape into the system, which was then, due to his negligence, out of order for eight hours, resulting in the airline losing all its reservations for that day worldwide.

Hard drugs or alcohol have never been the known cause of any crash of a passenger airliner in the United Kingdom or Europe. However, this is not evidence of abstinence, merely proof of good fortune.

A British Airways stewardess told me about a drugs party just before Christmas 1988, in a bedroom at the five-star Sheraton Skyline Hotel,

Heathrow. The room was occupied by the flight crew of a Middle Eastern airline. But among the twenty-odd revellers that night were two BA pilots, one of whom was on duty the following day on a European route.

'I went to the party with one of the BA pilots,' the stewardess explained. 'He's married; I'm not. We'd been having an affair for about three months; we're not any more. As the night wore on, the party spilled into about three rooms. At first it was just booze that was being handed around, but after midnight everyone was sniffing cocaine. It wasn't being sold; it was being given away by one of the foreign pilots.

'This was nothing new. We were there for the coke. It was happening all over the world whenever we were on stop-overs. Usually the foreign flight crews bring the drugs into Britain. Overseas, it's no problem: anything you might ever want is freely available, especially in the United States.

'Both the BA pilots got high on a mixture of coke and alcohol. By two or three o'clock in the morning, the whole thing had degenerated into an orgy, which was par for the course. Most people in the airline business live on their nerves, so they're always searching for ways to unwind and drugs do help . . . short-term.

'One of the BA pilots – my lover, in fact – crashed out sometime between four o'clock and six, yet he was at the controls of a passenger aircraft that same afternoon. We actually had to drop him into a bath of cold water to revive him. My flat was not far away and we used a taxi to get him back there. We actually carried him out of the hotel, pretending he had a damaged foot.

'At my place, I fed him like a baby, but he couldn't keep any of it down. I tried to persuade him to report sick, but he wouldn't hear of it. In the end, he slept restlessly for a couple of hours, then woke up, had another bath – this time a hot one and of his own volition – took aspirin, shaved and put on his uniform.

'He was utterly incapable of driving a car, but felt confident to take up an airliner full of passengers, so I had to drive him to the airport. When he came back to me that night, he said his flights had been uneventful; nothing but routine.

'I was at a number of those sort of parties, but mostly abroad; usually in the States. There are drugs at almost every party these days. When you're overseas for the night, it's only natural to let your hair down.

There are parties every night; you don't have to look for them. You know exactly who to call. Sometimes there's a message waiting for you at the hotel when you check in.

'I've often been on flights when every stewardess has been hungover from the night before. That was dangerous: if there had been an emergency, we'd never have coped. Of course it's more serious if the flight crew are alcoholics or dabbling in hard drugs, but the only passengers being carried on any flight should be those who have paid for the privilege!'

Laurie Taylor served on committees which considered the question of pilots resorting to drink and drugs as a release from exhaustion. 'Sleep deprivation is an inevitability of modern airline schedules and the crossing of time zones,' he conceded. 'Pilots are always discouraged from taking drugs because of the side-effects, but sometimes they are the lesser of evils. If a pilot is not sleeping, he is advised to seek medical advice. It's a problem that comes with the job, so it's nothing to be self-conscious or defensive about. It's important for a pilot to plan his rest before a flight, but this is easier said than done, especially when you're on a one-night stop-over and your body's not attuned to the climate or the time cycle.

'Meditation techniques are taught, but they do not work for everybody. Some, it is inescapably true, become secret drinkers. There are those who turn to alcohol as a relaxant, hoping it will help them to sleep, while others look to it as a stimulant to keep them awake, enabling them to get through a shift that would otherwise be too daunting. These are not the only reasons, of course. Pilots have the lifestyles of high-powered executives and all the offshoot complications. There is frequently enormous responsibility and considerable knife-edge tension. Domestic disruptions and a blitzed social life are other influences. Where there is that kind of highly-strung and taut lifestyle, whether it be in the boardroom or the cockpit, there are going to be occasions when somebody snaps; when they come apart. But only as a very last resort will they be drummed out of aviation.

'It takes a small fortune to train each pilot. No airline wants to see all that money written off. The first pilot advisory group began in the USA. Now they exist in 65 countries. They are there for the treatment of pilots with either a drink or drugs problem, or both.

'Usually the tip-off will originate from a relative, a wife, or a concerned colleague. The subject is immediately removed from flying duties, investigated, and then given all the appropriate help that is required. He will be allowed back in the air only when everyone is satisfied he is no longer a risk to himself or those in his care. It is a big decision and, therefore, never taken lightly. Many pilots' careers have been saved due to prevailing enlightened attitudes and a sincere policy commitment to rehabilitation.

'After a long flight, all pilots are wound up like a coiled spring: I always was. It's impossible to go straight to bed and expect to sleep; you're wasting your time. I would always have a couple of beers after every flight, whatever the time of day, even if everyone else in the hotel was having breakfast. I would invite the flight-deck crew to my room and privately we'd crack a couple of cans of beer each, exchange stories about the flight, recount anecdotes, joke a bit and generally unwind. What we did was healthy. Our drinking was out in the open, and was, without a doubt, therapeutic. Two beers was my maximum and that self-imposed rule was never broken. But one never knows for sure what's going on in the heads of others.'

As mentioned earlier, 'pilot error' is the conclusion most often reached by investigators putting together the jigsaw of an air crash. The Safety Advisory Committee of the International Air Transport Association (IATA) studied for an attributable cause 38 accidents or serious reported incidents during 1984, and the human factor soared way above all else with 68 per cent, though the figures indicate that there was frequently more than one incriminating element. Aircraft and systems failures were in second place at 21 per cent, a long way behind. Bad weather, air-traffic controllers and airports came third with an 18 per cent score. In the United States mistakes by pilots contribute to the cause, on average, of at least 65 per cent of all accidents in each year.

In themselves, the figures mean little more than saying that all deaths last year were the result of hearts ceasing to beat. But what made them stop? 'Pilot error' is an outcome, not an explanation. How were the mistakes made when there is so much human and technical back-up; so much automated and inbuilt insurance? That is the real question which has to be addressed. The answers may enable lives lost in the past to result in lives saved in the future.

It is important, of course, not to become paranoid. For every inadequate pilot, there are a thousand irreproachable ones: typified by Eric Moody when he was in charge of British Airways Flight 009, a 747 en route from Kuala Lumpur, Malaysia, to Perth, Western Australia, on the night of 24 June 1982.

During the smooth, uneventful climb to a cruising altitude of 33,000 feet, there was no hint of what was to come. Dinner was served and cleared away. The 247 passengers prepared for the movie. Lights were lowered. For a number of the crew members, too, it was a chance for them to put their feet up.

Jakarta, Indonesia, was about 130 nautical miles to the north-west when British-born Captain Moody decided on a tour of his aircraft. He had just reached the first-class cabin when a message was conveyed to him that he was needed on the flight-deck. Still smiling and unruffled, he climbed the spiral staircase in the manner of a surgeon called to a cardiac arrest; hurrying without rushing. The ping of the 'fasten seat-belts' signs lighting up suggested to him that they were about to enter a zone of unforeseen turbulence.

Moody was puzzled, rather than alarmed, by the scene he encountered in the cockpit. Visibility from the windscreen had been reduced to zero by a rainbow glare resembling St Elmo's Fire. The captain settled himself into his harness and commenced a swift run-through of the instruments, paying particular attention to the weather radar. Despite the blinding glow outside, there was no instrument evidence of any mechanical malfunction, nor any warning on the radar of freak atmospheric conditions. Even so, there was no escaping the pungent smell permeating the aircraft. On leaving the first-class cabin, Moody had observed a white cloud – could be smoke, he thought – wafting from the ankle-high vents.

Suddenly the flight engineer shouted, 'Engine failure Number Four!'

Moody immediately went into the fire drill and everyone on the flight-deck followed to the letter his crisp, cogent orders.

A 747 can fly and land on three engines, two engines, and even one engine, if necessary. The odds of a four-engined modern jet airliner losing total power in all engines simultaneously are millions and billions to one.

In quick succession, Flight 009 suffered a second engine failure, then a third – and finally the 'impossible', being converted at 37,000 feet into a gigantic, eerily silent glider. Moody, like the captain of the

Titanic, found himself thrust into the very crisis which he had been led to believe, along with all his peers, was inconceivable.

In order to keep the aircraft under control, Moody tilted his 747 into a shallow nosedive, at the same time putting out an SOS signal, giving their bearing.

At 26,000 feet, the pressurization plummeted on the flight-deck and the crew put on oxygen masks, which immediately led to a further crisis. The first officer's mask proved defective and came apart in his hands and he began to lose consciousness. Now Moody had the choice of maintaining altitude for as long as possible, which would mean the loss of the services of his right-hand man, or hastening the descent in the hope that his first officer would be back in action within a few seconds. Moody opted for the second choice among evils.

After a steep fall of a further 6000 feet, the co-pilot recovered and was able to mend his mask, enabling Moody once more to reduce the angle of declination.

The entire flight crew were doing everything in their power to re-start an engine. Any engine. All they needed was one. One out of four. If not, they were doomed. And time was running out.

At 14,000 feet, the oxygen masks in the passenger cabins dropped from the overhead units. It was at this point that Moody decided the passengers should be told something, and also comforted. His five pithy sentences will go down in aviation history as a memorial to a breed who earn in one crisis every penny they will ever be paid in a lifetime.

'Good evening, ladies and gentlemen, this is your captain speaking. We have a small problem. All four engines have stopped. We are doing our damnedest to get them going again. I trust you are not in too much distress.'

Moody, his entire crew and all the passengers lived to relate the events of 24 June 1982. Engine Number Four was re-started as the aircraft was about to dip below 12,000 feet, getting perilously low. Ninety seconds later, the other engines spluttered back to life and Moody was able to start a steady climb to safety, at the same time making a run for the nearest place to put down, Jakarta.

Despite the restoration of power, Moody was flying virtually blind-fold; the windscreen had become more of a mask than a window on the world. As the plane came in to land, Moody had to squint through two minuscule clear specks in order to locate the runway lights. Even so, he made a classic touchdown, to a spontaneous round of applause from a grateful payload.

It was a further two days before the cause of the phenomenon was determined: they had flown into a dense cloud of volcanic dust, spilt into the atmosphere during the eruption of Mount Gallunggung in Indonesia, fouling the engine-blades and blanketing the windscreen.

All the fears about drunken pilots proved justified when the three members of the flight-deck crew of a Northwest Airlines Boeing 727 had their licences invoked in March 1990 for flying in the United States while under the influence of alcohol. The two pilots and a flight engineer were arrested in St Paul by an FAA agent, following a telephone tip-off to the agency. The aircraft, carrying 91 passengers and six crew, had just landed from Fargo. A few weeks later, a Northwest Airlines pilot was arrested for driving while drunk as he drove to the airport in St Paul, Minnesota, where he was due to take command of a passenger aircraft.

During the summer of 1990, commercial airline pilots were quizzed about their sex-lives and drug-taking habits. The sensitive, personal questions came in an eight-page questionnaire, composed jointly by the International Federation of Air Line Pilots' Associations, representing 70,000 pilots worldwide, and the RAF Institute of Aviation Medicine. The researchers were anxious to discover if there was a link between jet-lag, stress, alcohol and drugs, such as marijuana and cocaine, and the relatively premature death of pilots; 60 per cent die before they reach retirement. On average, commercial pilots die eight years earlier than other workers.

7 HUMAN FATIGUE

Fatigue wears out planes eventually and they crack up if not carefully nursed. The same applies to humans.

Airline pilots, weary from flying many hours across multiple time zones, often wander out of assigned air space, land on wrong runways and even fall asleep at the controls of planes carrying hundreds of passengers.

In 1988 the Associated Press conducted an investigation in the United States of the danger of tiredness on the flight-deck. A review of sleep research, and interviews with researchers and pilots, revealed that crew fatigue was a growing menace. Many of the respondents blamed deregulation in the United States for the increasing reports of air-crew fatigue there.

Deregulation brought a competitive 'Big Bang' in air travel and pilots accused airlines of trying to lower costs by working them harder, sometimes with schedules that kept them flying all night and into the next day.

US Government documents in the possession of Associated Press described some 600 incidents during a five-year period in which air crew cited fatigue for potentially dangerous mistakes in navigation, communications and piloting.

Fatigue had never been listed in the United States as the official cause of an air accident, although it had been linked with several major incidents. However, the Canadian Aviation Safety Board was citing fatigue as a relevant factor in the crash on 12 December 1985, at Gander, Newfoundland, involving a charter plane carrying 248 US servicemen and a crew of eight. The servicemen were on their way home for Christmas from the Middle East. The crew of the Arrow Air DC-8 had flown an exhausting schedule in the previous twelve days, including short lay-overs, multiple time zones and gruelling flight hours. Investigators concluded that icing and crew fatigue were joint causes of the fatal crash as the DC-8 was taking off at Gander on the last leg of its flight to Fort Campbell, Kentucky.

'When you're fatigued, you get distracted easily,' said Dave Linsley, a United Airlines captain and a spokesman for his union. 'You'll miss a radio call, or enter the wrong data or read it wrong. Then you get into physical problems, hitting the wrong switch, over-controlling the aircraft, sometimes turning the wrong way or busting [violating] an altitude. It comes down to both of you sitting at the controls and shaking your heads to stay on top of things.'

Some two dozen pilots were interviewed by Associated Press and many of them admitted falling asleep at the controls.

'I've flown trips that weren't safe because we were all so exhausted,' said a Northwest Airlines captain. 'I've flown trips that leave at midnight with three legs [take-offs and landings] and you arrive at noon, feeling like a piece of dog-meat.'

Throughout the world pilot fatigue has become recognized by the experts as an underestimated danger. 'I am convinced that serious errors occur that are facilitated by fatigue, sleep loss, jet lag, whatever you want to call it,' said Curtis Graeber, a psychologist with NASA, the US space agency.

According to the US National Transportation Safety Board, the crew of a China Airways 747 from Taipei to Los Angeles on 19 February 1985 relied too long on autopilot to adjust the plane's bearing after a simple engine flame-out. When the captain finally took over, the 220-ton aircraft rolled into a six-mile nosedive, approaching the speed of sound before control was regained 9500 feet above the Pacific. The aircraft was extensively damaged and two people were seriously injured.

Fatigue was also suspected of having been a significant factor when on 25 September 1978 a Pacific Southwest 727 collided with a private plane near San Diego, California. The previous night the crew of the 727 had been off duty for barely seven hours. Sleeptime was estimated at a maximum five and a half hours. On the morning of the crash the captain was heard saying on the cockpit tape-recorder, 'I'm dragging. It was a short night.' The crash killed 146 people. 'Pilot error' was the recorded reason for the accident, which is true but not the whole truth.

'The problem with fatigue is it's not a bent piece of metal,' said Dr Stanley Mohler, a former FAA official, who has been in charge of

Aerospace Medicine at Wright State University in the United States. 'It's not a liquid that can be analysed in the laboratory.'

Some 600 accounts of missed approaches, near misses and narrowly avoided 'tragedies', all attributed to fatigue, came from voluntary pilot reports filed with the Air Safety Reporting System, an office run by NASA for pilots who want to confess to mistakes and report treacherous conditions, without fear of retribution.

Here are three examples of typical accounts logged with NASA:

1 The co-pilot of a 'cross-country' 747 in February 1987 looked up from his coffee cup to see that his captain was asleep at the controls. The aircraft was already well into its descent into Boston.

2 In March 1987 an airliner bound for Baltimore from Los Angeles dropped 4000 feet below its assigned altitude as the crew slept, the plane getting so close to another aircraft that alarms were set off in air-traffic control.

3 In November 1988 the co-pilot of another jet airliner began a take-off roll at Fort Lauderdale, Florida, without having set the wing-flaps. He was warned by the cockpit sirens and the take-off was aborted just in time.

'It is quite sobering to consider that the combination of fatigue and distractions could so easily cause a breakdown in my own cockpit discipline,' wrote one co-pilot, who had flown for three days with little sleep.

Aircraft do not crash because pilots are tired, most experts are agreed. Fatigue becomes a killer when it coincides with some other problem, such as freak weather or mechanical failure.

The Associated Press summed up its survey this way: 'On paper, FAA flight rules seem favourable to pilots. Domestic pilots are limited to eight hours' flight-time a day; overseas pilots fly no more than twelve. All pilots must get at least eight hours of rest between flight sequences. However, the regulations count only scheduled flight-time, not the hours spent on the ground between flights. So scheduled turn-arounds and unscheduled delays can push a crew's day up to sixteen hours.'

The consequences of human fatigue have been known to the airline industry for many years. Much research has been conducted at the Institute of Aviation Medicine, attached to the Ministry of Defence at Farnborough, Hampshire, and in the United States at the aerospace medicine unit at Wright State University. Progress is being made as pilots become more willing to report themselves, as well as their colleagues, on condition that the information is treated in confidence.

One British Airways 747 pilot declared himself unfit to fly at the climax of a three-week period during which he had passed through 56 time zones. In a report to his union, he said, 'Our licences give us responsibility towards our passengers and air safety, and I feel unable to discharge this duty in my zombie-like state.' His complaint was respected and he escaped punishment.

One must admire the probity of pilots who are prepared to make a stand, and sympathize with those who are victimized when they do. One pilot employed by an African airline was suspended from duty and officially charged with 'sabotaging the economic interests of the state'. There had been long delays and the pilot unilaterally decided to ground his aircraft so that his crew could rest because they were 'asleep on their feet'.

Another African airline, which thought nothing of imposing a twenty-hour daily flying shift, sacked a pilot for making an emergency landing when the entire flight-deck crew were seeing double owing to excessive tiredness. Both the pilot and co-pilot were accused of 'economic sabotage' and the pilot was even threatened with execution if found guilty. After protests from their representatives in the industry in their own country, they were released from jail and never brought to trial, though a permanent ban on flying remained, effectively reducing them to poverty.

In another incident, a British Airways captain, who had not slept for twenty-four hours, fell asleep just as his 747 was starting its final approach to Los Angeles.

Both pilots in the cockpit of another transatlantic flight in 1981 were asleep for twenty minutes before waking with a start when bells sounded, warning them that they were travelling too fast. This was revealed the same year in a confidential report made to the Institute of Aviation Medicine, Farnborough. 'I shudder to think what could have happened,' one of them wrote in his frank summary to the Institute.

These were the words of a British Airways captain in one of his 'voyage reports', regular summaries handed in after each flight: 'I am now seven hours into a Seattle flight. I feel tired, dried-out and numb. The danger is that you make incorrect decisions when tired. Please take notice to stop this dangerous practice at once.' By *dangerous practice*, he meant the rostering of flight duties which made for difficult sleeping patterns.

Having time off between flights is counter-productive if the crew are jet-lagged and therefore cannot sleep. The result is that they are twice as tired when eventually they return to the flight-deck than if they had turned round and flown home directly after their outgoing journey. Sleep and effective recovery are the crucial factors, not rest periods – which can be a misnomer. Sleep is not guaranteed just because a rest period is set aside.

In 1981 a report on crew fatigue was presented to BALPA, the British Air Line Pilots' Association, by Neil Shaw, then chairman of the British long-haul pilots' group. At BALPA's conference that year, Shaw said the fact that pilots had been prepared to put their signatures to such a strong critique was 'alarming proof of the situation that exists in civil airlines; political dynamite, in my opinion. If we released any of these, I think there would be a public outcry.' Strong stuff indeed, especially when considering the conventional reticence of the profession. Neil Shaw implored pilots to unite to 'put a stop to the economy-minded madness which is beginning to erode all our safety standards'. The British Civil Aviation Authority (CAA) received a copy of the report on pilot fatigue, but chose not to act upon it: Lord King, chief executive of British Airways, was also lobbied, but did not respond. A CAA official commented at the time, 'Pilots, like everybody else, make mistakes; but few of them complain to us. What bedevils the system is that there has been no objective research into the causes and effects of long-haul fatigue.'

The CAA did recruit the help of the Farnborough Institute, where it was disclosed, 'We've had reports from wide-body, helicopter, charter and air-taxi pilots about whole crews being asleep and many reports detail errors that could be attributed to tiredness and the low motivation and level of care that it carries in its train. We have also been disturbed by the number of calls from crews who sound at their wits' end with fatigue and frustration because they feel nothing is being done for them, yet feel unable to tackle their companies for fear of being branded as troublemakers and jeopardizing their jobs.'

A statement from the CAA claimed there was 'no evidence available to show any particular group of pilots' was being 'pushed regularly to the limits' of what was permitted, which appeared to be in conflict with the opinion of those at the sharp end of the industry. In the wake of that statement by the CAA's director general, a charter pilot wrote to his union: 'The only effective means of learning what is going on would be for him to attach himself to a crew for a week in the summer period and experience at first-hand all the frustrations, excessive hours and the inevitable roster changes that we experience throughout the day and night. Everyone at the operating end is under enormous pressure. The ground engineers work with the lack of spares and lack of aircraft-time on the ground. Consequently, the flight crews – already over-worked and ridiculously understaffed – have to take into the air aircraft that have page after page of "allowable" defects. It can take twenty to thirty minutes to read and assimilate them all and discuss the abnormal operating techniques required as a result of each one of them.'

Because of scheduling, pilots are frequently taking planes into the air just at the hour their heads are ready for the pillow. If a pilot on a long-haul service reaches his final destination late at night, it could be another twenty-four hours before his next flight. On paper, that seems reasonable, even generous, but in practice it is flawed. 'The worst possible set of circumstances,' said Laurie Taylor. If he is lucky, the pilot falls asleep almost immediately, maybe even achieving a straight eight hours. The trap is that he has then been awake for sixteen straight hours when it comes to his next take-off. And it would be another eleven hours, maybe, before he is landing again.

Captain Douglas Wyles was, until October 1981, the safety representative of British Airways' long-haul pilots. He is on record as saying, to John Pilger in the *Daily Mirror*, 'Pilot fatigue is a timebomb. It was only due to massive complaints from pilots and a story in the Press that a whole crew had fallen asleep on the flight-deck, that an inquiry was set up in 1972. The experts found that a Britannia crash, which killed 100 passengers, was almost certainly due to flight fatigue, and this contradicted the official finding. Our real problem began in 1979 when, instead of reducing the work-load with the new long-range aircraft, the union and British Airways agreed to increase productivity, which allowed the normal working period to increase from twelve to thirteen hours. Before that, a pilot got acceptable periods of time off between flights, but as the fuel crisis pushed up the price of fuel, the object was to get the maximum out of the crew.

'Of course flying is tiring, but what the rostering pilots now have to endure can produce an unusual type of fatigue; the feeling of a head cold, very low body temperature and, in extreme cases, nausea. You have a condition as if you are in limbo and you only really recover during annual leave.

'I was the captain of a 747, flying with an engineer who had crossed 33 time zones in nine days. We were approaching Washington and I asked him for the Let Down Charts. I quickly realized he had given me the charts for Los Angeles. I sent him to lie down for two hours. The man was exhausted.'

In 1980, Captain David Miners, a British pilot, wrote a memo to his union, which included this sweeping condemnation: 'The 1979 agreement was the biggest confidence trick in BALPA history and the most devastating setback to our working conditions ever. The psychological demands of the agreement have eroded safety levels to an unacceptable degree. To the United States pilots' union, we are a joke.' Miners became chairman of the British long-haul pilots' group. He was vice-chairman when he wrote in a report, entitled 'Pay and Productivity 1979/80,' of the 'unbearable level of fatigue', which he went on to attribute to the 'new scheduling agreement'.

'When we discuss fatigue, we don't talk to pilots, we talk to industrial relations managers, who, in their own words, admit lack of knowledge in the field,' Neil Shaw wrote in a 1981 issue of *The Log*, the British pilots' journal.

When questioned in 1983 about pilots' complaints and fears, British Airways countered with, 'BA operations are well within limits laid down by the CAA and the Flight Time Limitations Board. The interests of our flying crew are protected by a long-range agreement concluded with BALPA. Pilots have an arrangement with the airline under which they choose which flights they will undertake. This is known as the Bidline System. We have no shortage of pilots who choose to operate on long routes. Any member of a crew can remove himself from a trip if he feels he is too tired.' The last sentence of that statement provoked a scornful reaction from pilots, one of them putting in writing: 'The occasions of fatigue are too numerous to mention. If we did things like this of our own volition [removing themselves from a flight due to tiredness], we would be accused of being negligent and stupid, with no thought of passenger safety.'

The use of powerful drugs by pilots to overcome insomnia due to jet-lag is something of a modern trend. The older type of barbiturate-based sedatives were hardly ever chanced by pilots because of the savage side-effects, including residual drowsiness and the equivalent of a hang-over for the most part of the next day. But a new generation of tranquilli-zers, the offspring of Valium, has changed all that.

By the late 1980s research by the Farnborough Institute scientists showed that the medical officers of most of the world's leading airlines were prescribing tranquillizers and sleeping tablets to pilots who were unable to beat jet-lag without help. A medical officer with a US inter-national carrier explained his own policy to me: 'Businessmen are advised not to do business within 48 hours of dramatic time-zone manoeuvres. Yet a pilot can be expected to fly again within half that period. You can't run from jet-lag. We know it's there. It clobbers everybody, to varying degrees. When people cannot sleep, and know in advance because of their metabolism they're not going to sleep, they can do stupid things, like turning to alcohol or buying drugs on the black market, and that's dangerous. We're talking about "D for Dead" dangerous. Our pilots fly to places where hard drugs are easily obtain-able on street corners, in bars and even in hotel lobbies. For a man who hasn't slept properly for several nights, the temptation can be irresistible. Much better, therefore, that the whole issue should be out in the open. I'd rather fly any day with a pilot who's had a good night's sleep, even though it was drug-induced, than one who's crashing out, even before we're in the air. As long as they're taken in moderation, no pilot will become addicted to the drugs I prescribe.'

There were mounting fears by air crews that the drugging of pilots by airline medics would be a means of extracting excessive flying hours from them. 'We take yellow pills to go to sleep, then take red pills to stay awake,' said the senior captain of an international charter company. 'The RAF gave those pills to their transport crews during the Falklands War, but they soon looked like zombies. We want to know the long-term effect of guzzling those things. Only the other day, I found that one crew had totally mismanaged the balancing of fuel in the aircraft's tanks. I knew we were all tired, but when I checked I found we were 3000lb lighter in the centre tank than the two outers. Had we hit turbulence, the wings could have folded.'

A result of the pressure from so many quarters was the announcement in January 1989 by the CAA of new regulations to stop over-tired pilots flying when they should be resting. The aim was to prevent the creeping practice of airlines extending flying duties as part of routine, rather than in exceptional circumstances. There was no change to the maximum flying hours for flight crews of 100 hours per month and 900 hours per year, but commanders would not be allowed to extend flight duty periods if it would result in crews having a shorter rest allocation. The maximum crew standby period of twenty hours was to be reduced, and staff who planned duty rosters would have to be made fully aware of all the existing, and new, regulations.

The CAA also stipulated that duty rosters should be published in sufficient time to allow staff to plan rest and off-duty periods. A CAA spokesman said, 'We have to make sure that there is not an erosion of safety by people flying when they are too tired to do so. Extending flying duty hours has been overdone. We believe some operators are building these extensions into their schedules.' The CAA's new guide-lines also required airlines to consult their operational crews on new roster patterns.

A few months later the CAA made it known that the Farnborough Institute had been asked to develop a failsafe warning system to wake pilots who began to doze on the flight-deck. This move came in April 1989 in the immediate aftermath of a captain, in charge of a transatlantic flight, opening his eyes with a start to see that he was into the final stages of his descent into Gatwick, London; in sleepy confusion he operated the wrong controls. The equally startled co-pilot corrected the error just before touchdown, thus avoiding a certain crash involving a full complement of passengers.

The warning system the CAA had in mind would see all long-haul crews wired to hi-tech alarms, which would result in a bell ringing in the cockpit the moment anyone closed his eyes. Further indications of drowsiness, such as the head rolling forward or tilting to the side, would be detected by other sensors fastened to the body. Cockpit cameras recording all activity by the flight-deck crew was another CAA idea for consideration. A statement on behalf of the RAF scientists at Farnbor-ough said, 'It may sound a crazy idea, but we will be exploring head tilt, eye closure, physiological and activity monitors for the aviation industry.'

James Reason, a professor of psychology at Manchester University, is an authority on human fallibility. Much of his research has been on the subject of risk and how it is handled, and he specializes in the human factor in accidents. 'Fewer people are controlling more and more potential danger, and they're doing so often not under the best conditions,' he argued in *The Times* in April 1989. 'Immediately after an accident, there is always great emphasis on what the driver or pilot did. It gradually unfolds, however, that they are only the inheritors of a lot of pathogens that had been in the system a long time. One finds that there is a concatenation of diabolical coincidences. In retrospect, we exaggerate what people should have known. Few people have over-all views. Even if they had, many of the things that contribute to a disaster are not in themselves particularly unusual or dangerous. Even the best intentioned and most highly skilled people make mistakes. Indeed, if often goes with being highly skilled. Decision-makers must decide how to allocate their resources. If they give money to production, they can look to their productivity figures for immediate feedback. But the pursuit of safety gives negative feedback: you are winning when you hear nothing. It is not a very compelling reason for investing in safety.'

Laurie Taylor made this germane observation in his book on air safety: 'It is interesting to note that in the USSR, where the profit motive is not a factor, the crews of Aeroflot, the national airline, are required to stay at a "prophylactic sanatorium" for about twenty-four hours before a long flight, in order to undergo simple medical tests and to obtain rest in medically supervised conditions. Similar medically supervised conditions are imposed on the crews at their places of stop-over along the route, and it seems in some respects that the flight crews of the Soviet Union are better protected against fatigue than their Western counterparts, although at some loss of personal freedom.'

The late Captain John Maus has been blamed for the crash at Detroit on 16 August 1987 of Northwest's Flight 255 to Phoenix, Arizona. There is no doubt that the pilot's mistakes led to the McDonnell Douglas MD-80, one of the most sophisticated and computerized aircraft in service, failing to climb away from the Metro airport. The aircraft, carrying 147 passengers, six crew and two off-duty Northwest pilots taking a ride home, ran into difficulties the moment its wheels left the runway at 8.42 p.m. Maus's control-column began vibrating violently, the aircraft rolled to the right, then almost 30 degrees the other way. A computerized female voice on the flight-deck was warning, 'Stall!

Stall! Stall!' Fourteen seconds later, the plane was a mere 45 feet from the ground, when it should have been at an altitude of at least 600 feet. A split second later it struck lamp-posts in two car rental parking lots, finally cartwheeling on to the I-94 freeway. There was only one survivor, a four-year-old child. Two motorists were also killed.

In the subsequent investigation, experts of the National Transportation Safety Board (NTSB) could not at first believe the evidence salvaged from the wreckage: the flaps and slats on the wings had not been set for take-off.

The extending of flaps and slats prior to take-off and landing is as automatic to a pilot as it is for a car-driver to make sure the gear is in neutral before switching on the ignition. Extended flaps are necessary for extra lift at the two crucial points of any flight – the beginning and end.

Jim Cash, one of the NTSB's investigators, listened to the Cockpit Voice Recorder tape and was astonished to find no record of the crew's having performed routine instrument checks before take-off. The airline's rules demanded that the captain should call for a checklist run-down as they made their way to the runway. If for some reason the captain failed to initiate this procedure, it was the duty of the first officer – David Dodds that Sunday evening – to remind the pilot. Dodds had not done so.

The Digital Flight Data Recorder (DFDR) verified that the crew had performed all their duties punctiliously during their previous six take-offs and landings that same day. Something else emerged: on the way to Runway 3 Center, Maus had made a wrong turn to a taxiway and had also overlooked a radio frequency change, which should have been made on the ground. The errors were becoming a catalogue.

Autopsies were ordered on the pilots. Had they been drinking or taking drugs? No, those tests were negative. So, too, was the exploration for disease which might have affected their judgement and performance.

Maus had been a pilot for 32 years, with 20,859 unblemished flying hours to his credit. Confidential assessments of him by his peers had evoked such epithets as 'perfectionist', 'meticulous', a 'slave to the book' and 'painfully methodical'; scarcely the image of a slipshod man.

The investigators probed further. Maus had been a captain with Republic until the merger with Northwest in 1986, when he was one of 1000 pilots to be downgraded. His annual salary had been reduced by $2500, though this should not have meant any hardship; it still left him with an income of approximately $90,000 a year. Later, he had applied for the post of chief pilot in Las Vegas for Northwest, but was passed over.

Dodds had one small black mark on his record, but so minor as to be dismissed as inconsequential: in 1976 the FAA had fined him for flying over a football field without permission. Apart from that one indiscretion, he had been faultless since beginning his career.

Yet, on the evening of 16 August 1987, both these talented and responsible professionals made crass mistakes and neglected procedures which should have been executed as a reflex, even by novices. So rudimentary is setting the flaps for take-off that, at first, the investigators discounted this theory as a possible cause of the crash. 'For a long time we couldn't believe the guy didn't set the flaps,' said Ben Lightfoot, vice-president of technical services for Northwest. 'I think the evidence supports that now.'

No one will ever know for certain why those elementary mistakes were made, nor the reason for the crew's negligence in omitting the checklist routine from the pre-take-off preparations. Educated speculation is all we are left with. In view of the history of Maus and Dodds, and the testimonies of witnesses who were on earlier segments flown by the same crew, one is swayed to the view that the *real* cause of this crash was crew fatigue. There is no accusation, in this case, of the airline's having imposed excessive hours on the crew. But boredom can lead to drowsiness, or a lack of concentration, just as much as long working hours. Maus may have accepted that his career prospects had levelled out. Perhaps in that state of mind, even the routine of flying, for which he had lived so long, was becoming tedious. Add to that the fact that he had done it all six times previously the same day. Possibly he had become as automated as his machine.

Aircraft like the MD-80, which do almost everything for the crew, are seen by many pilots as hazardous rather than helpful. Their self-sufficiency can be taken for granted and over-relied upon, leading to a mental block or 'brain paralysis'.

An automated recorded voice, similar to the one which warned of the stall, should have alerted the crew to the non-extended flaps as they applied the power for their take-off roll, giving them ample time in which to abort safely, but the robot servant proved itself as fallible as its human master.

'With the increasing automation of the cockpit, the crew has been trained to depend more and more on the airplanes to tell them what's wrong,' said Lightfoot. 'In this case, there was no warning light, no indication of any failure. You come to rely on the plane to do that.' It is not unknown for pilots to disconnect these cockpit warning systems, considering them a nuisance, especially if they have been giving false alarms.

The American pilots' union (ALPA) dismissed as 'unthinkable' the proposition that Maus and Dodds may have pulled the circuit-breaker just to give themselves a quiet life. The members of the NTSB specializing in crew behaviour shared the view of ALPA. Certainly there was nothing tangible to bolster any supposition that Maus and Dodds had been reckless and cavalier.

There is an international agreement on the fitness requirements of a pilot. Once a pilot has passed the age of 40, a twice-yearly medical check-up is usually mandatory. The nature and regularity of proficiency tests are determined by individual countries. Once again, though, two a year is the norm for pilots above the age of 40.

One British pilot was frank enough to admit on television in 1989 that flights gave him the opportunity to catch up on sleep and that he always took his bedside alarm-clock in the cockpit with him to wake him in time for landing.

Dr Ian Parry, a senior medical examiner for the CAA, told a story which typified the latent danger in crew fatigue. 'A man who was flying an aeroplane into one of our well-known airports found that his first officer had nodded off and he suddenly thought, "My goodness, I've got to land this aircraft within the next minute" and when it was actually landing he thought, "Am I at the right airport? Is this the right runway?" because he felt so tired.'

Henry Duffy, the president of ALPA, had this to say in 1987: 'First, drugs are not yet a major problem for airline pilots. Second, that does not mean we are ignoring the problem. Frankly, the prospects of drugs in the cockpit scares us and we need to do something now. Third, random testing, the popular "quick fix" being promoted by some, has far too many disadvantages.'

ALPA's main objection to random testing was its 'repugnance to the

US Constitution and . . . conflict with the basic principle of presumption of innocence,' which seems both illogical and inconsistent: there was no constitutional crisis over random drug-testing of Olympic athletes. Only the drug-users, the maniacs, had anything to fear, though ALPA insisted that drug-testing was 'notoriously inaccurate', a claim without much enthusiastic support from the medical profession, prompting one US senator to remark, 'The position taken by these union representatives is the most ludicrous I have heard in my ten years in the Senate.'

In the same year, the new administrator of the FAA, T. Allan McArtor, predicted tough measures in the pipeline. 'If you are not medically qualified, if you are not drug-free, if you are not technically proficient, if you cannot demonstrate your skills, you will not fly in national airspace.'

Many commercial airline pilots in the United States, afraid of the long-term consequences of dependency on drugs, secretly turned to aromatherapy for help. Seldom did they confide in their families that they were receiving this treatment and never to their colleagues, because of the negative macho factor.

Airline medical officers would never recommend aromatherapy because there remains an air of mystique about it and it suffers from sketchy images of quackery and the deep-rooted prejudices against alternative medicine, especially within the medical profession.

In lay language, aromatherapy is massage with sweet-smelling essential oils. Some oils stimulate, while others sedate. Camomile, for example, is reputed to have hypnotic powers and is therefore ideal for insomniacs, whereas rosemary, from Spain, sharpens the mental faculties and strengthens the heartbeat. Aromatherapy is the oldest 'new treatment' in the world: the basic concept was known to the ancient Greeks, making it somewhat longer established than Valium and amphetamines, though no less controversial.

Even so, pilots' visits to aromatherapists tended to be surreptitious, which saddened international expert Michele Elizabeth, a doctor's daughter, who was trained in Britain at the world-famous Elizabeth Jones School of Aromatherapy.

'It does help, no matter what the sceptics say,' she said emphatically. 'Don't forget, I see the results first-hand. Most people come to me after drugs have failed them miserably or have been only marginally effective, but at a price: that of debilitating side-effects.

'"Ah!" cry the critics, "but it's all in the mind." Exactly! Aromatherapy relies on much more than physio-chemical powers. The massage soothes while the oils blitz the senses. The very essence of the treatment is a combined manipulation of both mind and matter.

'It can help men just as much as women, but in general they are more tentative about experimenting with something like this because of its feminine undertones, which are mythical. But for many men it's tantamount to an underground activity and that is unnecessary. After all, essential oils were used by Dr Jean Valnet in the Second World War to treat wounded soldiers.' Dr Valnet is generally recognized as the godfather of contemporary aromatherapy, but the basic philosophy can be traced to 430 BC, when Hippocrates encouraged the Greeks to burn scented bonfires in the streets. Later, in the fourteenth century, herbal fumigation was used to some apparent effect against the plague in England.

'The essential oils, very potent, are diluted in a vegetable oil base,' Ms Elizabeth explained. 'When applied in massage, they penetrate the skin into the bloodstream and reach vital organs within 30 to 100 minutes.

'The first session with a new client always begins with a half-hour consultation. It's important for me to find out as much as possible about the client before I embark on any treatment. I'll try to discover what's at the root of the problem. Most of the people who come to me are suffering from tension and stress, and therefore cannot sleep. Many of them have been on drugs and are at the end of their tether, looking for a more positive solution, rather than simply masking the symptoms. Only after the initial consultation can I come to a decision on the treatment I think would be most beneficial. We never claim to cure, only to help. We're one weapon in the overall armoury.

'If pilots, suffering from jet-lag, can overcome fatigue or be helped to conquer insomnia, without drugs, then it must be good news for everybody, especially those people who fill the passenger-seats.'

John King, a doctor of psychology, has researched at Warwick University the scientific basis of the use of fragrance in relaxation therapy, being quoted thus: 'Fragrance is added to many commercial products, and often subconsciously determines why people choose, for example, one shampoo over another. That kind of power to influence people, without their being aware of it, could be used in a beneficial clinical way.'

One senior pilot with United Airlines eulogized aromatherapy as his 'salvation', explaining, 'I was becoming a write-off, filling myself with chemicals to pick me up and shut me down. I turned to aromatherapy in desperation and I've never swallowed a drug since. I just tell the therapist whether I want to be relaxed or revved up. No one else knows. My wife would be suspicious if I mentioned massage and most of the other pilots, well . . . I guess they'd just come apart at the seams.'

He was nowhere near as alone as he thought.

As if drug-taking and drinking by pilots were not intimidating enough, there is also the spectre of mental illness, which, although it must be kept in perspective, is by no means unheard of. In fact, of all the reasons for the premature retirement of pilots, mental illness is the second most common.

The people whose job it is to draw up pilots' timetables believe that they are often the front-line defence against mental illness on the flight-deck. The first clue frequently is a succession of co-pilots making a special request not to be paired with a certain captain. If one name keeps emerging as a commander a large number of other pilots want to avoid, then there is cause for disquiet, but all too regularly those early signals go unheeded.

The mental disorder of a captain has already been confirmed as responsible for one fatal crash in modern times. The company was Japan Air Lines, which has a superlative reputation for safety. The location was Tokyo Bay, in 1982, just as the jet airliner was turning into its final approach to the city's airport. Without warning, the pilot slammed forward the control-column, sending the plane into a dive. Then he shut down the engines before re-starting two of them, but only to throw them into reverse thrust. The aircraft was too low for the co-pilot to do anything and the plane went down into the bay, where many lives were lost.

For two years or more previously, that commander had suffered from a mental disorder which had manifested itself in anti-social behaviour and he was suspended from flying while undergoing psychiatric treatment. Later he was allowed to resume his flying duties, though only in the co-pilot's seat. But after a year of demotion, he was reinstated as a captain, the consequences of which are now grievous history.

Naturally, the company had a lot of explaining to do. Japan Air Lines maintained that the captain would not have been returned to the flight-deck if their medical team and management had been properly briefed, implying that vital information had been withheld.

There is a camaraderie among air folk and their families. Many commercial pilots have been headhunted from their country's air force, where team spirit, pulling together and barrack-room loyalty have been drilled into them. That blind fidelity lingers on in a form of freemasonry. You do not tell tales. If your colleague is wounded – physically or mentally – then your job is to get him back to base: you carry him, in the hope that he would do the same for you should the need arise.

The wife of an American pilot faced this dilemma after their only child was killed in a road accident on her way home from school. The pilot, who idolized his daughter, was devastated. He was given two months' compassionate leave in 1989, but was eager to return to work, unfortunately for the wrong reason: he hoped flying would be a palliative, affording him release from his mourning. He was not sleeping, and at night he would pad around for hours downstairs in the dark, then go to his daughter's bedroom and kneel at her bed, talking to her as if she was still there. If his wife tried to entice him away, he became aggressive and abusive, threatening to kill her and then himself. The next development was a level of social withdrawal which the wife described as 'unnerving'. He ate very little, seldom spoke and was 'so distant' that, for his wife, it was a marriage 'with a ghost'. When he complained that he had nothing left to live for, his wife decided it was time to consult their GP, but he said there was nothing he could do unless the husband took the initiative and sought help. The pilot, discovering his wife had been discussing him with their physician, 'went crazy' and threatened to take his own life and that of everyone else on the next aircraft he captained if she ever again talked about him with a doctor 'behind (his) back'.

He was not drinking or taking drugs, but he was so mentally unstable that he had become a danger to himself and the public. What should a wife do? 'If I go to a doctor, they'll ground me,' he warned his wife. 'Our whole lifestyle will be on the line. Even if they let me fly again some day, I'll miss out on promotion. There'll always be a question-mark against my name. Just give me time. I'll work it out for myself.'

Instead of improving, his mental condition deteriorated. Other pilots would telephone the wife to say things such as, 'I'm worried about your husband. He was really strange yesterday . . . frightened the hell out of me . . . I'd get him to a doctor, if I were you, before someone turns him in. I don't want to have to be the one to do it.'

Scared for many different reasons, some of them conflicting, the wife made an anonymous call to her husband's airline, though, in view of the details given, there could have been little doubt as to the identity of the caller.

The pilot was grounded, whereupon he walked out on his wife, and three days later leapt to his death from the tenth floor of a hotel in Los Angeles. His widow was to say, 'Only then did the airline realize just how close to the edge he'd been. There's no doubt in my mind that he'd have done something terrible in the air if he'd been allowed to go on flying. Of course I have regrets – a million of them – but not for doing what I did. I saved the lives of others, but not my husband's. Some people in my family have accused me of being responsible for my husband's death. Some really dreadful things have been intimated, from my wanting him dead for his insurance money to my clearing the way for a marriage with someone else. I can live with those lies, however cruel and hurtful they might be. But I couldn't have lived with myself if I'd kept silent and my husband had killed three or four hundred people.'

We have already established that age is a factor in aircraft safety: so, too, it is with pilots, but in reverse. The statistics illustrate conclusively that granddad is a safer driver in the sky than grandson. The age group 30–34 is the most prone to accidents. From then on, however, the figures improve with age, the over-sixties topping the safety chart. Despite this consistent graph, which has fluctuated very little over the years, the FAA decrees that 60 should be the retirement age for airline pilots. The airlines of some other countries, including British Airways, compel their pilots to retire even younger, at 55. More logical, in view of all the evidence, would be the forced retirement of machines rather than manpower.

Often overlooked is the conflict which can ferment on the flight-deck, simply through the mismatch of personalities. When schedules are planned, no thought is given to compatibility. Names are virtually drawn from a hat, like pitching teams against each other in a football knock-out competition. Some chemistries do not mix, as most of us know from office life. In the claustrophobic closet of a cockpit, everything is magnified and exacerbated. Tempers boil at a much lower temperature.

Some captains and first officers find themselves competing against one another on the flight-deck, as if involved in a contest. Not so long ago, there was a survey in which captains were questioned about co-pilots, and vice versa. The objection most levelled against captains was 'over-confidence'. After 'too competitive', the second feature most complained of by captains about their first officers was – 'over-confidence'.

Bombs, like the one stowed aboard Pan Am 103, are not the only explosive forces which imperil commercial aircraft: there are those inside the heads of some pilots, and they are no less threatening.

8 BURNING ISSUES

Most passengers are soothed when the captain purrs into the public address system, 'Good evening, ladies and gentlemen, this is your captain speaking. On behalf of the flight-deck crew, I welcome you aboard.' That must have been the case as Flight SV 163, of Saudi Arabian Airlines, from Riyadh to Jeddah, prepared for take-off on 19 August 1980.

The 288 passengers had no means of knowing that the captain of their Lockheed L1011 Tristar, Mohammed Ali Khowyter, aged 38, had consistently failed his training tests. His records showed him a 'slow learner', needing more time to qualify than most other pilots, and he had 'difficulty adapting to changing circumstances'.

Khowyter's first officer was Sami Abdullah, aged 26, who had been stood down from his training programme for making 'poor progress', although he was later reinstated after representations from his union.

The third and final member of the cockpit crew was 42-year-old flight engineer Bradley Curtis, an American. In the United States, Curtis had flown DC3s – Dakotas, the workhorses of early civil aviation. But when he had applied to be upgraded to fly big modern jets, such as the Boeing 737, his training was terminated and he was declared unsuitable for either captain or first officer of *any* aircraft because his instructors had discovered he was dyslexic.

Flight SV 163 was a mere seven minutes old when the flight-deck crew were alerted by flashing lights to smoke on board. Information on the engineer's panel was more specific: Curtis, the dyslexic, should have known immediately that the smoke was emanating from C3, a small cargo hold, which was usually heated and pressurized, especially if animals were being transported.

The cockpit triumvirate devoted the next three minutes to thumbing through the airline's manual to determine what action they should take in such an emergency.

A further eighty-one seconds elapsed, while checks were made to see if the alarm had been triggered by a faulty transmission system. And all the time the aircraft was heading inexorably away from the airport.

Curtis, unable to find the appropriate page in the manual, asked the captain, 'Should I just go back there and see if I can find anything or smell anything?' This question was immortalized on the cockpit voice-recorder.

Twelve minutes had passed between the initial warning and Khowyter's decision to make a U-turn back to Riyadh, although the American engineer was reassuring him, 'Okay, no problem, no problem, so we are going to be returning. Everybody's panicking in the back, though. No problem. No problem at all.' All this time the passengers and flight attendants were being poisoned by toxic fumes seeping into the cabin.

Flight SV 163, which had originated in Karachi with 82 passengers, was equipped with oxygen masks, but for a reason which will for ever remain a mystery the pilot failed to order their use.

Panic spread as the cabin staff, in three languages, instructed the passengers to prepare for 'a possible crash landing'.

In 28 minutes and 24 seconds from take-off, the smouldering L1011 was back on the ground at Riyadh, with Khowyter saying over the radio, 'We congratulate the passengers for the safe landing. We are now trying to open the doors to let out the passengers.'

The normal procedure in such an emergency would be for the pilot to throw engines into reverse-thrust on touchdown, brake hard and initiate a speedy evacuation, via the escape chutes, the moment the aircraft came to a standstill. Inexplicably, Khowyter allowed the plane to continue along the runway as if making a standard landing, then negotiating a 180-degree turn, before taxiing back towards the terminal building. It took the Tristar 2 minutes 40 seconds to stop. Even then, the captain did not shut down the engines; they continued rotating for a further three minutes.

Seconds after the engines were finally stopped, there was a flash fire along the cabin ceiling. This is a phenomenon stimulated by gaseous products of the burning furnishings, concentrated near the ceiling, becoming further heated and igniting, causing a massive rise in temperature, with oxygen levels tumbling to a mere fraction of normal. It was impossible to survive these conditions for more than a few seconds.

Outside, seventeen firemen in nine vehicles were waiting, but the doors of the aircraft remained closed. Many of those firemen had never been trained to tackle an aircraft fire and had no idea how to break into a sealed airliner. From the moment the aircraft came to a standstill, it took twenty-six minutes for the emergency services to prise open a door, by which time all 301 people on board were dead.

For months the details of this accident were kept secret, although the investigation into the causes was conducted by the US National Transport Safety Board, the British Accident Investigation Branch, Lockheed, Scotland Yard's Forensic Science Laboratory and the Royal Aircraft Establishment at Farnborough. A confidential report was prepared for the Presidency of Civil Aviation in Jeddah. Two of the conclusions were, 'The crew responded appallingly slowly to warnings of imminent disaster and made inexplicable errors of judgement'; and 'cabin furnishings rapidly burned to give off dense smoke and incapacitating toxic gases.' But the lessons were not learned.

Fire on aircraft is a killer: not so much the flames, but the toxic fumes from hostile fabrics. Of 1000 deaths in air crashes, approximately 200 will be the victims of fire. Half the people asphyxiated by poisonous gases die needlessly, most researchers into air safety believe, including Frank Taylor, director of the Cranfield Aviation Safety Centre, Bedfordshire.

Dr James Vant, of Linacre College, Oxford, said that much had been learned from a study of accidents between 1964 and 1975 involving airlines within NATO countries. For instance, a majority of the people killed or injured were the victims of fire and its fumes, starting after the crash, rather than of the impact itself.

Several accidents have highlighted the virulence of toxic smoke. There was the Varig Airlines plane in 1973 which made a controlled crash landing just four miles short of the Orly runway, near Paris, when choking and blinding smoke, coming from a lavatory, filled the cockpit, immobilizing the crew. Of 134 people on board, there were only eleven survivors, ten of them members of the crew. The crash itself did not result in any deaths. Smoke, as at Riyadh in 1980, was the killer. But it took the fire on the British Airtours Boeing 737, on 22 August 1985 at Ringway airport, Manchester, to apply minds to an issue which had been begging for action for years.

Captain Peter Terrington was in the left-hand seat on the flight-deck of Flight KT 328 as the 737 picked up speed on its take-off roll. The time was 7.13 in the morning, and 151 passengers were looking forward to a holiday in the Mediterranean on the Greek island of Corfu. The plane had covered two-thirds of the 10,000-foot runway and was just passing the control-tower at 100 mph, almost at the point of no return, when the crew heard a dull thud, the noise apparently coming from the port side. Another two seconds and Terrington would have been committed to taking off, whatever the circumstances.

There was nothing on the instruments to tell the crew what was wrong. Terrington's gut reaction was that a bird had been sucked into one of the two engines or a tyre had burst. Either way, he had to abort take-off, which he did, radioing his decision to the tower.

Unaware of the reality of the situation, Terrington was not savage on the brakes, allowing the plane to run 1000 metres, then pulling it to the right to stop on the threshold of the Link Delta turn-off. There was no flat tyre, nor had the aircraft run into a flock of birds: the combustion chamber of one of the engines had exploded, puncturing the fuel tank, and the port wing was ablaze.

It was to be ten seconds after the explosion of the port engine before the fire bells sounded on the flight-deck. If Terrington had known at the outset that the port wing was ablaze, he would not have reduced speed as smoothly and neither would he have made the right turn, because it placed the aircraft upwind of the fire, which was fanned by the seven-knot breeze.

The airport's firemen were at the aircraft within thirty seconds of its stopping and were quickly getting to grips with the outside flames. Inside the plane, no one was either killed or injured. In theory, a totally safe evacuation should have been expected, but fifty-three passengers and two crew were to die within the next few minutes: no one, not even after the scandal – there is no other word for it – at Riyadh had appreciated fully just how quickly conditions could deteriorate in a plane fire.

Fuel was gathering under the tail section as the blaze began burning through the aluminium fuselage, the flames licking into the cargo-hold. Within another forty seconds, the fire had spread to the floor of the passenger-cabin, setting alight some of the seats and cushions. The firemen were winning the battle outside, not realizing that the plane inside was fast being turned into a gas chamber. Side panels, overhead lockers and the ceiling began to melt, giving off the toxic gases which brought such swift death to so many. Pathologists were later to discover that twenty of the dead had inhaled far more hydrogen cyanide than necessary to kill them instantly.

No one can legislate against panic, which inevitably takes its own toll. Can anyone wonder that passengers incarcerated in this deadly gas chamber were climbing over the backs of seats, fighting each other, stampeding towards the only three usable exits out of six and trying to claw their way to freedom from the shrivelling metal shell?

So intense was the fire that the rear section had withered away and collapsed to the ground after only two minutes, while inside the plane gangways were blocked by bodies as the acrid smoke not only poisoned passengers but also reduced visibility to zero. The flaring upholstery was giving out ammonia, carbon monoxide and hydrogen cyanide, all highly toxic gases.

Evidence from survivors revealed that smoke not only temporarily blinds but also soaks up sound. Debilitating bronchial spasms rooted people to the spot. The overhead lighting was useless; none of it could be seen, including the emergency exit signs.

Ninety seconds has been the legal maximum time allowed for evacuating an aircraft in an emergency, but this was fixed before it was realized how quickly people could be overcome by toxic fumes in a compact, enclosed area.

Because of the findings of the official inquiry into this accident, aircraft seat cushions were replaced with materials that could resist flames for two minutes at 1100° C, which should allow passengers in a similar emergency more than 90 seconds for a safe evacuation.

Ronald Ashford, the CAA's director of safety regulations, reported that computer studies indicated that if the new materials had been developed before the Manchester fire, and had been incorporated in the cushions and other fittings, 44 per cent of the people who died would have lived. The CAA also believed that another 5 per cent of the victims would have escaped if there had been floor-level lighting, which became mandatory on all aircraft in December 1987.

Nevertheless, the compilers of the official report into the Manchester incident were not convinced that floor-lighting was the answer, arguing the case for an 'audio attraction' mechanism, such as bleepers, which would lead passengers by sound instead of having to rely on their impaired vision.

A burst tyre has caused an airliner to disintegrate in mid-air. That was on 31 March 1986, and the plane in question was a Boeing 727, owned by Mexicana Airlines. When the tyre burst during the flight, after the landing gear had been retracted, ducts for fuel, water, electricity and pneumatics were ruptured. Escaping hot air initiated a fire and the aircraft began to come apart at the seams at 15,000 feet, at which point the tail fell off and the crew had no means of keeping the plane airborne. No one on board survived.

Smokehoods would have undoubtedly saved more lives at Manchester, the investigators speculated, but only if the equipment had been perfected. Nothing on the market at the time of the accident would have sufficed, they emphasized.

The inquiry by the Department of Transport's Air Accidents Investigation Branch lasted thirty-two months and the key elements of thirty-one recommendations were: smokehoods for every passenger, the development of sprinkler systems, the creation of audio signalling devices to guide passengers in smoke, more stringent evacuation tests, changes in aircraft ventilation so that air escaped through the roof of the cabin (the Manchester Boeing 737 drew in air through the roof, fanning the smoke and fumes from the front section) and the introduction of regulations for aircraft interior materials, specifying the amounts of smoke and poisonous fumes they could give off when they burned (old standards referred only to the speed at which materials caught fire).

In the spring of 1988, before the report on the Manchester fire was published, the British government approved a design for a smokehood which was 'guaranteed' to save lives; manufacturers estimated that they could be mass-produced for £50 each, but most of the world's airlines were indifferent. Some were opposed on the grounds that smokehoods would increase the risk to passengers by delaying evacuation. Other airlines were doubtful about the extent of protection. The hood envisaged would provide total protection from poisonous gases for thirty minutes. The CAA was censured in Parliament for dismissing as 'impractical' the pressure for aircraft to carry enough smokehoods for all passengers. But even if the CAA overnight made smokehoods compulsory for all British carriers, most airlines flying out of United Kingdom airports would automatically be exempt because their safety standards were regulated by the appropriate authorities in their own countries.

The FAA was also sceptical about the effectiveness of smokehoods. Everett Pittman, the FAA's international airworthiness programmes officer, said, 'We have liaised closely with our British and Canadian counterparts to improve passenger safety, but at present we feel that smokehoods are not a viable proposition.'

It was routine for British Airways aircraft to carry smokehoods for its crew, but the airline did not favour their introduction for passengers until they became obligatory. Dan Air was also against smokehoods, along with Swissair, Iberia, Sabena, Air India, Qantas, Pakistan International and Cathay Pacific. Less equivocal was Air Europe, Britain's largest charter airline, which issued this statement: 'We have been waiting for the Civil Aviation Authority to approve a standard design for smokehoods and if they are available and meet the standard approved by the CAA, then we will almost certainly carry them for the safety of our passengers.'

Despite the strong argument for smokehoods and the belief that, in the future, they could prove life-savers, most expert opinion remained sceptical about the contribution they could make to safety on a mass scale. The CAA, the British Safety Council, the International Airline Passengers' Association and professional fire officers, at the time of the publication of the official report into the British Airtours blaze at Manchester, were not convinced that a satisfactory smokehood was yet on the market. When flight attendants were subjected to speed tests, they took between 40 and 100 seconds to put on the smokehoods which had been aboard the British Airtours 737 for the crew.

There was also considerable disagreement between the experts; very few aspects of fire safety, even after the Manchester inquiry, produced unanimity or anything remotely definitive. For example, David King, the air accident inspector, recommended that more room should be made around the central wing exits, a view opposed by Ronald Ashford, who argued that research commissioned by the CAA had proved that space in the vicinity of exits became congested when passengers were engaged in 'competitive behaviour' (an airline euphemism for panic) and that limited mobility was an advantage rather than a hindrance.

Soon after the Manchester incident, both the FAA and the CAA ordered modifications to be made to the front doors of the Boeing 737.

Below:
The USS 'Vincennes', from which two Standard missiles were fired at Flight 655, an Iran Air jetliner bound from Bandar Abbas to Dubai on Sunday 3 July 1988

Right:
Captain Will Rogers III, the captain of the USS 'Vincennes', who ordered the shooting-down of Iran Air Flight 655 in the Persian Gulf, killing all 290 civilians on board

Right:
The huge crater
at Lockerbie, Scotland,
pinpoints the spot where
the main fuselage of Pan
Am's sabotaged Boeing
747 landed just before
Christmas 1988. Of the
270 people killed, eleven
were on the ground

Below:
One of the most poignant
pictures in the annals
of air crashes: a Scottish
policeman's vigil at
Lockerbie beside the
severed nose-cone of
'Maid of the Seas', which
left London Heathrow for
New York as Flight 103 on
21 December 1988
carrying a Semtex bomb in
the luggage-hold

Right:
A Toshiba radio/cassette
bomb, similar to the one
believed to have blown
up Pan Am Flight 103
over Lockerbie, Scotland.
This device was seized in
October 1988 by West
German police during a
raid on a Palestinian
terrorist cell

Below:
A hangar full of coffins at Tenerife airport in the Canary Islands tells its own chilling story. Two 747s – owned by Pan Am and KLM – collided in fog on the runway

Right:
A stark memorial to the dead on the Tenerife runway in the jumbo pile-up which occurred during poor visibility and was aggravated by less than maximum assistance from the airport's technology

Debris is sorted and packaged at the site of the crash of a Turkish Airlines DC10, just north of Paris, which killed 346 people. There were no survivors when a cargo door burst open shortly after take-off in March 1974

Above:
Debris litters the 1-94 freeway just outside Detroit's Metro airport on 17 August 1987, the day after Northwest Flight 255 came down just seconds after take-off. There was only one survivor of the 155 people on board and two passing motorists were killed

Below:
The taut but calm atmosphere of the control tower is captured in this photograph of ground-controllers handling air traffic at London Heathrow, the world's busiest international airport

Below:
London air-traffic controller Jim Cozens fears that the skies are becoming too crowded and a high-risk place to be. Mid-air collisions, he says, are often being avoided more by luck than judgement

Right:
Unfinished planes, looking like bullets, lined up in Boeing's Seattle manufacturing plant. Boeing have come in for harsh criticism for alleged sloppy workmanship in the past

Below:
These are the intimidating controls a 747 pilot faces every time he takes to the air. Here a maintenance engineer double-checks to see that everything is in order

Left:
The woman at the controls of this aircraft simulator in the United States is undergoing therapeutic treatment for the fear of flying. By the look on her face, she needs treatment for her fear of the therapist!

Right:
Therapy treatment in the United States for frightened flyers recreates with claustrophobic authenticity the atmosphere of a modern jetliner's passenger cabin

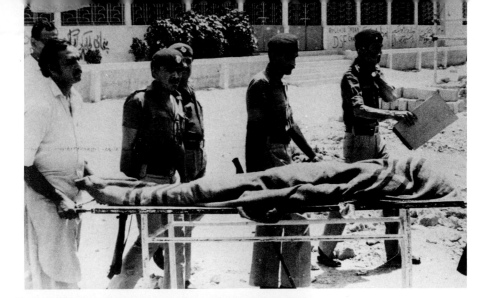

Above:
The first victim of a hijacking siege in Karachi, Pakistan, is carried from Pan Am Flight 073. The aircraft was captured in September 1986 by four terrorists, and the first shooting was of a Californian, just after dawn

Left:
The harassed-looking Paul Channon, when he was Britain's Minister of Transport, just after the crash on the M1 in Leicestershire of a British Midland Boeing 737. Forty-four people lost their lives in this accident in January 1989, when the pilot, Captain Kevin Hunt, shut down the wrong engine of two en route from London Heathrow to Belfast, Northern Ireland, after the instruments warned him of a fire. Speculation centred on faulty wiring

This followed the jamming on the British Airtours jet of the front right-hand door, which was later forced open after the opposite door had been successfully opened.

The CAA supported the suggested introduction of a water-sprinkling system for all passenger aircraft which, in their view, could possibly have saved another 20 per cent of those who died at Manchester. The FAA, the CAA and various other interested parties in Canada and Europe launched a highly intensified research programme into sprinklers, which they trusted would make a breakthrough by the early 1990s. Only when there was an international agreement on an approved design would water-sprinklers become mandatory for all passenger aircraft.

A few statistics are worth bearing in mind at this point. Between 1966 and 1985, there were 74 aircraft fires among the West's leading commercial carriers, involving 8610 passengers, 2500 of them dying as a result of the blaze – mainly because of the poisonous gases – and unrelated to impact. In 1977, 583 people died in one crash – when two 747s, one owned by Pan Am, the other bearing the KLM logo, collided in fog on the runway at Tenerife and burst into flames.

We are all prepared to accept there will be no survivors when an aircraft is blown up at 33,000 feet, but there is a feeling in the air industry that modern technology should be sufficiently advanced to make death from toxic fumes a thing of the past.

William Beckett, co-chairman of the Survivors Campaign to Improve Safety in Airline Flight Equipment (SCI-SAFE), was not satisfied that progress was either fast enough or sufficiently radical. 'We feel that cost is still equated to safety improvements, measured by the number of deaths at the end of the runway.' Mr Beckett's daughter died in the Manchester fire.

SCI-SAFE wanted smokehoods to be immediately available to all passengers, believing that at least forty-eight people died unnecessarily at Manchester.

Tony Parry, the chief fire officer for Greater Manchester, favoured the introduction of smokehoods and sprinklers, but warned that, in themselves, they would not be enough. Of equal urgency was the improvisation of quicker means of evacuation. He explained: 'Death from toxic fumes generally comes before death from burns or heat, but in fires like the one at Manchester escape routes would need to be improved. Otherwise, you merely replace one way of dying with another.'

But Mr Beckett countered, 'All we want is for the CAA to meet their responsibilities and act effectively and efficiently to at once implement the recommendations made after this most detailed investigation into how and why the disaster occurred. Only then can we return to our families and resume anything like a normal life. Until that happens, every survivor and relative of those killed daily have to live with the nightmare. It is unjust and irresponsible of the CAA, who we had all previously presumed had our best safety interests at heart.'

The thirty-one recommendations in the official report were as follows:

1 The crew should always position an aircraft on fire so that the wind would blow the flames away from the aircraft.

2 All flight-deck crews should have unobstructed views of the outside of their aircraft from the cockpit, possibly by means of cameras or even simple car-type mirrors, enabling them to estimate swiftly the extent of any damage.

3 Crews should always stop at the earliest point and estimate damage while still on the runway, rather than taxiing off first.

4 Evacuation alarms should be fitted to aircraft to warn the cabin staff automatically of an impending emergency.

5 All emergency equipment for use by the cabin crew should be stored near their feet, rather than in overhead lockers.

6 The dissemination of safety information from the manufacturers should be improved and co-ordinated at international level.

7 Information on the maintenance of critical components should be more explicit and devoid of ambiguity.

8 No more repairs to combustion cans in Pratt and Whitney JT8D engines. They would have to be replaced.

9 Airlines should refrain from altering their technical manuals before consulting the aircraft and engine manufacturers.

10 The internal configuration of the Boeing 737 should be re-designed to afford the cabin crew an unimpeded view of their territory. More space should be allocated between the forward galleys, and a row of seats next to the wing should be removed.

11 All routes to the exits should be kept clear.

12 Public address systems should be independent of engine power.

13 Crew members with most experience should be spread evenly throughout the cabin area.

14 There should be better communication between all the emergency rescue teams at airports.

15 Management techniques should be made more efficient through amended training and recruitment procedures for fire officers at airports.

16 Firemen and other rescue services at airports should be equipped with more breathing apparatus.

17 The officer in overall charge of the rescue operation should be immediately recognizable by his distinctive clothing.

18 A review should be made of methods for tackling fires on aircraft.

19 Water sprinkler systems should be developed as a matter of urgency and introduced at the earliest opportunity on all passenger aircraft.

20 Research should be directed towards ways of strengthening the aircraft hull and preventing a collapse in critical areas during a fire.

21 The access to external fuel tanks should be hardened.

22 A strict control should be exercised on the carrying of aerosols on all aircraft.

23 Emergency oxygen cylinders should be fitted with pressure relief valves and stowed in protected areas.

24 Urgent consideration should be given to formulating a requirement to provide smokehoods.

25 Cabin crew should be trained in the use of smokehoods so that they are at their 'maximum optimum' during an emergency evacuation.

26 Cabin materials should be so made that they do not give off toxic gases.

27 The effect of water sprinklers in an airline fire should be properly researched.

28 The problems of exits being blocked and doors jammed should be introduced into trial runs by cabin crews.

29 All seats alongside exits should be strengthened so they could withstand great force and abuse before breaking.

30 An audio system should be devised to help 'blinded' passengers find their way to the exits.

31 Research should be undertaken on aircraft air-conditioning to prevent it becoming fouled by smoke.

The sudden rupturing of a combustion chamber in the port JT8D engine was officially blamed for the accident. The guilty can, which fractured, had been repaired by means of a welding technique which was approved by the CAA and other safety authorities. However, a different type of welding method was outlined in the manual of the engine manufacturer, Pratt and Whitney; these instructions had not been followed.

On the morning of the Manchester fire, the repaired can broke away and penetrated the fuel tank, igniting a blaze underneath the fuselage. Of this event, the official report said it 'changed the nature of the incident from a purely engine-related incident into a catastrophic accident.'

There had been three previous reports of combustion cans fracturing, but no fuel tanks had been punctured. The investigation did reveal that there had been many problems with these cans, without their actually rupturing, and these difficulties had been written off as the consequence of improper repairs, thus avoiding service bulletins or airworthiness directives. In one sentence, the report highlighted a breakdown in communication between the operators and the engine-makers: 'It has become evident from the complete absence of dialogue between British Airways and Pratt and Whitney on the subject of combustor-can potential failures that, on the one hand, the manufacturer believed that his messages were being understood and acted upon, and on the other that the airline interpreted these messages as largely inapplicable to them at that time.'

In the first seven months of 1985, sixty British Airways pilots complained of slow acceleration from the Boeing 737, while eighty-five other BA crews, in the same period, had protested about 'throttle stagger'. It was unfortunate, said the report, that British Airways had not presented the catalogue of pilots' complaints to the manufacturers.

Even the Civil Service language of a formal official document seemed to change genre as it set the scene inside that aircraft that August morning: 'She [stewardess Joanna Toff] cleared the jam by pulling one young passenger forwards and the flow started. Later she saw a young girl lying on the floor of the forward aisle. She pushed another youth back, pulled the girl forward by her collar, and pushed her down the slide. As the passengers came forwards through the bulkhead aperture, so the smoke built up in the forward galley area. She recalled feeling a body slump against her legs, bent down, and, due to improved visibility near the floor, saw that it was another girl passenger. Her face was black with soot, her eyes were fixed and dilated, and there were no signs of breathing. The stewardess considered giving her the kiss of life, when a fireman down below shouted for her to throw the girl down to him. With great difficulty, she lifted her by the waist and threw her into the chute. The stewardess felt around for other passengers back as far as the galley cabin entrance. She was considering getting her smokehood, when a fireman shouted to her to jump. Having been unable to locate any further passengers, she went down the slide.'

There are always recriminations and bitterness after any plane accident – they are to be expected – but in this case they were amplified by the sure knowledge and acceptance that no one need have died at Manchester; everyone should have escaped alive.

William Beckett, joint founder of SCI-SAFE, made this appeal: 'For too long the CAA has done little more than pay lip service to calls for life-saving improvements. Now it is time we forced them to put things right.' And John Beardmore, co-chairman of SCI-SAFE, was even more scathing. 'They [the CAA] have let us down by certifying that aircraft as safe when it was a death-trap. Now they have let us down again by not taking enough action to improve matters in the most important matters, which we are certain are smokehoods and larger exits.'

John Guntrip, vice-chairman of the Guild of Air Pilots and Navigators, believed the proposed water-sprinklers would be 'the greatest step forward in aviation safety for many years', but warned that they would 'mean a penalty in terms of weight, fuel consumption and cost'.

Christopher Tugendhat, chairman of the CAA, said that consumers would have to decide whether they were prepared to pay for increased safety through dearer fares. He defended his organization, saying, 'We must learn from these terrible events and I believe that is what we have done.' He wanted it recorded that the CAA had 'fully accepted' twenty-five of the thirty-one recommendations, ten had already been acted upon and the remainder, which 'mainly concerned reviews, requiring extensive research or call for internal action', were in the 'action file'. In addition to banning the repair of combustion chambers in JT8D engines, wing access panels had been strengthened, fire-blocking standards for materials used to make seats and walls had been upgraded, an order had been made for oxygen bottles to be fitted with vents to stop them exploding, and all British airlines had been made to follow the US international carriers in respect of installing smoke-detectors in all toilets. The position of emergency equipment to be used by cabin crews had also been moved to provide greater safety and a seat had been taken from the area of a wing exit.

But on the question of smokehoods, Tugendhat reiterated, 'We've agonized over this a great deal, but if a hood does not meet all the requirements, we were afraid there could be cases in which it might even cost life, rather than save it.'

It became evident from leaked information from the Department of Transport that passengers could not expect to be issued with smoke-hoods for at least two years from March 1989, and the wait for sprinklers would be even longer.

Six years after the one incident which did more than anything to educate the airline industry to the requirements for surviving an air-plane fire, the very two essentials which could have saved everyone on the Manchester flight will still be missing from commercial aircraft.

9 DEADLY CARGO

Bombs and overheating engines are far from the only reasons for explosions and fires on planes. Pilots are becoming increasingly worried about the hazardous goods which find their way on to passenger aircraft, sometimes – but not always – innocently.

Some of the reports filed read like extracts from fiction. A missile engineer boarded a civilian aircraft carrying a rocket motor filled with explosives. On another flight, a passenger had tear gas in his cabin baggage. A customs officer, examining luggage from an incoming flight, found three bottles of nitric acid and a bottle of hydrochloric acid.

One passenger, who was stopped by security officials during the boarding process of an aircraft, was concealing in a suitcase 144 quarter-litre bottles of hydrochloric acid. The fumes were so overpowering that four of the officers were detained in hospital for four days.

The floor and sub-floor of an MD80 aircraft in 1987 were seriously damaged when hydrogen peroxide leaked from a consignment of chemicals in the luggage-hold. The plane had to make an emergency landing at Nashville, Tennessee. The despatching company had falsely labelled the cargo; their selfish, criminal action could have cost lives.

A British Airways jet, bound for Manchester in February 1986, made an emergency landing at London Heathrow because passengers were overcome by fumes from two bottles of ethyl chloronate. The bottles had been taken on board by a passenger, who was fined by magistrates, but that was all.

During two domestic flights in the United Kingdom in January 1984, the respective pilots were informed by children that there were fireworks on board. The fireworks were not only in the passenger-cabin but also in suitcases in the hold. Six more similar cases were reported in the February and March of that year. In one incident alone, 12 large and 2500 small fireworks, including bangers, rockets and jumping crackers, were confiscated on board.

The flight-deck crew of a Pan Am Boeing 707 cargo aircraft lost control as they approached Boston in December 1973. The plane crashed and all on board died. The subsequent investigation showed that the crew had been 'blinded' by fumes from nitric acid, which can react with other materials to produce melting heat and acrid smoke. The weight of the chemicals on the aircraft came to 15,000lb, and more than half of the load was improperly packaged and had been incorrectly labelled. Many of the chemicals were disguised as electrical appliances.

Six months later, seventy-five passengers on an Aeromexico DC9 had a lucky escape when a shipment of nitric acid flooded the cargo-hold.

Laurie Taylor wrote, 'As current trends are to relax the original ICAO (International Civil Aviation Organization) Technical Instructions for the Safe Transport of Dangerous Goods by Air, and to allow more "exempted" dangerous goods on board aircraft, the risk seems likely to increase. These small quantities of exempted dangerous goods will not carry the normal labels, and thus the pilot-in-command will not be aware of the presence of dangerous goods that may be mixed in with other non-dangerous, as well as with dangerous goods. There will, therefore, be a reduced level of safety that will require an increased awareness of all persons concerned, if risk is to be contained at an acceptable level.

'As so little effort is expended by the UPU (Universal Postal Union) in informing the general public about the risk to air travel posed by using airmail to send dangerous goods around the world, it seems that this particular risk will be present for many years to come.'

It is estimated that millions of packages sent airmail every year are lethal enough to bring down a 747. An example was a package from Taiwan to a sporting arms dealer in Brisbane, Australia. The package was cleared by customs, without being opened, then fell from a counter, whereupon it detonated. Although there were no warning labels on the parcel, it contained 44,000 starting-pistol caps.

'People just do not think,' said Taylor. 'They don't set out to endanger people's lives, I'm satisfied of that, though that's no consolation when you're at 30,000 feet. There's not enough policing, not sufficient warnings, inadequate inspections. This whole area of operation is much too slipshod; terrifying. The mere thought of the range of dangerous goods unwittingly carried every day on passenger aircraft, all over the world, scares the hell out of me. It's true to say that on any large aircraft there's sufficient illegal materials to ensure its destruction, should there be a mishap.

'There are strict regulations regarding how all potentially dangerous materials should be packaged, but the shippers are left to conform with very little monitoring by the authorities. Detective work is non-existent. Different types of chemicals are carried, and when mixed, they can be highly volatile and inflammable. There has only to be a spillage, which is not an uncommon occurrence, and a disaster is on the cards. The corrosive nature of some of the chemicals transported on passenger airplanes is an outrage: they're capable of burning through the floors and filling the cabin with deadly fumes. If passengers knew what was under their feet half the time, they would be running scared.

'One becomes tired of the number of sportsmen – big-game hunters and rifle-range marksmen – who think nothing of loading their luggage with live ammunition. You would think those people, trained to be so cautious, would know better, but so many of them are utterly reckless. There are easier ways of committing suicide and without taking a plane-load of passengers with you.

'Every year there are 100 dangerous substances added to the list of those which are transported as cargo on passenger aircraft. Some are even radioactive and can be despatched ordinary airmail, without anyone checking. Pilots feel very strongly about this issue: I certainly do. One day an airplane, maybe a fully loaded 747, is going to go up in smoke in mid-air, but the "bomb" will not be the work of terrorists; it will be a consignment of chemicals, paid for and despatched by a large company and welcomed on board by the airline's accountants.

'The truth is that today almost every passenger aircraft takes off laden with commercial "bombs", of which the travelling public is totally oblivious. Most people, I'm certain, would assume that all potentially dangerous goods are screened and barred from airplanes, especially those carrying passengers, but that's not so. I've said it before and I say it again, the public has to become political, lobbying the politicians and withdrawing their patronage unless the rules are made more strin-gent and are rigorously applied. In the past, law-breakers have been aided and abetted by ignorance: the ignorance of a public which had no idea what was going on. Now the public knows the facts and it's up to them, and flight crews, to do something about it. The public has economic clout, which is the best muscle there is.'

Combi-aircraft – an unholy alliance between cargo and human livestock – are the bane of all pilots' unions. These aircraft have mobile bulkheads on the main deck, behind which are sections where unusually large loads of cargo can be stocked. Within those compartments run flight control cables, yet there is no fire-resistant lining material. In addition, there is no way in which ventilation can be restricted, which means, according to the pilots' unions, that combi-aircraft are fire-traps.

Pilots have been campaigning for years to have stricter rules restricting the carriage of dangerous materials, but projected trends would indicate they have been losing the argument. The amount of dangerous goods transported by air is predicted to increase by 20 per cent each year. In the face of mounting criticism, the airlines are planning even more combi-aircraft, and flight crew organizations are predicting a 'holocaust' as a direct result, particularly because of the lack of access to the special cargo compartments and the absence of automatic fire-fighting equipment.

A combination of ventilation and oxygen in the main deck cargo compartments of the combi-aircraft would almost certainly make a fire uncontrollable, it was argued, but there was not much sympathy from the boardroom accountants.

The Federation of International Airline pilots, at its 1987 conference, called for dangerous goods to be restricted to all-cargo planes, but feared that there was little likelihood of those aims being achieved in the foreseeable future. The pilots' federation pointed out that if there was an accident during take-off or landing, and the aircraft was carrying dangerous goods – perhaps corrosive or radioactive materials – the rescue services would first have to deal with the toxic levels, and the passengers would come second; bad news for the public.

'If I was offered a free first-class, round-the-world ticket on a two-engined, extended range (ETOPS) combi-aircraft, operated by a financially-strapped company based in the Third World or South America and scheduled to cross hostile territory, I should decline it,' said Laurie Taylor. 'They represent all the ingredients I'd advise people to avoid, but the public have very little pre-knowledge of the aircraft in which they will be travelling. They fly blind. The industry, sadly, seems only to learn from ambulance-chasing and going to funerals.'

*

Airline food can be as life-threatening as dangerous goods. The problem is such that at the end of June 1989 a meeting was convened in London for the ten biggest airline caterers in the United Kingdom to discuss food poisoning in the air, which public health officials described as a greater threat to safety than hijacking. The meeting was deemed necessary because the Central Public Health Laboratory had amassed evidence to demonstrate that almost a quarter of all airline meals were contaminated with excessive levels of bacteria. During the survey, public health inspectors sampled 1013 meals from the ten mass-production kitchens. Surface colony counts of more than a million organisms per gram – ten times the permitted level – were found in 241 of the meals. A fifth of the meals tested were infected with unacceptable amounts of *E.coli*, the bacteria linked with faecal contamination. Salmonella enteritidis was present in four of the inspected foods, three of them hors d'oeuvres.

The investigation of the Central Public Health Laboratory followed one of the worst outbreaks of food poisoning caused by airline meals. The Center for Disease Control in Georgia, Atlanta, was informed on 15 March 1984 that eight passengers had been taken seriously ill following a British Airways flight from Heathrow to the United States. That same day, the Communicable Diseases Surveillance Centre in London was informed by local public health authorities of cases of gastro-enteritis among the flight staff of British Airways. Around the world, more than 750 British Airways passengers and staff were to be struck down by food-poisoning.

Kim Wan Chan, a citizen of Hong Kong who was working in London, died in hospital. So did Ali Alireza, the former Saudi Arabian ambassador to the United States, who suffered a heart attack while being treated for food-poisoning. The contamination was traced to an aspic glaze served with hors d'oeuvres to first-class and club passengers.

The threat to safety posed by poisoning from inflight meals has always been recognized, explaining the policy of captains and their co-pilots having to eat different types of food while in the air. Incapacitation during flights among air crews is not at all rare and symptoms related to conditions initiated by food contamination head the list: diarrhoea, nausea and stomach cramps.

Hundreds of pilots in the United States have reported 'memory loss, confusion, visual disturbances, headaches and gastro-intestinal reactions leading to in-flight safety problems' after consuming low-calorie soft drinks containing the artificial sweetener aspartame, marketed under the trade name Nutrasweet. 'If pilots quit using these products their symptoms ease, but return if they start consuming them again,' said Mary Stoddard, of the US Aspartame Consumer Safety Network. Pilots need to consume a lot of liquid whilst airborne as a defence against dehydration and diet soft drinks are appealing because of the low calorie count.

Between January 1961 and April 1968 seventeen pilots worldwide died on flight-decks: as a direct result of those deaths in the cockpit, there were five incidents which led to a number of passengers losing their lives and a total of 148 casualties. One survey in the United States revealed that 1500 pilots out of 4500 had been so ill during a flight that they could not continue at the controls, and 28 per cent reported that their illness had endangered the safety of the aircraft. When a pilot is taken ill at the controls, he is helped from his seat and replaced with an untrained flight attendant, often a stewardess. On the flight-deck of a 747, for example, it is impossible for one person to see and operate all the instruments. If it is the captain who becomes ill, then the co-pilot assumes command and calls upon the services of a flight attendant to sit in as understudy and follow orders. This happened in 1975 on a National Airlines DC10 from London Heathrow to Miami. In mid-Atlantic the captain began to run a fever and complained of stomach cramps. A little later, he began vomiting and suffered double vision, finally slumping forward. He spent most of the remainder of that flight in and out of a toilet and was replaced at the controls by a 26-year-old stewardess who did not even have a driving-licence. Her role in that emergency was to operate the instruments beyond the reach of the first officer who was then in charge. A full-scale Arthur Hailey plot almost unfolded when the first officer also started to feel sick about half an hour from Miami. The captain and co-pilot had followed the rules, choosing different foods from the flight menu, but earlier they had both eaten eggs, bacon and sausages for breakfast at the same London hotel.

When the captain was taken ill, the senior flight attendant asked over the public address system for any doctors or nurses on board to make themselves known. The request was made very low-key to avoid alarm-ing the passengers: no one would have guessed from the nonchalant manner of the staff that it was the pilot who needed urgent medical attention. Two British nurses and a physician from Miami responded to the call for help and the doctor promptly diagnosed food-poisoning.

Just north of Palm Beach, a stewardess returned to the doctor to whisper to him that the co-pilot and the flight-engineer were now beginning to develop symptoms similar to those experienced by the captain just before collapsing.

As soon as the doctor reached the flight-deck for the second time, he could see that the first officer was in considerable distress. One of the nurses prepared an ice-pack for his forehead, but there was not much else that could be done.

The time factor now became crucial. The doctor warned that the first officer could lose consciousness at any moment; his pulse-rate was rapid and erratic, and his breathing had become shallow, which was reducing his concentration, meaning that more responsibility was having to be shouldered by the stewardess in the co-pilot's seat. The flight-engineer was becoming dizzy and disoriented. Fortunately, they were able to land the plane at Miami before the situation deteriorated any further, though the senior attendant of that flight was beginning to worry about the reaction among the passengers if she had to ask over the PA system, 'Excuse me, but is there a pilot on board?'

10 CROWDED SKIES

The captain of the northbound Boeing 747 from London Heathrow was eager to reach as quickly as possible the rarified air of high altitude, where less fuel is burned. 'If I can't climb, I won't make Los Angeles,' the pilot complained to ground-control.

The laconic reply, as spontaneous as a ricochet, went, 'If you climb now, you won't make Manchester!'

That pithy exchange typifies the bargaining that goes on day and night throughout the world between flight-deck crews and ground-controllers for the ever-diminishing space along the crowded sky-lanes. The potential for mid-air collisions has troubled most responsible minds in the industry for years and has been the staple diet of the front pages of daily newspapers. In fact the first reports from Lockerbie alluded to the possibility of a second aircraft having been involved.

Throughout the eighties, *near miss* seemed to be the tenor of almost every other air scare story in the press. 'Near miss' is a misnomer, of course, and never used by pilots, who more accurately refer to *near hits*. The near-hit syndrome has arisen at a time of an expanding industry and a reduction in the numbers of controllers to manage and safeguard the extra volume of movement on the ground and in the air.

Facts and figures mean very little in this conundrum of air safety. What is critical is the performance of the air-traffic controllers; how they match up to the soaring demands and pressures, and whether they believe they are coping. They are the best judges of the system and, with flight crews, are on trial whenever there is a collision, whether the accident be in the sky or on the ground.

When two aircraft of a similar type are taking off in the same direction, the separation time is usually two minutes. When they are going opposite ways, the time gap is normally one minute. As soon as a plane has taken off and is climbing safely on its Standard Instrument

Departure, it is transferred by the air controller to the first radar sector for clearance to its ultimate cruising altitude.

At the busiest airports, there will be as many as 2000 aircraft movements every day. Most large international airports have two control rooms. Controllers in the upper, glass-domed room direct aircraft for take-off and landing. The complex below, usually lit only by the radar-scopes, is where controllers guide incoming aircraft on to the runways.

Through the working life of one controller emerges a vivid picture of a life-and-death game of roulette. Every ground controller, however stoical, has a horror story to tell, but is usually too reticent or afraid to do so, unless it is unattributed.

Jim Cozens is an exception. He was prepared to collaborate with me during the preparation of this book because of the promptings of his conscience. Cozens had always loved his job, even after fifteen daunting years, and intended his criticisms to be constructive. He was a man who cared – about his profession and about other people. 'My idea is not to sensationalize,' he began. 'But if the truth is sensational, then it would be dishonest of me to dress it down to look something different.'

Cozens, who was a controller for fifteen years until resigning in 1988 to pursue a musical career, would start his morning shift in the control-room of the West Drayton air-traffic centre, near London's Heathrow airport, at 7.30. From the control-room, divided into nine different segments known as suites, 3000 planes could be managed every day.

Cozens would be one of seventy controllers on duty at any time of the day or night. After plugging in, he would listen for about five minutes, until he was confident that he 'understood the overall picture'. Directly in front of him would be a 23-inch radar screen, and to his side a keyboard, making it possible for him to adjust the screen to concentrate on one particular area of the sky or to superimpose the coastline.

All aircraft were identified as little orange dots. The movement of aircraft would be shown on the screen every six-and-a-half seconds by the changing of the pulses and dots. Each controller is an anchorman, talking with pilots, receiving messages from flight crews in one ear and being updated in the other ear by their opposite numbers in other sectors about aircraft being 'passed over'.

Here is a typical sequence: an orange dot appears on Cozens's screen. 'Good morning, this is Speedbird 101 at 350.'

Cozens tunes in. 'Good morning. Maintain that level. Squawk ident.'

Squawk ident meant that the controller was asking for an automatic transmission of the aircraft's callsign and height to appear on his own screen.

'You're cleared direct to Biggin for Heathrow, landing on 27 Left. Go to 130 when you're ready.' In the language of the sky, that meant the plane was cleared directly to the Heathrow holding zone, where the airport's traffic-controllers would take over. 'Go to 130' was an instruction to the pilot to descend to 13,000 feet.

After two hours, controllers at West Drayton were given a half-hour break. 'It's hard to keep concentration non-stop for that long, just watching dots on a screen,' said Cozens. 'Two hours is over the natural limit. One-and-a-half hours would be safer.'

Cozens described the scene as his screen filled with eight or ten aircraft. 'It's a real bees' nest. They're buzzing round each other in complex patterns. I have to make very quick decisions, talk fast, run with it. I daren't take my eyes off the screen for a second. When you're so overloaded, it scares you.

'In the summer months, when the skies are mad with planes, you can get scared any time. You keep fear locked away: if you think about it, you could lose control.'

Twice in a short space of time Cozens had to order two planes under his control to make 90-degree turns in order to avoid collisions with military aircraft. Lunch for Cozens would come none too soon at 12.30, allowing him one hour in the nearby canteen.

'There's an acute shortage of air-traffic control staff at a time when there's a dramatic increase in the number of planes in the sky,' he complained. 'There are a lot more near-misses than the public hear about. We have our own system of reporting. I have reported things that were outrageously dangerous, real screamers that almost caused me to have heart-failure. Yet I don't think they were included in the air-safety statistics. When you've had a heavy day, you feel as if you've been in the boxing-ring for ten rounds. The job is probably no more stressful than that of City whizz-kids, but if they make mistakes they just lose a lot of money. We're dealing with lives every second of the day.'

Cozens's work rota would consist of two morning shifts, then two night shifts, followed by three days off, returning to two afternoon shifts.

'In 1988, the maximum capacity we were supposed to handle was regularly being breached,' Cozens alleged. 'I know from my own experience. I'm talking first-hand, not hearsay. There were times when I was losing the picture.

'You're trying to be a juggler and you're afraid you're going to drop one. It's a terrifying feeling. You go cold rather than sweaty. In a day, you can go through a hundred deaths. You keep breathing a sigh of relief. The whole system has been pushing its luck for years.

'By 1986 the traffic was building faster than predicted, while at the same time the number of controllers was falling, as a direct policy of trimming and streamlining. Around that period, KLM, worried about safety, began pressuring its government to hire more controllers in Holland. The Dutch government were persuaded and went to tender for ten air-traffic controllers and the CAA made a bid, eventually winning the contract. The upshot was that ten experienced controllers were sent to Holland from Britain on the eve of the Great Sky Rush. The Dutch could see it coming and cashed in at Britain's expense, leaving us further depleted. Can you imagine anything so daft? We're talking about mismanagement on a grand scale.

'In many respects, the pressure on a controller is no different from that on a journalist who has to meet a deadline or a businessman having to work out his VAT tax returns before a certain date. There is pressure to perform faultlessly and accurately within a tight timescale. A failure to do so has its consequences and penalties. The businessman could end up paying more tax than was due or even go to jail. Our failure is measured in human lives; that's the difference. We cannot afford to make mistakes, but we all do; every day.

'The system is not safe. The numbers game is false accounting: by that I mean you cannot use statistics to show that flying is no more risky today than it was ten years ago.

'Just because the number who die in air accidents every year average out about the same, it doesn't follow that the safety factor is constant; that's because the figures are doctored.

'Very often aircraft are missing one another more by luck than judgement. You can close your eyes and fire a gun at random into the air and the odds are you won't hit anything or anybody, but no one would argue what you're doing is safe or that you should continue behaving that way because of the statistics and odds. Yet that's the way air-traffic control has developed. We gamble that our winning run will keep on.

'All the controllers I've ever worked with have all had a profound sense of dedication and commitment. You don't come across skivers: they wouldn't be tolerated by their mates or management. There's a real Battle of Britain spirit, backs to the wall stuff, all the senses and emotions blitzed, but you just have to hang in and hope. This must sound all very melodramatic, but it's the way it is.

'When the shit hits the fan – the way it did in the summers of 1986 and 1987 – no one has a clue how they're going to get through. By the end of your shift, you're ragged; you're one of the limping wounded and all you're fit for is going straight home and crashing out. You haven't the energy for a social life. There's a drag and drain on all your resources.

'I should guess most people have the notion that there's a great deal of direct supervision in the control-room, but there isn't. A controller is left very much to his own devices.

'We're in the business of providing a service to commercial companies, keeping them on the move and helping them make a profit. We're very much involved in the profit-making process for others: the optimum cruising altitude for jet airliners is as high as possible; 37,000 to 43,000 feet. The longer they have to fly at lower altitudes, the more it costs them. That's why there's so much negotiating for those top corridors: we're not really talking altitude, the real issue is profit margin. The captain who's stuck down in the clouds can see all the profit on his flight disappearing in his jetstream and he's not a happy man. Pilots are company executives and they're expected to do their sums just like any other member of the management team.

'All controllers take a pride in providing a good service. We always do better than the minimum required of us. The only thing ever on our mind is how to keep the buggers away from one another!

'One minute everything can be ticking over sweetly, then the next minute you suddenly have eighteen orange dots demanding your attention all at once. You have to remind yourself that each dot represents three or four hundred people. It's mad!

'We don't have strategic planning. What we have is hit and miss. So many planes turn up simultaneously, you can be running very hard. You can very quickly reach a situation in which a pilot calls and you don't know who he is and you're rapidly losing the picture. At that point, you cannot guarantee safety. It doesn't mean there's going to be a crash. It means you don't know what's going to happen and that is not providing safety.

'I would shout, "Oh, my God! What's happening? Quick, help me out!" The real danger is when there's a lack of communication; when a controller tries to hide the fact that he's overloaded and he's lost the overall picture. If you shout, someone will always come running and you'll get out of trouble.

'Visualize a large, empty car-park and suddenly, simultaneously, two vehicles enter it from opposite entrances. It's dark and neither car has lights on and the two drivers aren't aware of each other's presence. Even so, the odds are against a collision. In blissful ignorance, they will pass one another in the night. But the fact that there's no collision is not proof of good safety management. The law of chance is on their side and that's how it is so often in the air. Figures prove only whatever argument you're trying to justify; they're used for illusions.

'The CAA has been putting out propaganda to the effect that the number of near-misses is decreasing, but that is duff information. There are many near-misses which pilots never know about, often because they're in cloud at the time and see nothing. The only people who know the real score of the game are the ground controllers. But to make a report on a near-miss involves an hour of paperwork in your off-duty time. In reality, it means working overtime, without pay, to write about what are often your own shortcomings. Human nature being what it is, there's a tendency to avoid making a report, if at all possible. Only a fool is going to blow the whistle on himself after he's done it once and has been verbally kicked around for it.

'A lot of doubtful data were being put out by the authorities and a number of people decided in 1987 it was whistle-blowing time. There were a number of moles among controllers around the world who were desperate for the truth to get out so that something might be done, but I wasn't one of them. I always played by the rules.

'I saw one controller sitting transfixed as two dots on his screen were converging. He had frozen. The planes were going to collide – there was no doubt about that – and at that moment he was the only person in the world who could prevent it, unless someone intervened. "What are you going to do?" I shouted. There was no answer; he was still mentally and physically paralysed.

'I plugged in and pulled the planes apart. My colleague's hair was standing on end and he was flushed, like a naughty schoolboy caught cheating in class. It's a terrible feeling when you lose control and hard to explain, but you have to ride it out and run faster and faster until you catch up. In the end, the strain gets to everyone. One controller almost starved himself to death. He worried so much about his job that he couldn't eat and his bowels withered. He was in hospital for six months and it was all put down to pressure of work. All the sharp, jagged edges of tension are there to be seen. The atmosphere's volatile; there's intolerance and shouting, and relationships are strained. You become a grey person, beaten to a pulp. You reach a point where you say to yourself, "If I get one more plane, how will I cope?" You feel that one more pilot calling in will break you. "Will it call? Won't it call?" You're like a fully wound-up spring that's being ever further tightened by the minute, until you're at the absolute limit.

'I never believed that the system was ever protecting me, which is bad for morale and confidence.

'You'll always find a lot of compulsive smokers, even if they're banned from smoking at work. Most of us would light up the moment we stepped into daylight and a cigarette would be burning until bedtime. I've never witnessed alcoholism, though. Most controllers would be too tired to have the energy to go boozing after their shift: bed tends to be the first and last stop.

'We did resent being branded a bunch of skivers by the CAA because you couldn't come across a more conscientious bunch who really cared about the service they were giving.

'Because there's no obvious profit in safety, no commercial value, it will always be the last item on any agenda. People have to be made to realize that we're in a pre-disaster situation; we're very close to the edge. The numbers of controllers are improving, but they're not keeping pace with expansion. The industry's crying out for more runways and more airspace. It's a crisis and money must be thrown at it.

'Just half an hour before Paul Channon [then the Secretary of State for Transport] paid us an official visit, there was almost a head-on collision, which would have been the fault of the controller next to me. I was looking after the Dover sector while the person next to me had control of military aircraft over East Anglia. Just by chance, I spotted that he had two planes on a collision course at 27,000 feet. I asked him, "What are you going to do about it?" I didn't get an answer. His eyes had glazed over and I could tell he was in a state of brain-freeze.

'By that time, the planes were about thirty seconds from disaster, so I had to intervene. I plugged in and took over. When the emergency was over, the guy beside me was shellshocked. It can happen to anyone, no matter how experienced. A great actor can go on stage and suffer a mental blank, so why not an air-traffic controller?'

Let us study in closer detail the anatomy of a near-hit. Any day would do, the occurrence is so prevalent, but let us settle for 1 July 1987. It could be any country, but for the sake of accuracy we are talking about the United Kingdom.

Flight BA 473, a British Airtours Tristar, was descending at 2.15 p.m. over the south of England for a landing at Gatwick. As it approached Britain's second busiest airport, the captain made contact, using its callsign, Speedbird 73 Lima.

Fifty miles to the west of Gatwick, the crew of a British Airways 747, Flight BA 073, were preparing to take off from Heathrow for Toronto, Canada. The captain was given the callsign Speedbird 73. This meant that, when abbreviated on the controllers' radar screens, the Tristar descending into Gatwick and the 747 about to depart Heathrow would both have appeared with the matching '73' label, which should not have caused complications because of their different headings and the miles between them.

The Tristar was cleared into its finals for landing when there was a major hiccup at Gatwick, where a navigation light had gone on the blink and the airport's only runway, at one of the peak times of the day, had to be temporarily closed. For the controllers, it was a test of initiative and improvisation. Incoming aircraft had to be deployed in airspace all over the Home Counties, using every corridor of available stacking territory.

Meanwhile, the 747 to Toronto took off, but was held down by controllers at a low, uneconomic altitude and the captain was anxious to negotiate permission to climb. There were now two Speedbird 73s in the air and a freak set of circumstances was conspiring to bring about a dangerous encounter.

A tired, overworked controller, nearing the end of an exhausting shift, could very easily have sent the two of them into an identical holding position. Cloud would have robbed the crews of any faint chance of seeing one another.

Laurie Taylor, also on his way to Toronto in a 747, once came so close to another plane as he was passing through cloud that he got a clear view of the other pilot. Mark 1 Eyeball is the pilot's term for the last line of defence: in clear visibility, when all else has failed, there is the outside chance of one pilot, or both, being able to take avoiding action, usually diving or climbing. 'In my near-hit drama, it was too late for that,' Taylor recalled. 'It was all over in the blink of an eyelid. Our missing distance could be measured in fractions. Luck kissed me that day.'

But on 1 July 1987, at West Drayton, a hawk-eyed controller was quick to pick up the two Speedbird 73s blinking at him from the same screen and he took the necessary action to ensure that there would be no further confusion, which was fortunate because of their close proximity. It is on that sort of day that there will be an aluminium shower, the euphemism among controllers for the unthinkable.

The authorities claim that the way the two Speedbird 73s were spotted was evidence that everyone was doing a good job and the system was working.

In Britain, for example, the CAA and its functional limb, the National Air Traffic Services (NATS), pointed to a steady decline in the number of mid-air near-hits since 1977. But this was denied by most controllers and pilots for the reasons already stated: flight crews are often unaware they have nearly been involved in a collision, and controllers are either reluctant to report themselves or are discouraged from doing so by their superiors.

In 1987 the chairman of BALPA, Mike Clarke, reflected pilots' suspicion of statistics when he commented, 'We have no doubt that air-misses have been falling over the years. But we have to ask whether the precise figures are useful or rubbish.'

In the same year, Keith Mack, the head of the National Air Traffic Services (NATS), remarked that the whole of the United Kingdom was effectively 'one big terminal area', while explaining that the air-corridors over southern England were practically the most congested in the entire world. And a pessimistic retired supervisor was warning that every plane in the air over southern England was in a 'potential conflict situation'.

In September 1986 a DC9 and a small private plane, a Piper Archer piloted by Los Angeles businessman William Kramer, collided with fatal consequences over southern California, prompting a traffic controller to state publicly, 'When there's good flying weather in southern California, there are so many aeroplanes in the sky there's absolutely no way you can possibly keep track of them all.' This controller, based at the FAA's Palmdale control centre, added, 'It's a miracle there are not more collisions.'

The DC9 was owned by Aeromexico and there were no survivors among the sixty-four passengers and crew. The three people in the light aircraft also died and there were fatalities on the ground. After the crash, the FAA instituted a six-hour spot check at twenty-three airports in the Los Angeles Basin and recorded 175 violations of restricted airspace in that brief period.

That summer, thirty-four controllers at the Palmdale ATC Center had been suspended from duty following allegations that they all used cocaine and hashish. Thirteen of those suspended controllers had been offered special leave to undergo drug rehabilitation, causing Congressman Guy Molinari to demand that all US traffic-controllers should be compelled to submit themselves for drug and alcohol tests. However, 'air-traffic control limitations' were cited by the National Transportation Safety Board as the probable cause of the collision.

In the United States, many of the air-traffic problems date back to 1981, when President Reagan dismissed all controllers who had gone on strike. At a stroke, the air-traffic control network was decimated. The system was maintained by non-strikers and chaos in United States' airspace persisted throughout the decade, despite a new recruitment drive.

Five years later in the US, there was only half the number of qualified controllers there had been in 1981, despite the fact that there were more flights to manage than ever before. The FAA insisted that safety would be maintained by vigorously controlling traffic-flow at peak periods, until more controllers had been employed and fully trained. Despite these assurances, there was little comfort for anybody. Throughout the mid-eighties, the number of near-hits in US airspace soared at an alarming rate: 592 in 1984, which was then a record; 758 in 1985; 867 in 1986.

'Critical' near-hits in 1986 numbered 141, which meant that collisions were avoided by luck and not judgement, substantiating the unacceptable roulette ingredient in modern air travel.

To be fair, the FAA recognized the need for updating the system and moved fast, initiating a modernization programme scheduled for completion in 1993. Old prototype ATC computers were to be replaced with high-tech models which would do the job ten times as quickly as their predecessors. The new generation of computers could accept seven million instructions per second and store sixteen megabytes in their memory. The updating process was to include greater centralization and consolidation. Some 200 separate radar control centres were to be merged into 23 zone areas, each equipped with a new computer. Contemporary software would also be on its way.

These achievements and the considerable subsequent progress must not be minimized, but the controllers and their representatives, backed by pilots' unions, continued to stress that the provision of new technological hardware was tackling only half the problem. The other half was a human one. A brilliant machine could still be let down by a tired and overworked operator.

Laurie Taylor's accusation that commercial aviation had evolved through the influence of ambulance-chasing and attending funerals was borne out by the development of the air-traffic control system, which was not properly organized until 1956 as a response to the collision of two airliners over the Grand Canyon. It has taken more ambulances and funerals to induce the political will for further legislation and innovation.

The CAA also announced in the late eighties an update of the British equipment, but in many parts of the world the facilities remained so primitive – almost non-existent – that pilots in certain regions had to keep announcing their altitude and heading over the radio, in the hope that other crews in the area would be listening in and picking up the signals. Pilots dubbed this 'DIY trafficking'.

Any accusation of scare-mongering against the controllers in the United States would be unjustified. Every year the number of reported near-hits in the US has risen steeply. California has been a particular black spot, with near-hits doubling between 1981 and 1986, reaching crisis point when there was a report every two days. Of the 709 incidents listed in California during those five years, 155 were categorized by the FAA as 'critical'; the planes had come within 100 feet of each other. But several of the near-hits involved aircraft which missed one another by ten feet or less.

An obstacle to tighter legislation in the United States was the political strength of the private plane owners, a wealthy and articulate lobby of more than 250,000 members and as influential as the firearms pressure group. The lobby fought strenuously and successfully any attempt by the FAA to ban light aircraft from the commercial routes.

When the DC9 collided with a private plane, there were more than ten other similar 'fun' aircraft in dangerously close proximity to commercial flights.

Dennis Cottle, a former commercial pilot who had moved to a ground job at Palmdale, said, 'Even if you see every plane up there, you can't possibly track every one. It's impossible.'

Frustrating for controllers was the lack of transponders on so many small privately-owned family planes. It is the transponder which identifies the plane to the controllers and Cottle said, 'It's almost impossible to see an aeroplane not equipped with one.'

Most controllers are, as Cozens said, devoted to their vocation, but not all. In 1989, Captain Gaetano Comignano and his crew were just three minutes from touchdown in the middle of the night at Reggio Calabria's Tito Minniti airport in southern Italy, when all the runway lights went out. On board that domestic flight from Rome were 124 passengers. Comignano had the wheels of the ATI C9 down and was committed to land, but suddenly there was not a light to be seen. The pilot's immediate assumption was that there had been a power failure, so he radioed the tower for information and assistance. He could scarcely believe the reply: Comignano was told that the controllers had warned that they would close down the airport at 1 a.m. 'on the dot'. It was then a minute past one o'clock and they were 'off'. The controllers then unplugged and Flight 314 was left to its own devices, with the ground rapidly approaching.

All Comignano could do in the unprecedented circumstances was attempt a last-minute overshoot. In pursuit of that end, he restored full power and put the aircraft into a steep climb. ATI Flight 314 was helped that night by a favourable wind which gave it lift just at the critical moment, and Comignano was able to fly away to safety, eventually landing 100 miles further along the coast, where the standard of service was more civilized.

The following day an investigating magistrate learned that Flight 314 had been subjected to a similar ordeal at the same airport twenty-four hours earlier. On both those nights, Flight 314 had been delayed at Rome. On each occasion, a controller at Tito Minniti had contacted the captain to remind him that the airport at Reggio Calabria closed at midnight and that it would be kept open an extra hour, 'but not a minute more'.

On the night before Comignano was in command, the pilot changed course several miles from Tito Minniti when he failed to raise the airport on the radio and saw that it was in darkness. But Captain Comignano believed he could beat the 1 a.m. deadline. On his final approach, he was in constant touch with the tower at Tito Minniti and they gave him his last-minute landing instructions.

'We were about to land, with the wheels down, and on the stroke of one o'clock, out went the lights,' he told a press conference. 'This could never have happened in any other airport in Europe. I would have thought from a human viewpoint that air control would have stayed on a bit, knowing we were coming in. How anyone can turn off lights when a jet airliner is minutes from touchdown is incomprehensible. The rules seem to be very rigid. Had a south to north wind been blowing, the situation would have been critical and possibly disastrous.'

Passengers screamed and there was some panic when the plane overshot. 'We did have to take pretty drastic action and a number of people did think we were going to crash and they were going to die,' said the pilot. 'It was a close call. And it would not have been an accident. We would have been sent to our death.' A magistrate investigated a possible charge of 'criminal irresponsibility', but there were no arraignments.

There are exceptional circumstances when a pilot has to make do without runway lights. Laurie Taylor was at the controls of a Boeing 707 on the ground at night at Caracas, Venezuela, and the passengers were filing towards the aircraft across the tarmac from the terminal building, when there was an earthquake. 'The ground moved and the passengers fell,' Taylor recalled. 'The plane shook as if in a hurricane storm and all the lights went out, not only at the airport but throughout the city and all around for miles.

'I got out of the aircraft and commandeered a car and drove the whole length of the runway, looking for cracks or ravines, but I couldn't see any damage. After picking themselves up, the passengers had run for cover inside the aircraft.

'I made an instant decision. I told the airport chiefs that I was going to attempt a take-off. They thought I'd gone crackers.

'"You can't, all the controllers have gone home!" I was told. "Everyone's going home! You must get out of the airport."

'"That's exactly what I intend doing," I said. "Upwards!" It seemed to me that we'd be better off in the air without controllers than on the ground in an earthquake.

'It was about midnight when I made my take-off roll in pitch darkness, as if there wasn't a light in the world, just the aircraft's lights. I laid it on the line to the passengers, giving them the choice of taking their chance with me or staying with the earthquake. I think they all came. I'm sure I made the right decision. I shouldn't like to have to do it again, but we got away safely. The worst part was the runway roll. There was always the possibility that it would open up in front of us if there were more earth tremors.'

Over the United Kingdom, 27 August 1986 was a bad day for air-traffic flow, but useful for academic study of the dangers of having to rely on antiquated hardware. The preamble to a potential disaster began over the North Sea at a point in the sky named Blufa, an airways frontier. Blufa is a reporting point for all aircraft entering the London flight information region. Two DC10s, within a minute of one another at 1.10 p.m., were passed from Amsterdam control to West Drayton. Both DC10s were cruising in airway UB1, one of the numerous freeways in the sky in British airspace. The controllers who handled the British North Sea sector – one of the most congested in the world, with at least 70,000 movements a year – are based not in London but at Eastern Radar at RAF Watton, near Norwich, in East Anglia.

The first of the two DC10s to check-in to Eastern Radar did so from 28,000 feet, heading for the Ottringham beacon on the River Humber and then on to Manchester. The second DC10 was cruising at 24,000 feet and making for yet another check-point, Dogga, where it was scheduled to make a right turn and head up to the east coast on airway UB13.

Nothing was untoward at this stage. The vertical separation between airliners had to be a minimum of 1000 feet and this was being observed, although the DC10 at 24,000 feet was expecting to be cleared very soon to a higher and more economic altitude.

Both aircraft were given their squawks, but the equipment at Eastern Radar was so obsolete that it was unable to translate information automatically. The flight details of the two DC10s had been passed from London to Eastern Radar via datalink. It was then the responsibility of an air-traffic control assistant at Eastern Radar to record those details on an illuminated board with a chinagraph pencil.

After the controller identified the planes on his screen, the assistant attached a store dot, an electric flag giving the details of each aircraft so that they could be easily identified as they worked their way across the screen. But there was an inbuilt flaw: the store dot could not automatically follow the trace. This had to be done manually. Using the chinagraph pencil, the assistant had to keep updating, on a display board, the altitude and heading of all aircraft in their sector. Horizontally, the two DC10s were so close that the radar failed to separate them, giving 'garbled returns'. It was totally incapable of distinguishing one from the other.

At this point, although hectic, everything was still under control, a situation that was to change dramatically. A trainee assistant at Eastern Radar volunteered to make himself responsible for moving the store dots and his help was appreciated. But a few seconds later there was a breakdown with the datalink and information dried up on all other aircraft poised to cross the threshold into that sector. The trainee was told to seek help from trained staff, while the assistant tried to restore the link, without which radar traces would appear on their screen but without identification.

Unfortunately, the instruction was not heard by the trainee. As a consequence, the store dots became attached to the wrong traces and the display board showed incorrect information.

Because the overall picture was becoming confused, the controller requested one of the DC10s to switch off his transponder. The object of this manoeuvre was to procure an unequivocal response from the other DC10. Everything from here on, however, was flawed, because the store dot of the Ottringham-bound DC10 had been transferred by mistake to a completely different aircraft. The time was 1.16 p.m. and events were conspiring to bring about a crisis which could very easily have had a fatal denouement.

The lower DC10 was cleared to 28,000 feet, the same altitude as the other DC10. It was about a further minute before the captain of the aircraft heading for Ottringham started a steady left turn, just to the east of the Humber estuary. At that moment, he caught a shimmering metallic glimpse of the other DC10, took immediate, reflex avoiding action, and radioed Eastern Radar. The two planes missed one another by 'a few hundred feet'. If they had been in cloud, this could have been an account of the first mid-air collision between two jet airliners in British airspace.

Just one month earlier, the ten controllers of North Sea airspace had warned NATS in a letter that their equipment was 'archaic'. The letter had succinctly spelled out the difficulties, including defective radars, outmoded working methods and repeated interference on the airwaves.

In an effort to pacify the disgruntled controllers, Keith Mack, the head of NATS, and Tom Murphy, managing director of the CAA, hired a conference room at a London hotel for four hours to bring everybody together. Approximately 200 controllers attended the meeting, at which Mack is reported to have taken considerable flak during his twenty-minute address. The CAA had promised an initial £26 million improvement programme and had followed the Americans in introducing flow-control whenever there was a danger of controllers being overloaded. Mack continued to put forward the official line that 'serious' near-hits in the United Kingdom were going down in number the whole time. Quoting CAA figures, he said that between 1980 and 1985 the number of 'serious' mid-air incidents had dropped from 31 a year to 21, during which time aircraft movements had risen from 2 million to 2.7 million.

At 6.30 a.m. on 15 November 1986 there was a total black-out at the West Drayton London Air Traffic Control Centre, just as the incoming rush of transatlantic flights was beginning. It was a total power-failure, which crippled even the back-up generator. Everything was wiped from the radar screen covering England and Wales south of Newcastle. After the IBM 9020 computer, a model of the mid-sixties, broke down, eclipsing the progress of all flights, controllers had to return to writing data by hand. Batteries, which would last for only half an hour, kept the radios functioning so that controllers and flight crew were still able to retain communication.

Once again 'a freak sequence of events' was blamed, initiated by the failure of a small capacitor. One controller said of that morning, 'There were many air misses, all due to equipment failures. We were lucky. If the same sequence of events occurs in the summer, the effect does not bear thinking about.'

The engineers managed to restore power to the computer just five minutes before the batteries were due to run out. For twenty-five minutes, airliners had been stacked over London without ground controllers having any radar scrutiny of their movements.

A speedy modernization programme would have seemed essential, but it was not to be because the CAA's negotiations for a new £13 million machine were delayed by the insistence of the manufacturers that the CAA, which was covered by insurance for claims of up to £450 million, should indemnify them against the cost of any litigation.

Saturday, 6 February 1988 was a day none of the controllers at West Drayton, nor Captain Clive Richardson, will ever forget. Winter weekends were usually slack, but because of the increasing popularity of ski holidays in Europe, flights to snow resorts had proliferated almost into a shuttle service. Adding to the congestion was the fact that Gatwick had closed again, this time at 10.50 a.m., to allow runway landing lights to be repaired. Simultaneously, one of the Heathrow runways was out of action and so a quiet Saturday soon became mayhem.

Flights into Britain across the Channel from mainland Europe were being stacked near Gatwick and Lydd, Kent. No restriction was placed on the air-flow, but the controller looking after the Lydd sector began to realize that the build-up was becoming too much for him and he called for help, his plea being answered by a colleague who plugged in.

Two bleeps on the screen, both at 18,000 feet, represented a Bulgarian airlines TU54 and a British Airways TriStar, piloted by Captain Richardson. At 11 a.m. these two blips were heading inexorably towards one another.

Another controller, witnessing what was happening from his own screen, rushed to the Lydd control panel, but by the time he got there to shout his warning it was too late. The two blips had merged, becoming one.

The controller of the Lydd sector was 'devastated'. At that moment, he believed that every controller's nightmare had become his reality.

On those two aircraft there were more than 500 people.

For twelve seconds, the two blips remained locked as one on the screen, with the controllers watching in shocked silence, waiting for the dots to disappear. But they suddenly separated.

Richardson, en route from Paris to London, had seen the Bulgarian aircraft and had swung his TriStar to the right. Experts were later to confirm that a delay of another second – or even less – and both aircraft would have been on their way down in pieces to the Kentish countryside.

The controller in charge of the Lydd sector that morning was to admit in his report that he 'simply forgot' the two aircraft heading for each other at 18,000 feet. Another controller, also on duty that morning, said, 'We've all had incidents, even bad ones, which we still get away with without reporting. The system leads you on until you are forced into an error.'

Two weeks later it was happening all over again with the pilot of a Pan Am 727, making for Heathrow, having to take avoiding measures narrowly to miss a British Caledonian BAC 1-11 going from Gatwick to Amsterdam. The captain of the Pan Am aircraft, which had 147 passengers and seven crew on board, took his plane down to 25,000 feet when the instructions were to descend to 26,000 feet. At 25,000 feet, he was at the same altitude as the BAC 1-11, which was carrying 65 passengers and five crew. Both planes were on course for a beacon at Clacton, Essex, an extremely hectic sector of the British network of air corridors.

By 1988, NATS had come to the conclusion that the long-term solution for Britain was a total reorganization of the air-traffic control over London and the south-east, emulating the system which had been adopted for New York airspace, an even busier hub.

Keith Mack was confident that the new system, known as Central Control Function – to be introduced before 1995 – would make it possible for 30 per cent more flights to be handled. The airspace for restructuring came under the heading of London Terminal Manoeuvring Area (LTMA), stretching from the capital, through most of the Home Counties and covering the altitudes 2500 to 13,500 feet. Aircraft served by the LTMA were to be those using Heathrow, Gatwick,

Stansted and Luton. The concept was to make the job simpler for the controllers.

In the old system, any aircraft heading for London would be handled by someone at West Drayton looking after one of the five outlying sectors. Pilots were then given directions and told at what altitude to fly. Aircraft taking off would be controlled by staff at the airport tower until being passed over to the LTMA shortly after becoming airborne. The ten on-duty LTMA controllers could each be handling up to fifteen aircraft at any one time. Central Control Function was designed to change all that.

The area covered by the LTMA was to be expanded by 50 per cent, taking in altitudes up to 19,000 feet and segregated into approximately 30 sectors, and creating a one-way system in the sky over south-east England. Each sector was to have its own controller. Corridors, some hundreds of miles in length, would be reserved for planes flying from or to specified airports, with no trespassing or deviation tolerated. Because controllers would be dealing with traffic heading in one direction only, the hope was for a less complex working practice and a reduction in the amount of communication and co-ordination necessary.

There was to be no change to the stacking procedures and organization in which aircraft queued: Heathrow had four stacks, Gatwick two, and Luton and Stansted shared a couple. However, they were to be pushed further back, thus enabling aircraft taking off to climb quickly above the stacks, rather than be forced to duck under them. This streamlining of the system was designed to allow jet airliners to attain their economic cruising height much more rapidly. Better cohesion was to be effected by the transfer of approach controllers at each airport to West Drayton, where they would be placed beside the LTMA controllers, who would be handling distant incoming flights. Extra miles would be added to some flights, but the bottom line was expected to be improved safety.

Alan Parker, who had been given the task of making the Central Control Function operational, likened the plan to a one-way route in a town or city: some favourite short-cuts would be declared out of bounds so that everything was kept on the move, free from the danger of meeting anything head-on. He was to say, 'We are going to have three very busy airports and a tremendous criss-crossing of traffic between them. Somehow we have to try to accommodate it all.'

Meanwhile, Mack was cautious about the outcome of the £200 million being spent on the five-year improvement programme: 'That should enable us to meet the demand safely. But I won't say there will not be any near-misses: I could never guarantee that.'

It is wrong, however, to believe that a mid-air collision occurs only near airports. On New Year's Day 1984, a Pan Am DC10 had to dive 600 feet to miss another Pan Am aircraft, a 747, when they were over the southern Atlantic, 200 miles from Miami. Two giant modern airliners – each weighing something in the region of 240 tons – could hardly get closer without impact: when the pilot of the DC10, doing a charter run between New York and the West Indies, put his plane into a nose-dive, seven miles high, only fifty feet separated them.

The 747, Pan Am Flight 99, was out of London Heathrow for Miami. A collision would almost certainly have produced a death toll of 499.

Jim Reilly, the manager of the Miami air-traffic control centre, acknowledged that the mistake was made on the ground. 'The jets shouldn't have been assigned the same altitude. Somewhere along the line, we goofed up here. Somewhere there was a lack of co-ordination.'

And a Miami controller agreed with Reilly: 'There's no question that the error was here. The two flights were in radio contact, but too far out to register radar. The controllers involved weren't trainees. They have some 30 years' experience between them. But it happened.'

Another controller said that the incident could be directly attributed to the sacking by President Reagan of the 11,000 striking air-traffic staff.

One person was injured, though not seriously, in the DC10. A passenger from that plane described the experience thus: 'It was more of a shock than frightening. For a minute we felt like astronauts, weightless as the plane dropped. None of us saw the other aircraft. We're very grateful to the captain.'

By 1989, the worst mid-air collision remained that of a British Airways Trident and a Yugoslav DC9 over Zagreb in September 1976. All 176 people involved died.

Of one incident over north London, on 29 July 1986, an aviation expert commented, 'The two planes were closing at a combined speed of almost 500 knots [nearly 600 mph]. Technically, they should have collided.' Both planes were making for Heathrow: a BAe 1-11 shuttle from Edinburgh and a Boeing 737 out of Munich. At 10.30 a.m. both captains were given identical instructions; to fly to a point just above

Stanmore, in north London, where they would make turns to bring them on to their landing approach. Subsequently, it was the 737 from Munich, with 70 passengers, which was 'overlooked'. When the controller realized his mistake, he radioed the captain of the 737, but it was too late. The blips on the radar screen had already converged. A collision was averted at the last split-second by the pilot of the 737 pulling back on the controls, putting his aircraft into the steepest possible climb and leapfrogging over the BAe 1-11.

Although a catastrophe had been avoided, it was no credit to the system. Investigators learned that the controller who made the mistake on this occasion had two VIP visitors with him in the control-room, both peering over his shoulder and plugging into the system when the near-hit occurred, which could well have distracted him. The official report made the observation: 'It is possible that the presence of two visitors, who were listening to the radio-telephone and were watching his screen, may have contributed. It is noteworthy that Heathrow radar control receives an almost constant stream of official and unofficial visitors, and it is common practice for them to plug in to the RTF beside an active controller. It is, however, the right of the controller to send them away if he thinks that their presence is interfering with his concentration. This does not normally occur.'

Robert McCrindle, the Conservative Member of Parliament for Brentwood and Ongar, and chairman of the all-party House of Commons Aviation Committee, wrote to the CAA to demand an immediate ban on visitors using equipment in airport control towers. Michael Spicer, the British Government's Aviation Minister, also called for the papers on the case, to see if Parliament should intervene. However, the CAA did not believe a 'blanket' ban was necessary because any controller had a right to refuse to allow a visitor use of air-traffic control equipment, though this was not as easy in practice as in theory because most guests tended to be VIPs. The government did not see fit to act on the matter.

Sometimes it is not so much the actual circumstances of a near-hit as the protagonists themselves that give it status among the statistics. For instance, on 25 July 1985 the British people almost lost their Prime Minister.

Margaret Thatcher left the House of Commons at 3.30 p.m. to be driven in her official car to nearby Chelsea Barracks, where a Puma helicopter was awaiting her. Flying the helicopter was Squadron Leader Paul Buckland.

In Mrs Thatcher's party that afternoon were Charles Pole, a private secretary responsible for foreign affairs; Stephen Sherbourne, a member of the Prime Minister's political office; Jean Caines, a deputy press secretary; a clerk; and two detectives acting as bodyguards. This was to be the start of Mrs Thatcher's journey to Washington for a two-day political conference.

Ground controllers directed the Puma to the VIP bay on Heathrow's south side, where the Prime Minister's RAF VC-10 was parked.

Meanwhile, Captain Peter King, on the flight-deck of a British Airways 757, was being cleared for take-off on Runway 10 Right. Seconds later he began his take-off roll, with the 126 passengers on board expecting Frankfurt, West Germany, to be the next stop.

The Puma carrying Mrs Thatcher and her party was flying parallel with Runway 10 Right. There was no risk until the helicopter suddenly turned across the runway. At that moment, the British Airways 757 reached 138 mph and was about to leave the runway.

A controller spotted the danger and shouted to Captain King over the radio, 'Abort! Abort!' The warning coincided with King's own sighting of the helicopter. He slammed on the brakes and threw the engines into reverse thrust. Luggage fell from overhead lockers but no one was injured and Flight 728 stopped safely before the end of the runway, though the aircraft had to be left for an hour to allow the brakes to cool.

A Heathrow official was to claim, 'The jet was just seconds away from smashing into the helicopter. We were on the brink of a major disaster, which could have involved more than 150 people.'

If the 757 had been travelling another 27 mph faster, it would have been committed to take-off, having passed the point of no return, and a collision would have been almost inevitable.

After the jet came to a standstill, there was a blistering exchange of words between King and a controller, though it was not until much later that the captain of the British Airways jet was aware that the helicopter was carrying the Prime Minister.

A CAA spokesman confirmed that a complaint had been lodged and a report would be made available to the aviation industry, 'but would not be for public consumption'. He did venture that 'I don't think air-traffic control is involved in this case.'

King was later to tell reporters at his home in Maidenhead, Berkshire, 'I thought it would be a routine flight and I would be back in time for a round of golf.'

British Airways stated, 'We had a 757 on its way to Frankfurt. It was cleared for take-off. An instruction was given from traffic control to abort, which it did safely. Later, it returned to the runway and took off for Frankfurt safely.'

Flight 728 had been running approximately 20 minutes late, otherwise it would have been well on its way to Frankfurt long before the arrival on the scene of the Prime Minister's helicopter.

Recognizing the expanding needs for air-traffic facilities in British airspace, the CAA pledged a further £300 to £400 million investment on top of the £200 million already guaranteed between 1987 and 1992. The extra cash was to be injected into the system between 1992 and the close of the century. Priority was being given to enlarging and streamlining West Drayton, replacing obsolescent radar, providing a new computer and setting aside £21 million for Central Control Function. The additional funding from 1992 would be to finance three major projects: the construction of a completely new London Air Traffic Control Centre on a new site, costing a least £190 million; the upgrading of the Scottish Air Traffic Control Centre at Prestwick, Ayrshire; and finally the introduction of microwave landing systems, futuristic technology making provisions for more aircraft to utilize existing runways.

The development during the eighties of TCAS, the Traffic Alert and Collision Avoidance System, was hailed in the United States as a panacea for all the worst air-traffic ills. Many experts confidently predicted that the device was so revolutionary that the risk of mid-air collisions would be eliminated completely. The main impediment was the price, each system costing £300,000 to buy and fit. It consisted of a cockpit display screen linked to an onboard computer. Antennae were attached to the outside of the aircraft to scan the sky for 'bandits' – literally any other plane – and a transponder transmitted signals to be picked up by all airplanes in the region. Should a plane come within forty-five seconds' flying time of an aircraft equipped with TCAS, an amber light flashed on the screen and an alternative approved route was displayed automatically. If the situation deteriorated further and a 'bandit' was no more than thirty seconds away, then a red alert flashed and a speech synthesizer directed the crew to take immediate avoiding action.

Sperry Dalmo Vickers and Allied Bendix, the American manufacturers of TCAS, had their product on the market in 1988, but not to universal approval by any means. The CAA, for example, were none too enthusiastic and were quickly accused by many pilots and controllers of obscurantism. The CAA's view was put this way: 'What could be useful in the wide open spaces of the United States may be completely unsuitable for the congested airways of south-east England. If all pilots were to decide they were on conflict collisions, it could cause greater chaos with everyone diverting at the same time. If the Americans were to force this one through, there would be complete fury. They are always trying to force their standards on the rest of the world.'

Is that so dreadful, if those 'enforced' standards are high ones and in order to protect and preserve human life?

Piedmont Airlines played an important role in pioneering TCAS, which was attached to one of their Boeing 727s. After 360 hours of intensive testing, Ken Carlson, the airline's TCAS project manager in New York, had been won over. 'Every pilot that has used it is absolutely delighted. They're grateful for every bit of information they can get.' Talking specifically about the TCAS performance, he said, 'It works beautifully.'

The FAA, in response to pressure from government, the public and pilots to find a way to negate the peril of collision in the sky, dictated that by 1992 it should be compulsory for all aircraft making use of the United States to have the TCAS device on board, which should have been good news to everyone. Even if it was not to prove a magic-wand solution, at least it was a significant shift in the right direction. But there were those who remained not just sceptical, but downright scornful; almost, it would seem, resentful. Instead of new frontiers being conquered in a fraternal spirit of international harmony, rivalry between national regulatory bodies forced up fresh barriers.

Of course, a collision between aircraft on the ground could be equally serious as one in the air, as shown by the crash on 27 March 1977, on the runway at Tenerife, in which more people lost their lives than in any other two-plane accident.

If two planes collide when they are taxiing for take-off for long-haul flights, they are likely to be fully loaded with fuel as well as passengers, so the risk of an explosion is considerable. The increasing number of flights worldwide has aggravated the congestion on the ground as well as in the air. Therefore, the invention in 1987 of British scientist David Morton, with the sobriquet Tripwire, was not without significance.

Tripwire, in effect a system of electronic traffic-lights, was a new technique for monitoring all movements of aircraft on runways and taxiways. It consisted of a network of sensor stations placed at regular intervals along the edge of taxiways and connected to a computer in the control-tower. Through the sensors, an infra-red beam was transmitted, identifying the position of all passing aircraft on the ground. Any aircraft taking a wrong turning or passing a red light was detected through instant computer analysis. Controllers were alerted by visual and audible alarms. Immediately they knew not only the rogue aircraft but also its callsign.

Automated ground movement, managed by radar, had traditionally been restricted to the large airports because of the cost, which was roughly three times as expensive as the Tripwire technique.

Morton, a former Royal Air Force electronics specialist, said of his invention, 'Radar on its own does not solve the problem. As there have been no alarms or means of instant indentification of individual aircraft on standard ground movement radar, the system is only as effective as the operator.'

The inspiration for Morton's research came from a collision at Madrid airport, Spain, in which ninety-three people died. In 1985 he received a £10,000 prize from the Scottish Glenrothes Development Corporation, which was encouraging new technology in aviation. This body has been at the forefront of promoting experimental work in industries which rely on new technology, especially in the computer field, and has a keen interest in the aviation industry. Later Morton borrowed £60,000 to enable him to develop the computer software and to construct the prototype essentials. Tripwire then came successfully through all its laboratory tests and its practicals, which were implemented in Scotland at a regional airport owned by a local authority. Despite the success of the practical and theoretical tests, it seemed unlikely that the CAA or the FAA would be tempted to invest in Tripwire, simply because it was the brainchild of an outsider.

The collision on the runway at Tenerife, which serves as a constant reminder that care on the ground is as imperative as in the air, was between two Boeing 747s, one of Pan Am and the other of KLM. There were no survivors from the KLM flight and a total of 583 people were killed. Weather conditions were so foggy that no one in the control-tower actually witnessed the crash, although it occurred on the runway.

These were the final words at 5.07 p.m. on Sunday, 27 March 1977 between ground control and the aircraft:

KLM co-pilot: 'We are now for take-off.'

Tower to KLM: 'OK. Standby for take-off. I will call you.'

Pan Am co-pilot: 'Clipper 1736.'

Tower: 'Papa Alpha 1736, report runway cleared.'

Pan Am: 'We'll report runway cleared.'

Tower: 'OK. Thank you.'

On that note the KLM captain, Veldhuizen 'Jaap' Zanten, commenced his take-off roll with 229 passengers. Although no one survived from his plane, it is obvious that van Zanten mistakenly believed he had been cleared for take-off. How such a costly mistake could have been made will always remain a matter for conjecture, though one theory is that there was radio interference and he heard only the 'take off' part of the controller's instruction and not the 'standby'. There is also speculation that he missed a vital section of the message from the Pan Am co-pilot.

The Pan Am first officer had said, 'We'll report runway cleared.' If the KLM captain was confident he had been cleared for take-off, the words he would have been expecting to hear from the Pan Am crew were 'runway cleared'. *We'll report* in front of *runway cleared* could quite possibly have also been missed, owing to several abnormal circumstances that day.

The Pan Am first officer survived to relate, 'We saw lights ahead of us in the fog. At first we thought it was the KLM standing at the end of the runway. Then we realized they were coming towards us.' He recalled shouting into the radio, 'Get off! Get off!'

And as Captain Victor Grubbs rushed power to the engines and veered his aircraft towards the grass, he called the tower, 'We're still on the runway.' By then, the KLM's speed was 150 knots and the nose-wheel was already off the ground. Because the cockpit was elevated, the crew of the KLM would not have seen anything of the runway. For a split second the KLM 747 was airborne, but not enough to miss the Pan Am jet, and the collision was broadside.

Before the last words between the tower and the aircraft, this exchange took place with the KLM co-pilot:

KLM: 'The KLM 4805 is now ready for take-off and we are waiting for our ATC clearance.'

Tower: 'You are cleared to the Papa Beacon, climb to and maintain flight level nine zero, right turn after take-off, proceed on heading 040 until intercepting the 325 radial from Las Palmas VOR.'

The KLM co-pilot, double-checking, repeated to the controller the message he had just received from the tower.

Tower: 'OK. Standby for take-off. I will call you.'

Silence, then the tower came back, 'Clearance correct.'

These exchanges had taken the KLM to the stage known as *airways clearance*, just one step from permission to take off. Translated, the instructions from the tower to van Zanten were that he should climb to 9000 feet and then make a right turn, but still he had to wait clearance to roll. There followed the dialogue which one can only assume was misheard and misunderstood, leading to the mishap.

Even after the explosion, the tower did not know what had happened. A controller kept repeating, 'KLM 4805. PA 1736. PA 1736. KLM 4805. Tenerife, KLM 4805. Tenerife, KLM 4805, Tenerife . . . '

The captain of Iberia Airlines Flight IB 174 attempted to contact the tower, getting the reply, '174 please maintain radio silence. Maintain 70 . . . KLM 4805, Tenerife. Clipper 1736, Tenerife . . . IB 174, I think it's better to proceed to Las Palmas. I haven't . . . There is fire on the runway and I don't know what it can be. There were two planes taxiing.'

A British Airways Tristar on the apron added to the dialogue: 'Tenerife, Bealine Alpha Golf.'

Tower: 'Station calling?'

Tristar: 'Bealine Alpha Golf on the corner of the apron: are you on to the flames on the leftside of the main runway?'

Tower: 'Affirmative, sir. We saw it and the fire corps is going there.'

Two of Tenerife's three radio frequencies had been inoperative for six months. The only one in use that Sunday was the 119.7 megacycle frequency, which had been installed originally to guide approaching aircraft. Overcrowding of the simple frequency must have been a contributing factor in the misunderstanding by the KLM captain.

Although the airport, perched 2000 feet above sea level, was shrouded in dense fog, the central runway lights were defunct: van Zanten had requested that they be turned on, but was informed that they were down.

Even the commands to the Pan Am crew had been ambiguous. The tower had been expecting the American airliner to leave the runway at an earlier exit than the one it was heading for. If the Pan Am jet had taken the slipway which the controller understood he had assigned to Captain Grubbs, there would not have been any crash, even with van Zanten rolling without consent.

It would be a mistake to attribute an accident of this nature to inexperience. Captain Grubbs was a World War II hero; van Zanten had been with KLM since 1950, and in 1971 he had become the Dutch airline's instructor on 747s. Later he was chosen for magazine advertisements to foster the image of reliability and stability. Communication through one language, English, is complicated by the range of accents, especially for those crews for whom it is a second or third tongue. The muddle on 29 January 1971 at Sydney airport, Australia, was a classic example. A controller told the captain of a Canadian Pacific Airlines DC8 that he could, 'Take a taxiway right.' To the pilot, who had just landed, it sounded like, 'Backtrack if you like.' Consequently, the captain of the Canadian Pacific DC8 made a U-turn and began to taxi back along the same runway on which he had just landed. Simultaneously, at the other end of the runway, a Trans Australia Airlines Boeing 727 was being cleared for take-off.

Fortunately, visibility was good and the TAA plane managed to get airborne before the two aircraft collided head-on. Even so, the 727 struck the tail of the DC8, illustrating just how close they came to disaster. After dumping fuel at sea, the 727 returned to the airport for an uneventful landing. The cause of the incident was attributed to 'difficulty of accent or idiom'.

While the public debate raged in the late eighties about safety in the sky, Professor Paul Cook, a British international authority on lasers, was drawing to the attention of the aviation legislators yet another peril. His research seemed to indicate that as many as 30 per cent of all pilots could be suffering from night blindness, thus increasing the chances of a mid-air collision after dark. Professor Cook, who held the chair of Laser Technology at Brunel University in Uxbridge, west London, stated: 'The present eye tests for pilots are only applicable specifically to daylight and, no matter how stringent they are, they don't take into account the difference between day and night.'

Official vision examinations were suspect, he feared, because they excluded tests which determined a pilot's ability to see in the dark, cloud or twilight. Professor Cook noted noted from research in Scandinavia that 19 per cent of motorists there suffered from myopia at dusk: that figure soared to 47 per cent at night. All those people failed the standard European driving test and Professor Cook was confident that pilots must be similarly afflicted.

'Averaged out, I would say that 30 per cent is a fair figure for people who suffer from twilight and night myopia,' he estimated. 'Pilots are particularly vulnerable to it because they get in fog or cloud. Some of them would become acutely short-sighted.'

Professor Cook had been using his patented Laser Spec technique to detect fine changes in the eye lens and its ability to focus in dark or gloomy conditions. His work had interested many military air forces, but had been largely ignored by the civilian authorities.

In May 1988 a senior medical officer with the CAA, Dr Ronald Pearson, said that tests were not geared to look specifically at the question of night-sight. He did not think there was 'a real problem' and doubted a significant difference between a person's sight in the day and at night. Dr Pearson defended the CAA's medical standards, arguing that they were 'as high as any in Europe'.

By early 1989 there was so much dissatisfaction with the CAA in Parliament and the industry in general that there seemed little hope of its riding the pressure for radical change. The powerful House of Commons Transport Select Committee had been hearing a catalogue of complaints against the CAA. After assessing much verbal and written evidence, the committee saw a need for fragmenting the CAA and for the creation of an independent watchdog committee to monitor air near-hits. The committee considered it inappropriate for the CAA to continue to employ air-traffic controllers. Air-traffic management, it felt, should be hived off to National Air Traffic Services, the natural organization for this undertaking, because it already co-ordinated military and civil operations. A portion of the report said, 'Whether justified or not it is all too easy to accuse the CAA of being judge and jury in its own court. We recommend that free-standing air-miss investigative machinery be set up.'

On the prickly subject of congestion in the air, Captain Jim Taylor, of the British pilots' union, told the Select Committee, 'The system is adequate . . . just.' Then he asked, 'How are we going to cope with the future?'

Bill Brett, assistant general secretary of the Institute of Professional Civil Servants, representing the controllers, insisted, 'We are not crying wolf. We are crying for help. Unless urgent action is taken, the UK high safety record will be unsustainable.' The Institute feared that safety would be 'downgraded' unless more controllers were engaged.

By March 1989 the Transport Committee had concluded that the CAA was guilty of a 'lack of foresight' in respect of the number of air-traffic controllers employed. Members of the committee 'disagreed strongly' with the CAA's view that the volume of traffic did not compromise safety. In fact the committee accused the CAA of positively compromising safety: 'occasions had given rise to fears that, at times, air-traffic has been overloaded to a point where safety has been in jeopardy.' The committee believed that the CAA should be split to allow the National Air Traffic Services (NATS) to report directly to the Department of Transport, allowing for the formation of 'a rules and regulation body, remaining independent of the Government'.

Comment from the committee's chairman, David Marshall, the Labour Member of Parliament for Shettleston, was that it was 'regrettable' a summer of 'appalling' delays was needed to prod the CAA into action. Paul Channon, who was shortly to be replaced as Transport Secretary in Mrs Thatcher's summer Cabinet re-shuffle, assured the committee, 'We are making up for lost time.' Unimpressed, the committee reported, 'It is with regret that we have to accept that the lost time cannot be made up more speedily.'

The necessity to break up the CAA was articulated succinctly by Terry Dicks, the Conservative MP for Hayes and Harlington. 'We have had a cosy little club in aviation. Now we have actually got in among them.'

One chilling sentence in the committee's official report had this to say on safety: 'We have no evidence that the CAA were not doing all they could, but we were unable to avoid the awful thought that a mid-air collision might provide more incentive to greater efforts.'

Controlling the air routes through Europe was a £1 billion-a-year business, but the Association of European Airlines did their sums and amazed themselves with their findings: the average length of flights could be reduced by 10 per cent and fares could be cut by a similar percentage if only planes were flying in a straight line from A to B and not forced into tedious circumnavigation.

An interesting study came from the German Airspace Users' Association: the total cost of delays in 1988 came to £3 billion, three times as much as the overheads for actually providing the service.

Although the EC was supposed to be evolving into one Europe, in 1989 there were still more than twenty European countries looking after their own airspace. There was an international agency, Eurocontrol, but it had only one centre, based in Maastricht, Holland, serving nearby regions of Benelux and Germany. The European airlanes were the result of national boundaries and politics, and not the outcome of the requirements of international aviation.

In most countries, the tab for funding the air-traffic control system was picked up by the government and there was a persuasive argument for privatizing this part of the aviation industry, a system already being tried successfully by a number of Britain's regional airports. As John Kay, Professor of Industrial Policy at the London Business School, wrote in the London *Daily Telegraph*, 'Privatization would not remove the bargaining power of the air-traffic controllers themselves, but it would place responsibility for the issue with the new management. Once outside the public sector, the right answer is probably to pay up, computerize as much of the system as possible, and feel a little safer and more comfortable with the high quality of staff that enhanced salaries would attract. Such a solution to Europe's air-traffic control problem inescapably reduces the role and authority of national civil servants and regulators.'

However, the most potent preventative medicine for mid-air madness continued to be TCAS, the Traffic Alert and Collision Avoidance System, despite the CAA's persistently tepid response. Thankfully, the FAA showed no sign of relenting on its declared policy of compelling all aircraft using United States airspace to be rigged with TCAS. Rather churlishly, the CAA made it known that aircraft could be ordered to switch off TCAS while in British airspace, despite the enthusiasm for it among pilots of all nations who had put it to the test.

A director of flight operations enthused, 'Like most pilots, I did not at first like the idea of having another instrument on the flight-deck.

But this really does work. Often in cloud you have no idea what is around you, despite being guided by controllers on the ground. This gives you an extremely accurate picture of where all the other traffic is within a twenty-mile radius.'

The CAA obdurately made this response: 'We are now conducting our own tests to ensure that not only is the system accurate but that there are a minimum number of false alarms. A false alert can lead to distrust of the system and it may be eventually ignored. We certainly don't want something which allows pilots to do their own thing when they may be under direct control from the ground.'

In March 1990 the CAA decided that, for the first time, air-traffic controllers' working hours would be regulated. The Authority had heard evidence of controllers working a 72-hour week, having no holiday in six weeks, while at the same time being on emergency call.

For an industry which trades on its speed, progress moves painfully slowly.

11 BLOOD MONEY

It is axiomatic that the manufacturers of airliners are in the business of making money. They are also the cornerstone of safety, which is not always so obvious. First comes the machine, then the man; in that order.

Airlines buy new equipment assuming it to be airworthy: that confidence rubs off on the consumer. Sometimes, unfortunately, it is misplaced. Certainly that was the case on 3 March 1974 for the passengers on the DC10 of Turkish Airlines, flying between Istanbul and London Heathrow.

The Istanbul–Paris segment was uneventful, but shortly after departing Orly for London the DC10 came down in the Forest of Ermenonville, a favourite picnic area for Parisians, cutting a swathe almost a mile long through the woods. All 344 people on board the aircraft died.

Three weeks later and long before the investigation was completed, a press conference was convened by McDonnell Douglas, the makers of the DC10, at their plant in Long Beach, southern California, just down the coast from Los Angeles. Heading the press conference was John Brizendine, president of the Douglas division. Brizendine had a confession to make: Ship 29, the DC10 which had ended its life a premature wreck in a French forest, had been allowed to leave the Long Beach factory without a crucial modification to the rear cargo-door, yet, according to the company's record-book, the work had been done.

Brizendine won many admirers that day for his candour, though this in no way mitigated the lapse by Douglas.

Brizendine spoke with hand-on-heart sincerity: 'This is a circumstance for which we do not yet have an explanation. We are investigating this matter vigorously. We know that we have great responsibilities and we take them very seriously. You might remember – as we always do – that a Douglas aircraft is always a Douglas aircraft, no matter who owns it, how long it remains in service, or what is done with it long after it's beyond our control. Our planes are part of our lives and part of our identity; that's one reason why we develop and build them with such care.'

In 1972 a DC10 had almost crashed over Windsor, Canada, when its rear cargo-door blew out. It was after this scare that an order was made for the reinforcement of all DC10 rear cargo-doors by fitting a support-plate. Ship 29 had just been built and was awaiting a buyer.

Every aircraft has a personal record file, the same as any employee. The dossier on Ship 29 showed that the rear cargo-door had been appropriately modified on 18 July 1972. The investigators found the offending door among the wreckage. It had been blown out in an incident that was a carbon copy of the emergency two years earlier in Canada; the support-plate had not been fitted.

The more the investigators probed the background of Ship 29, the more they realized that something was very wrong. Three Douglas inspectors had verified that the work had been done. Each job had to be specified in writing. When completed, those papers would be rubber-stamped by three checkers. Each rubber-stamp was personalized so that it would identify the user. The names of those inspectors were Edward M. Evans, Henry C. Noriega and Shelby G. Newton.

The mystery deepened when the three Douglas inspectors were questioned. Not one of them, according to their original recollections, had been involved with the modification of any DC10 rear cargo-door during the entire year of 1972. Neither had there been any occasion when the three of them had inspected the same job of work. Further-more, they were adamant that they had not given the stamp of approval to Ship 29 on 18 July 1972, when the aircraft had been parked on the ramp outside Building 54.

Of the three men in question, Evans was the only one to be employed as a full-time inspector. On 18 July 1972, Evans left home at 6.30 a.m. The drive to work took about twenty minutes. From the factory in the evening, he went to college, where he was studying quality control. He did not return home until 10.30 p.m. His personal rubber-stamp had never left his pocket, except for his own use. Therefore, when Evans was shown the position of his official stamp on the job documents, he said he had no alternative but to accept that he must have inadvertently approved work which had not been undertaken. When questioned by a lawyer during the investigation, Evans suggested that he might have been dazzled by the sun, which seemed to offer little towards a plausible explanation. Here is a sequence of dialogue between the attorney and Evans:

Attorney: 'Is it possible that you just missed the ship completely? Just in the press of business, just didn't get to Ship 29? Have you considered that?'

Evans: 'No.'

Attorney: 'You know you did something with Ship 29?'

Evans: 'The papers say I did.'

Attorney: 'True, the papers also say a couple of things that apparently weren't on there. I mean, have you considered that as a possibility?'

Evans: 'No.'

Attorney: 'Are you sure Ship 29 was there at that time?'

Evans: 'I have no idea.'

Attorney: 'I see.'

Evans: 'Everything you have shown me says it was there.'

Referring to the possibility that Evans could have rubber-stamped vital adjustments which had not been done, the attorney asked, 'Is there a doubt in your mind that you did?'

Evans: 'There was.'

Attorney: 'And there still is?'

Evans: 'No.'

Attorney: 'No?'

Evans: 'No.'

Attorney: 'You believe now that you actually stamped that off with those parts not here?'

Evans: 'I have no reason to doubt it. I am sorry.'

Shelby Newton was a highly skilled aeronautical engineer. On 18 July 1972, a Tuesday, he had been supervising the work of twenty men several hundreds of yards away from Building 54. He testified that neither he nor any of his men had worked on Ship 29 and that he had not, at that time, been trained for modification work on DC10 cargo-doors. Nothing could have induced him to 'stamp off work' he had 'not seen done' with his 'own eyes'. Nevertheless, his personalized stamp was on the paperwork. When it was his turn to be cross-examined by the lawyer about the stamp, this exchange took place:

Attorney: 'Did you place it on there?'

Newton: 'No.'

Attorney: 'Did you ever lend your stamp to anyone?'

Newton: 'No.'

Attorney: 'You know that you never let go of your stamp on 18 July 1972: is that correct?'

Newton: 'Yes.'

Attorney: 'It was always in your possession?'

Newton: 'Yes.'

Attorney: 'You never lent it to anyone?'

Newton: 'No.'

Attorney: 'If you didn't put 2Q690 on it and it was your stamp . . .'

Newton: 'Who did?'

Attorney: 'If someone else did, he was breaking the rules of McDonnell Douglas with respect to the use of stamps, as you understand the rules?'

Newton: 'I see what you are saying basically, but I have no answer.'

Attorney: 'Did anybody else have authority to use your Q-stamp?'

Newton: 'No.'

Attorney: 'Whoever used your Q-stamp did so without your authority? Is that correct?'

Newton: 'Nobody else used my Q-stamp.'

Noriega was an electrician and not a qualified mechanic. In all his twenty-four years with Douglas, he had never been entrusted with a mechanical assignment, which made sense if he was not competent for that area of employment. All day on 18 July 1972 he had been working on the electrical fittings of another DC10. He swore on oath that he, too, had never been near Ship 29 that day.

Whatever the truth behind the rubber-stamping of work that had not been done, Brizendine disputed that McDonnell Douglas were to blame for the crash. Although he conceded there had been a failure to fit the support-plate, he disputed that this had caused the break-up of the Turkish Airline DC10 five minutes after leaving Paris Orly.

The make-sure safety device on the rear cargo-door had been lethally mis-rigged. Brizendine alleged that the blame for the mis-rigging had to be shouldered solely by Turkish Airlines, who, in turn, denied culpability, accusing McDonnell Douglas.

The world was robbed of a full-scale public trial when, in May 1975, Douglas and its three co-defendants offered out-of-court settlements to the relatives of the dead and abandoned their defence over liability. In many ways, it was a pity that the public airing did not go ahead.

In court, lawyers for the families would have been able to put on the witness stand as many members of the McDonnell Douglas workforce as they wished. All the minutiae of working practices within the commercial aviation manufacturing industry would have been stripped naked in public. In the long term, although initially costly to McDonnell Douglas, it could have been beneficial to the industry as a whole.

Brizendine claimed that the negligence over Ship 29 was a one-off lapse and not an indictment of the overall standard of workmanship in his domain. In the absence of evidence to the contrary, Brizendine's word had to be accepted, but other incidents of shoddy workmanship elsewhere have again placed the manufacturers in the critical glare of the public spotlight.

On Tuesday, 12 August 1985, a Japanese Airlines Boeing 747, loaded with 509 holidaymakers and 15 crew, crashed into a mountain near Tokyo. There were only four survivors. Flight 123 departed Tokyo's Hameda airport at 6 p.m. on what should have been a one-hour hop to Japan's second city, Osaka. Halfway into the flight, the captain made an emergency radio call, saying they were going down because one of the doors was not properly closed and the fault could not be corrected. Then came the words from the captain, 'Emergency declare', and 'unable to control'. When Tokyo ground control asked if he wanted to return, he answered, 'Please.'

Later, the pilot contacted control again, requesting his position, which were to be his final words. A message from a controller went, 'Hameda and Yokota [a US air base near Tokyo] ready for emergency landing. You can begin approach any time.' But there was no response from the crew of the 747. It was all over.

After an investigation spanning more than twelve months, Boeing were saddled with the blame because of faulty repairs dating back to 1978, after the aircraft's tail had scraped the runway as it landed at Osaka in the June of that year. The slipshod workmanship related to the 747's aft pressure bulkhead, resulting in metal fatigue and cracks. The aft pressure bulkhead is the point at which the cabin is separated from the tail. This bulkhead had ruptured, blowing off the tail-cone, as well as the upper half of the tail-fin and rudder. The pilot had managed to maintain some degree of control because the descent had lasted some thirty-two minutes before Mount Osutaka had come between the 747 and a possible life-saving emergency landing back in Tokyo.

The report by Japan's Transport Ministry Aircraft Accident Investigation Commission exonerated the maintenance department of Japan Airlines. The pilot had been mistaken about a rear door not being properly closed, but, of course, he had no means of seeing what was happening to the plane's tail section.

There is a disturbing parallel between this case and the McDonnell Douglas DC10 Ship 29. Although the plane had not been correctly repaired, four Japanese government inspectors certified that the work had been completed satisfactorily, without checking for themselves. One of the Transport Ministry inspectors committed suicide immediately after being questioned by the police. Boeing subsequently admitted that their repairs on the plane were insufficient.

Boeing is undoubtedly the success story of modern plane-makers. Based in Seattle in the north-west of the United States, the company cornered 56 per cent of the world market for new aircraft in 1988 and accumulated a record $54 billion backlog of orders for 1049 aircraft.

Good business is not always good news for everybody. Market pressures for new equipment led to Boeing missing a number of delivery deadlines. More relevant was the erosion of quality. In a four-year period from 1984, Boeing was fined fourteen times by the FAA for lapses in quality control. A specific example of bad workmanship was the installation in the flight controls of twenty-two Boeing 767s of defective self-locking nuts. For this the company was fined $145,000 in March 1988.

Faulty parts in exit doors were another reason for financial penalties being imposed. In those four years, total fines levied by the FAA against Boeing amounted to $245,000.

Boeing have come a long way since their humble beginnings, when struggling in competition with other early aircraft manufacturers for a share of a modest, limited market.

The turning point came in 1943, as the Boeing B-29 bombers began rolling off the Seattle assembly lines. The B-29 was to change the world beyond recognition.

It was a Boeing B-29 that was used to drop the atom bombs on Hiroshima and Nagasaki. But the B-29 was much more than a bomber;

this model crossed the most significant frontier in aviation since the Wright brothers. The B-29 may not have been the prototype all-pressurized aircraft, but it was the first to overcome all the obstacles and was the progenitor of the Boeing 707, 737, 747, and so on. As the Americans would say, the B-29 was the grandaddy of them all.

After World War II the B-29 became the Boeing Stratocruiser, redesigned and equipped with a cocktail bar. The heady days of high-flying in rarified air had arrived, with Boeing in the trail-blazing position which they were never to relinquish.

Even so, forty years later a letter was to land on the doormat of Boeing from the chief engineer for technical and quality services of one of the world's largest and most prestigious airlines, saying, 'My quality inspectors can only properly inspect a very small proportion of each aircraft. They should never ever come across missing fasteners, missing parts, cracks, bodged rivets, fasteners fitted the wrong way round. Yet we find instances of some of these on every aircraft. All these mistakes and the re-work that you have to carry out must be costing Boeing a king's ransom.' Referring specifically to the findings of the airline's inspectors, the letter continued, ' . . . underscores our fears that the underlying reason for Boeing Company's poor quality record is that the production workforce are in general inadequately trained, possess a low level of basic working skills, and, of paramount concern, seem oblivious that they are building aircraft where any mistake not properly corrected, or hidden, represents a direct compromise with safety.'

That scathing letter was written by D. K. Craig of British Airways. It went on to suggest that one mistake had 'left no doubt that the integrity of the aircraft structure had been compromised.' Strong stuff indeed. In essence, Craig was accusing Boeing of having sold British Airways an aircraft which was not safe to fly.

Full credit must be given to Boeing for their reaction to Craig's withering missive. There was never any attempt to gloss over the company's shortcomings or to mastermind a cover-up; quite the opposite.

Phil M. Condit, Boeing's vice-president, had the letter photocopied and circulated among the labour force to make them aware of what was being alleged by customers. Condit's commendable motive was to 'improve corporate communications'. It was also an example of open management and an exercise in public accountability.

What occurred next should have been no surprise to anyone: Craig's letter was leaked to the press. In the predictable furore that followed, Condit was to astound local Seattle reporters by remarking that the complaint was far from unique. At a press conference in Seattle, he was to volunteer that Boeing were frequently on the receiving end of criticism from customers. 'Some are polite and others pull our chain reasonably hard,' he said. 'British Airways uses the same John Bullish tone to all its suppliers, open and direct. I would hate to see BA inhibited because what they say appears in the press.'

Condit and Frank A. Shrontz, Boeing's president, embarked on a world tour to reassure all its valued customers that everything was not as bad as they might have read in the newspapers. Their message was that Boeing were at full stretch, but not over-committed.

Another Boeing executive, Dean Thornton, also tried to soothe potential buyers. 'An airliner like the 747 is a big and complicated piece of machinery and sometimes it seems like Murphy's Law takes over.' The faults which had been discovered were 'isolated incidents that shouldn't happen,' he said. 'We're gonna bust our butts to make sure they don't happen again.'

It transpired that British Airways were not the first to express dissatisfaction, though others had been less forthright. Susumu Yamaji, the president of Japan Airlines, had also written to Shrontz, listing a string of defects.

Boeing could not afford to ignore complaints from any of its customers, but especially from Japan Airlines and British Airways. JAL already boasted a fleet of 63 Boeing 747s, which was to be enlarged to 100 by the turn of the century. British Airways had placed an order for $4.1 billion-worth of 747s and 767s, a record for Boeing.

Seattle, basically a one-industry city, showed its gratitude to Boeing's big-spending patrons by naming special celebration days after them. On Japan Airlines Day, the streets were a kaleidoscope of Stars and Stripes and Rising Suns. Lufthansa had its own day, so too British Airways. Without the airlines, Seattle would be Hunger City. Hence the importance placed by Boeing on customer relations, which were not helped by events in Japan starting on Christmas Day 1987. A JAL Boeing 747-300, on its maiden voyage, had to return to Tokyo when a warning light on the flight-deck alerted the crew to oil-pressure failure.

Engineers quickly diagnosed the problem: a nut had not been properly tightened on a pressure-sensor.

Another JAL 747, this time on a training flight, developed what is known in the trade as a 'runaway' engine; the Number Three engine could not be controlled. The fault was traced to the thrust-control cable, which had been wrongly fitted.

The fire-extinguishers on newly-delivered Boeing 767s, the Seattle company's version of the European Airbus, had been installed the wrong way round, which meant that, when activated, they would foam a completely different area from that intended.

After the 1985 JAL mountain crash, the airline overhauled its maintenance methods. In the past, maintenance had followed conventional Western lines. A plane would arrive for servicing and whichever mechanics were available would be assigned to the job. That all changed in 1985, when a system, tantamount to an ethos, of 'personal, dedicated maintenance' was introduced. In practice, as well as theory, this meant that the engineers would have *their own* aircraft for life; they would always service the same planes through the entire lifetime of those airliners and be encouraged to treat them as their personal property, part of their family. Pride and personal responsibility were encouraged. It went further.

Engineers had to travel on 'their' aircraft on the first flight following any major maintenance, the most compelling reason of all for them to make absolutely sure that everything was right on the night. In addition, they were in a position to do 'running repairs' should anything untoward be detected in accessible areas during the flight. Credit was given and gratitude shown in the form of a roll of honour displayed on board each aircraft, listing all the engineers responsible for its maintenance.

After the leak to the press of the letter to Boeing from British Airways, newspaper reporters in Seattle began telephoning all the other international airlines. They discovered that a wing-flap of an All Nipon Boeing aircraft had crumbled to pieces on its maiden flight. American Airlines reported that they, too, had inherited back-to-front fire-extinguishers on their new Boeing 747s. Complaints to Boeing about their quality control had also come from Air India, Lufthansa, Aerolineas Argentinas and Northwest.

On one new 747, fuel escaped into the cargo-hold. Boeing investigated and attributed the fault to corrosion in sub-standard bolts, which had been supplied by a sub-contractor. This discovery led to radical action by the FAA, which issued an airworthiness directive ordering the checking 'before further flight' of the bolts in 317 Boeing 747-200s, the number of that aircraft known to be in operation at the time.

To enable Boeing to cope with orders for the automated 747-400 series, they hired 3000 extra workers. Boeing's target was five aircraft a month, a new production being started every six days. A priority was to reduce the amount of overtime being worked and to improve the overall quality of production. Boeing's labour force, old and new, was being channelled through a Skills Process Centre, where each employee was subjected to 200 hours of highly intensive additional training.

Describing Boeing's insatiable appetite for manpower, Condit said that 'a bubble of overtime walks through the factory' every time a fresh project went into production. Most of their production staff had either military or civil aviation backgrounds, but one Boeing inspector alleged to the local media, 'untrained people are turned loose on real live airplanes.' In addition, there were accusations of drug-taking and electricians swinging on wire to stretch it, when it had been too short, while equipping 747s.

The reaction at Boeing was, understandably, one of indignation. An executive responded, 'The media has gone right over the top. We've had our problems, there's no denying that, but we're not cowboys and we don't employ saboteurs. From reading some of the newspapers, you'd believe Boeing was full of people whose only object being here was to sabotage our planes. It started with one tabloid and then they all seemed to be competing to outstrip each other. Much of it was exaggerated, some of it was invented. One London paper made out we had a dope problem. The image was one of marijuana hot-heads knocking planes together.

'All right, there have been seven cases of cross-wiring in the 757, an engine dropped off a Piedmont Airlines 737 at Chicago, and there were those complaints from JAL and BA, but you have to look at the overall picture. We lead the field and rightly so. You have to judge our track-record as a whole, not in part. You will always have a handful of drug-abusers in a workforce of 100,000. You're talking about the labour force the size of a small city. It's a microcosm of human life. You have the brilliant, the average and the not so good; the conscientious and those who have to be watched and pushed; drinkers and those who won't touch the stuff; family men and those who play around. So what's new?

'The drugs incident was a minor problem, but blown up by the Press, which I understand because Boeing is always big news. It's the price you pay for being the cream. Everybody wants to skim you!'

Yes, indeed, and cream can all too easily turn sour. The Pratt and Whitney JT8D engine that fell from the Piedmont aircraft had been held on by three bolts. Fatigue had been detected in similar bolts on several other Boeing 737s. A number of inspection directives were issued and stronger bolts, the result of an advanced design, were swiftly developed, but not in haste.

Lee Speight, Boeing's engineering manager, attributed the fatigue in the bolts to being 'improperly seated or loose in the conical socket, usually as a result of improper torquing'. The Piedmont 737 had clocked 19,400 hours and had made 21,400 landings since being delivered to the airline in 1981. Another Boeing official said, 'We don't know what caused the incident in Chicago, but the engine is designed to fall off in case of excessive loads. Excessive loads can rupture the fuel lines.'

In January 1989, Boeing had orders on its books for 1111 airliners, worth something in the region of £30 billion to them. *The Times* quoted one fitter at Boeing's Everett plant as saying: 'The pay is great, but they work us hard and there's people out there like zombies. Twelve-hour days for weeks in a row without end.' One worker cost Boeing a fortune by drilling holes in the wrong places on an airframe.

Two months earlier, Dean Thornton, president of Boeing Commerical Airplanes, apologized to airlines for the late delivery of new 747s. 'We're being burned by our own success. We've got too much on our plate. We've got too many inexperienced workers – green peas, we call them – and not enough of the old-timers who know how to do things. We're stretched right now.' He lamented that it was becoming increasingly difficult to find competent staff, local resources having been siphoned dry. Every day Boeing were advertising for labour on all the radio stations throughout Puget Sound, the seaboard area of Washington State.

Charles Bremner, the well-connected Seattle correspondent of the London *Times*, gave this interesting insight into the intrigue at Boeing: 'Some middle managers complain that morale has suffered since Boeing brought in "money people" with Harvard Business School philosophy, intent on watching the bottom line and letting people take care of themselves. Constant pressure to cut costs meant that lower managers were unable to implement all the promises about quality decreed from the top, they say. Boeing is under pressure from customers to cut prices and sweeten financing, partly because of what the Americans see as unfair state-subsidized competition from the European Airbus consortium. Despite record orders, Boeing's profit margins have been almost halved over the past ten years and Boeing managers are anxious that, despite the boom, the company could lack the cash to develop a new generation of planes.'

But John Nance, a Seattle author and industrial analyst, was confident that Boeing was 'not in serious trouble at all'. He did not believe that the situation had 'deteriorated to the point of alarm, but they have let a few things slip by them'.

Seattle is a proud city. Rightly so. The community is irrevocably tethered to Boeing. Great-grandfathers, brimful with nostalgia, remember the first plane Boeing ever built in 1916. Seattle has always been the seat of the Boeing dynasty. Complete families are married to Boeing: daughters work in the typing-pool, sons are draughtsmen or mechanics or engineers or electricians, working alongside their fathers, uncles and brothers. It is impossible to go into a bar, restaurant or store and escape the Boeing tendrils, no more than you could expect a respite from car-talk in Detroit.

Seattle folk are understandably sensitive about what they see as a slur on their reputation. They saw the scandal stories coming out of their city as a threat – a threat to their prosperity, their stability and future. Anything that damages Boeing hurts everybody in Seattle; the ripples of retrenchment go from the core to beyond the city limits.

One Boeing mechanic told me that he had been offered $20,000 to botch a job on a Boeing 747-400. 'I'm not going to give exact details of what I was supposed to do because if I did, anyone at Boeing would immediately know the job I was doing and that would narrow the numbers for them. The offer was made in a bar. The bribe was offered by a man and a woman. They'd done their homework. They knew my wife had been ill and my son had been in some trouble; not big trouble, but enough to have me on edge. In short, they'd been a considerable drain on my fiscal and emotional resources. Because of my troubles, I'd started drinking a bit too much, and gambling.

'I was doing good with overtime, but it wasn't even getting me through the weekend. I played the dogs, the horses, the illegal crap games and cards. I was gambling when I was bombed, which meant I hadn't a chance. I was giving Boeing twelve hours of my day and the other twelve went on booze and gambling. I was in such bad shape, I wasn't fit to die, let alone make airplanes.

'The only surprise is that anyone felt they needed to pay me to sabotage a plane. Odds were I'd do it without knowing. Maybe I did! I was a wreck, mentally and physically. The word gets around fast in a close-knit community like ours. The strong carry the weak. We try not to abandon anyone. Such camaraderie is good for the community, but it might not be so hot for Boeing. It means passengers [incompetent workers] are carried.

'There's no hiding from the fact that I was a passenger. My God! But I was no crook. If I'd taken that money and deliberately put passengers on Death Row upstairs, I couldn't have lived with myself. I needed the money. Did I just! But not that way. "No one will get hurt," they said. "It'll be picked up by the inspectors. If they miss it, the airline's mechanics and checkers will be on top of it. All you'll be doing is embarrassing Boeing, slowing 'em down and costing 'em some bucks. You'll just be a thorn in their ass. The place is in bad enough shape as it is. You'll just be adding to the mess."

'These weren't Arabs; not Iranians. They were American; West Coasters, I'd say; a regular kind of guy who could have been with his secretary; that's the way they looked to me. They didn't seem to me like political fanatics, but you can never tell, can you? So, who were they? I've asked myself a million times. The whole intention seemed to be to clobber Boeing, rather than the flying public. I got the feel that some form of industrial sabotage must be at the root.

'It also occurred to me that Boeing must have intelligence sources. Because of my personal problems, I wondered whether I'd been earmarked as a potential risk and was being put to some kind of test, to see if I had a breaking-point. They say everyone has a price, but I don't think you could buy anyone's soul on the floor at Boeing. There's too much pride, too much history . . . and too much to lose. We're on a high roll and it looks like staying that way well into the next century.'

Did he report the criminal approach which had been made to him?

'Not on your life! Nothing was going to make me have attention focused my way. I didn't want the FBI poking around in my affairs; I couldn't afford that.'

But if the couple who made the appeal were security officers, would not his silence be self-incriminating?

'It was a chance I had to take. I made it clear if they came near me again, I'd report them. I think I did enough to keep my own nose clean.'

Another Boeing mechanic said he was 'set up' by a woman with whom he had a brief affair. 'It only lasted a month and all she was really doing was setting me up. Every time we were screwing in her apartment, we were being filmed and bugged. The equipment must have been rigged inside her wardrobe: she was very professional.

'About a month after I started screwing her, we met for a drink one night in a bar. Within five minutes, we were joined by this guy, and she just got up and waltzed out; not a f—— goodbye. That was the last I ever saw of her. This guy – he was fortyish – sat down and tossed me a manila envelope. I hadn't a clue what was going on. I opened the envelope and there were the pictures. They were sickening. I wanted to throw up. Then I wanted to kill him.

'I told him they were wasting their time because I was just an ordinary worker. I had no fortune. "Don't worry," he said, laughing. "These photos won't cost you a dime." It took him just a few minutes to outline what he wanted. If I'd done as he said, I'd have deliberately loosened nuts in a section of the Boeing 747s which could have made the tailplane vulnerable. I nearly killed that guy there and then. I got the impression he was not working for a rival company. Subsequently, I found out he was an ex-employee of Boeing in middle-management who had a grudge against the company. Can you believe anyone would go to those lengths and that expense? I've no idea who the woman was, whether she was his wife, girlfriend, or just a hired help, but she certainly made a fool of me.

'I didn't go to the police or the Boeing management because my marriage would have been threatened. If the cops had gotten involved, everything would have gotten out of hand. I walked away from it and gambled they'd see there was no percentage in sending the photographs to my wife. I don't think they ever did because I'm sure I'd have been the first to hear about it! I've often wondered whether they went to work on anybody else and, if so, what was the outcome.'

Trying to assess a drugs problem is never more than an educated guess, rather than a precise calculation. People with a vice, particularly one which endangers others as well as themselves, are not given to candour. Only three Boeing employees were prepared to discuss with me their drug-taking habits. All of them had been mechanics on the 747-400 series. None of them was a young tearaway and there was a definite parallel between their motives for using drugs and those of flight crews. Here is one story which I have no reason to doubt; I paid no money to the subject and he appeared not to be motivated by malice, explaining that Boeing was his life: past, present and future.

'It was the overtime that started me on drugs, which I've never taken for kicks, only for practical purposes. You can't say no to overtime; it's against human nature to turn it down. Overtime means money; big money, but you pay for it. After a time, your personality changes. Tiredness takes over. Your eyes won't stay open. And the more tired you become, the less you sleep. It's a vicious circle and there's no way off; you just keep going round and round, getting more dizzy. So, you get hold of something to keep you awake; an upper. That's fine, except now it's even harder than ever to sleep. So, you need downers as well. Uppers in the morning, downers at night. Up, down; up, down; up, down . . . And a few beers in between, of course. It isn't long before you're freaking out. Coke is delicious; that really puts me in heaven. When you're up, you feel great; when you're down, you crash out.

'The trouble with the uppers is that you lose all sense of caring. You're so abandoned, you don't give a shit. The longer it goes on, the harder it is to stop. Ultimately, you don't want to stop. All the overtime has induced you to over-reach with your financial commitments. Drugs make it possible for you to keep going and all the time you keep reassuring yourself that if you blow out, there'll always be a safety net.'

Les Warby, who was employed on the 747-400 production line at Boeing's Everett plant between May and August in 1988, claimed to the British newspaper the *Guardian* that he had been ordered by his supervisor to stretch a wire which was too short to reach its connection. He was told, 'Don't worry, if there's a problem or if it breaks, it will be caught in test.'

A former employee of Boeing told a Seattle television station, 'I saw one instance where a wire had been stripped of its insulation and instead of replacing the wire, a piece of tape was put on it. Nobody caught it.' He rejected the claim by his supervisor that the fault would be put right further down the line. 'It won't get caught until it shorts out or causes an electrical problem on the airplane, and it's gonna be in the air.' He was an employee of the Renton plant in Seattle, where the 737s and 757s were being produced.

Internal documents leaked from within the Boeing empire seemed to establish beyond dispute that in September 1988 at least twenty Boeing 737s were built with many of the vital parts poorly assembled. I have no evidence that any of those planes went into service without the faults being rectified, but the number of own goals continued to bother Boeing, and rightly so.

The defective parts in question belonged to the aileron quadrant assembly, which is connected to the controls. The plane is steered by the movement of the ailerons, which are attached to the wings. A number of these parts had been forced together – known as pre-loading – which could lead to stress. The leaked documents seemed to suggest that twenty-four Boeing 737-300s and 400s were affected. A Boeing print-out in October 1988 announced, 'Discrepancy no longer exists.' In November, however, inspectors uncovered another dangerously fitted aileron quadrant assembly. This discovery came during a flight test of a Boeing 737-300. The unit was cracked, an assembly-pin was protruding and the other key, a securing device, was missing altogether. The parts had been crushed together with such force that they had to be pounded and prised apart with a hammer.

Les Warby told Seattle's KIRO Television News programme that he regarded the Boeing workforce as being divided into three divisions. 'There are the people for whom Boeing can do no wrong, those whose fathers worked there and all that. Then there are the ones who treat it like a military thing, the tight schedules. They do not care if something does not get finished, for them it is just a job. And the final third are the paranoid, afraid of losing their jobs. They have been told that Boeing doesn't like troublemakers, but they know what quality is and they are worried.'

Lester Wendell, a Boeing quality control officer for thirty years, had this to say; 'We are going to have to slow down, get back to basics and use our manpower and knowledge as in the past. Until the government and the aircraft industry face the facts, people will continue to be maimed and more lives will be lost.'

Twenty years before the boom of the eighties, Boeing was cutting back on its workforce by as much as two-thirds as the world dipped headlong into a recession, explaining why the company moved cautiously when the order-book began to look healthy again. They preferred to rely on overtime and the flexibility of labour, interchanging men among the myriad assembly-lines, hoping to avoid the past pitfalls of over-reaching, only to be pole-axed by the next slump in the market.

Boeing executive Craig Martin went on record as saying, 'Our goal is, and was, to build steadily and not get into a situation where we build up, then demand falls off, where individuals are hired then laid off. We learned that lesson in the late sixties, when the company damn near died.

'Errors in installing the fire-suppressant system were made possible because the fittings were all the same and easier to hook up the wrong way. Testing didn't catch it because tests were designed to ensure the whole system worked, not which way the extinguishant went. So we redesigned the fittings, making left and right different and making improper connections impossible.

'A six- to eight-year quality enhancement programme was designed to change the way the company and our suppliers think about quality. When you increase the rate of production on an assembly-line, it leads to disruption. Your suppliers internationally and internally have to be in tune. Some don't make it. Parts then get installed in the wrong order by people who have to move up and down the line. Some of the workers will be less skilled. It all adds up to more time, but that doesn't lead to a reduction in quality.'

In theory, all applicants for a new job at Boeing were supposed to pass an assessment conducted over a period of 200 hours to decide whether they were acceptable. After joining the company, all new intakes should have gone straight through a further 200 hours of high-pressure training, but this did not always happen because of the scale on which Boeing suddenly found they had to employ. For many new employees, it would be several months after joining before they were shunted from mainstream production to the sidelines for special tuition.

Added to the list of disgruntled Boeing customers were Singapore Airlines, who were building a reputation for flying nothing but new equipment. 'We continue to be very disappointed in Boeing's inability to meet delivery schedules,' a spokesman declared after Boeing had cancelled its 1989 delivery schedule for the 747-400. 'With two delay notifications, we remain reluctant to announce start-up dates for our new series 400 services.'

Competition in the airplane market-place is as cut-throat as any-where. Despite Boeing's stranglehold on the market, their profits have been halved since the seventies. This is not to imply that Boeing have to watch their pennies. Share earnings were expected almost to treble between 1988 and 1990, and the company had a healthy bank balance of $4.2 billion in 1989. Despite widespread criticism, Boeing retained their supporters. Bill Whitlow, an analyst on the West Coast with Dain Bosworth, an investment house, was optimistic about Boeing's future. 'They are making the right move by saying, "Hey, we've a quality problem here, we're ramping up way too fast."'

To intimate that Boeing were beleaguered would be an overstate-ment, but they were becoming increasingly sensitive to the negative publicity and in August 1989 flatly refused to pay a $200,000 fine imposed by the FAA for the alleged failure of the company to report promptly wiring faults on two aircraft owned by Royal Brunei Airlines and Delta Airlines.

The FAA, which has the power to propose civil penalties instead of court action, stated that 'an unsuppressed fire, causing severe damage to the airplane' could have resulted and that the airlines should have been notified within twenty-four hours. The FAA said it had taken Boeing several weeks to inform them. 'Boeing has refused to pay the proposed $200,000 fine and has asked for time to bring forward docu-mentary evidence. It wants to discuss the matter further. In the past, it has argued down fines, but has still paid fourteen times since 1985.' Boeing later agreed to pay the $200,000.

The severest fine against Boeing in the years 1985 and 1986 was $12,000, but they subsequently became much bigger: $21,000 in Jan-uary 1987, after Boeing had used invalid and outdated drawings in production and trimmed certain parts without engineering approval; $125,000 in May the same year for the failure of Boeing suppliers to test lock nuts; $16,000 in January 1988, for omitting brake metering valve-guards on fourteen aircraft; $30,000 for the fitting of defective exit doors on forty-four aircraft (the doors had been accepted by Textron, a supplier of Boeing); and $20,000 after Northrop, another Boeing supplier, failed to include a machining process in the production of taper support brackets. Despite all the setbacks, however, Boeing remained the world leader in the manufacture of passenger aircraft with a reputation second to none for sturdy, durable equipment which could survive countless mistakes of man and many of the worst acts of God.

A new scare in the summer of 1989 was the allegation that passenger aircraft were flying with parts which had not been tested. This news came from the FBI, who were investigating certain supplier companies for possible fraud. One of the companies under scrutiny was suspected of falsifying engineering tests on thousands of fasteners which literally hold aircraft together. The sale of the untested fasteners was understood to have begun in 1977. These fasteners hold the skin of the plane to the airframe and secure the engines to their fittings.

In another case, Bruce Rice, president of the American company Rice Aircraft, confessed to falsifying test certificates for airline parts. The FBI feared at least one supplier of Boeing, McDonnell Douglas and the European Airbus consortium had been falsifying data, certifying components which had failed corrosion trials, and had not performed any of the statutory tests. One of the suppliers under investigation had been selling to the US Defense Department for most of their fleet, especially the Stealth B-2 bomber. The US Government cancelled its contract shortly after Defense Department officials were briefed by FBI agents.

McDonnell Douglas acted equally swiftly: they had been supplied with rivets from this suspect company. Bruce Carter, the assistant US federal attorney in charge of the inquiry, said, 'There is undoubtedly a potential threat to safety.'

Many airlines were concerned because of the lack of communication. A spokesman for one of the world's largest charter operators said, 'If there is a problem, real or potential, we would want to hear about it immediately.'

It was in January 1989 that the FBI received information from an employee of one of the rogue firms, telling about a non-existent 'phantom' inspector whose rubber-stamp certified rivets, nuts, fasteners and lock bolts as of a quality fit for aircraft production. These parts, said the informant, had either failed official tests elsewhere or had not been checked at all. At first the FBI could not believe what they were hearing. They assumed that the complaint was coming from a malicious employee who had a score to settle. However, because of the seriousness of the accusations and the possible ramifications, a joint task force was formed between the Defense Criminal Investigation Service and the Air Force Office of Special Investigations.

By mid-summer the joint investigators had substantiated the main substance of the allegations, much to their astonishment and the chagrin of the manufacturers. As soon as the FBI made one of the companies under surveillance aware of their findings, Boeing, McDonnell Douglas, Lockheed, Airbus Industries, the European consortium, and engine-makers Pratt and Whitney were warned. A spokesman for the supplier said, 'This has come as quite a shock to the management. But we have found no faulty fasteners and do not believe there is any safety problem.'

Mike Grayley, a stress analyst and head of Strength and Analysis at the Engineering Sciences Data Unit, London, warned that 'brittle fasteners' could snap at any moment. Defects, he said, might be un-detected once the components had been fitted.

Following the FBI disclosures, Boeing intensified its testing of parts from suppliers, but company spokesman Paul Binder made it clear that it was way beyond their capacity to check every fastener. 'We use those products on every aircraft we make and run tests on statistical samples,' he explained.

The failure of the smallest part, such as a nut, can be catastrophic. In 1979, an American Airlines DC10 crashed on take-off from Chicago, when an engine fell as a bolt sheared. Two hundred and seventy-three people died.

Airlines could do little more than hold their breath, trying to put out of their minds the prospect that some of their brand new airplanes might be nothing more than a collection of secondhand parts.

12 CUT-THROAT WAR

Deregulation in the United States polarized opinion, both public and professional. Opening up the market could only benefit the industry and the consumer, reasoned the champions of free enterprise. A free-for-all would be a licence to kill, the opponents retaliated. Only time would tell, opined those who could afford to be philosophical or who accepted, perhaps ruefully, that they had no choice in the matter.

The Airline Deregulation Act of 1978, in effect, lifted restrictions which constrained competition, making it possible for virtually any company to start an airline and compete on the United States domestic network.

A few years later, after enough time for deregulation to prove or hang itself, Senator W. V. Roth, chairman of a Senate sub-committee, had this to say: 'There is growing evidence that cost-cutting, over-scheduling and crowded conditions at airports may be eroding safety margins and posing a growing threat to the flying public.'

Members of the Senate committee had been hearing evidence on a wide range of air safety issues, including the crash in 1985 at Gander, Newfoundland, of a commercial airliner on charter to the US Defense Department. The death toll in the accident at Gander was 256, and two ex-employees of the airline told the committee that their former company made a habit of keeping maintenance to a minimum and delaying repairs. The same witnesses also told of pilots consistently working shifts of sixteen and eighteen hours, but the airline pointed out that no FAA rules had been breached. In effect it was the system, deregulation, which was on trial, rather than individuals and companies.

Aviation had become an emotive political issue, as demonstrated by Roth's statement, which went on to disclose that the Senate inquiry had 'revealed a number of instances in which airline personnel, such as pilots and mechanics, were the only people in a position to know about potential safety hazards, yet were reluctant to report those conditions because of fear of reprisals by their employers. This amendment would help ensure that such fears do not stand in the way of disclosing and correcting safety hazards before they result in tragedy.'

Some of the most unnerving evidence had come from two former FAA air safety inspectors. They claimed that in 1984 the FAA knew about an airline which had been using unqualified checkers to certify its pilots, but no action had been taken. The executives of that airline decided against appearing before the committee to give verbal evidence and to be questioned, instead preferring, as was their prerogative, to submit an on-the-record statement, which was received a few days after the hearings ended. The statement from the airline rejected most of the accusations which had been levelled against them by the ex-FAA inspectors and denied any conspiracy with the FAA.

Deregulation was sold to the American people as a panacea; fierce competition would incite jungle warfare, encouraging the proliferation of airlines, thus increasing choice and raising quality, and forcing down fares. Consumer power! Utopia! Reagan had found a new outlet and expression for the American Dream.

The reality did not live up to the rhetoric. A number of the bigger airports organized auctions for the franchise of their boarding gates. Naturally, it was the big airlines who won every time.

Anybody could start an airline, but not everyone could find a pitch in the market-place. Warfare did become cut-throat, but the outcome was more as projected by the pessimists than by the optimists. Airlines started pruning staff and lowering wages, producing skirmishes with the unions. New companies, seeing the opportunity to exploit the industrial strife which was debilitating their older, established rivals, leaned towards non-union labour. This produced antagonism after take-overs, when union and non-union employees were expected to work in harmony alongside one another, frequently at different rates of pay for the same job.

Some pilots, who were compelled to settle for a reduced standard of living, no longer enjoyed job satisfaction. Many had their eye on retirement, rather than more immediate horizons. Here was yet another symptom of compromised safety.

Gradually, in a spate of mergers and buy-outs, the weaker opposition was expunged. Instead of there being more airlines from which to choose, there were less than before deregulation, and the monopoly by the few was even more accentuated.

The American Dream had fallen flat on its face.

The pilots' association of the United States, so troubled by the complications of deregulation, circulated a statement. 'The proponents of deregulation continually point out that legislation only addresses the economic regulation of the airlines: the safety regulations will not be changed. We do not disagree with this assertion, but we do take issue with the conclusion that safety, therefore, will not be affected. To take comfort in the regulations and enforcement responsibility of governments is to avoid the safety question.

'The primary factor in airline safety is cost. Maintenance of high safety standards is extremely expensive, whether measured in terms of equipment, facilities, maintenance-reliability, or by operating procedures and conditions. This fact is often taken for granted because it is rarely visible to the consumer of airline services. Nonetheless, airline companies have invested millions of dollars in onboard safety systems, personnel training facilities and programs, and aircraft maintenance and overhaul bases, which for the most part cannot be translated into economic efficiency. It is simply the price which must be paid to achieve the highest possible degree of safety in airline operations.

'They [new airlines] will not bring with them into the business the enormous investments in safety facilities and programs, and experienced personnel, which have been a major part of the overhead of establishment airlines for many years. But, you say, these applicants would have to prove to governments that they are fit to provide service and that they have the financial resources to conduct viable, safe operations. Furthermore, they would be required to meet the same safety standards that govern existing carriers.

'First of all, this presumes that existing airlines operate at the minimum level of government standards. Nothing could be further from the truth. Most certificated airlines today operate according to standards which far exceed the minimums required by government.

'Second, it presumes that government has the ability, financially and administratively, to monitor air carrier operations sufficiently to protect the public from all manner of unsafe practices. Again, nothing could be further from the truth. As a matter of fact, under many systems, the airlines and their employees monitor themselves under a delegation of responsibility from government. Even with this delegation, the resources of government are stretched to the limit.

'Third, fitness tests, which are expected to screen out potentially unsafe new entrants, presume that the financial requirements to start up an airline operation between two points are so enormous as to discourage at the outset all those who do not have ready access to huge pools of capital. This is wishful thinking. The procurement of equipment, personnel and working capital sufficient to conduct a spartan point-to-point service is relatively easy in today's economy.

'Finally, we must be concerned about the effects on safety which can be expected when carriers, both new and existing, are faced with extreme cost pressures related to their struggle to survive in an intensely competitive environment. This phenomenon is difficult to quantify, but past experience and common sense tells us it does exist. New companies cannot be expected to invest huge sums of money to enhance the margin of safety when their principal objectives are to establish themselves in the market-place and to maximize the efficiency of their operations to recover their basic costs. There is simply no competitive advantage to be gained by investing in safety, and expenditures in this area would not contribute significantly to operating efficiency. Conversely, if a carrier is confronted with severe financial difficulties, where completion of every flight counts, the temptation to cut corners in safety would be overwhelming.

'Extraordinary vigilance by government should be mandatory in a deregulated environment to guard against a relaxation of safety practices and procedures, particularly in that segment of the industry which lacks experience in air transportation and a long-standing commitment to safety.'

J. Enders, the president of the Flight Safety Foundation, commented in 1985 at the Foundation's annual meeting, 'The architects of deregulation failed to apply the fault-tree analysis technique which the aircraft designer is expected to apply to an aeroplane.'

In 1987, at Caracas, the chairman of the technical committee of the International Air Transport Association had this to say to the 168 chairmen of airlines who attended: 'Currently, many engineering and maintenance departments are confronted with older aircraft types with a very large number of airframe hours, including re-engined airframes, extending their useful lives even further into the future. At the same time, new aircraft types, with highly sophisticated technology, are being introduced into airline fleets. Both of these trends will produce extra and sometimes new problems, which are often difficult to solve. At the same time, many airlines are reducing manpower. These reductions may seriously affect professional engineering staffing. There is no question that productivity of engineering and maintenance departments had to be increased and new technology has produced many benefits. However, we must recognize the trends and take positive action to preserve the levels of safety and reliability.'

More recently, deregulation was to the forefront when, on 19 July 1989, Captain Al Haynes had to try to land at Sioux City, Iowa, a DC10 of United Airlines without hydraulics: no flaps, no brakes and a rudder which would turn only right. The pilot's sole means of steering the aircraft was by varying the thrust of the engines, yet he almost managed a textbook landing. Unfortunately, just short of the runway, a wing dipped, clipped the ground and the plane cartwheeled. The captain was one of 186 survivors; 110 others were not so lucky.

There was immediate speculation of a failure in the APU, the plane's auxiliary power unit, which is tantamount to an extra engine but is usually employed to generate the air-conditioning while the aircraft is on the ground and to start the engines. Experts pointed out that if the DC10's APU had been in use during the flight, it suggested the aircraft was flying while in need of major maintenance, thus propelling deregulation once again into the public forum.

Much of my own view of deregulation has been shaped by personal experience. On a flight from the United Kingdom to the United States, I found a warning, written with a ballpoint pen and sellotaped to the inside of a rear door of the 747, which said, 'Do not touch, door may fall off.' I assumed it was only the inside panelling and not the complete door that was a mere touch away from destruction, but even so . . . On a cold March day in New York, my flight to Miami from JFK was delayed several hours. When we did finally get on our way, the captain of the wide-bodied L1011 explained that there had been a fault with the airframe. As we turned on to the runway early that evening, the New Yorker pilot announced laconically, 'The mechanics tell me they've fixed everything. I'm paid to believe them. So, with a heartful of turtles, here we go!' And a couple of minutes after take-off, he was saying, 'My God, it really seems they *did* get it right!'

Just before take-off from JFK to Los Angeles on a 747, I complained to a stewardess of smelling smoke. 'Yes,' she said, sniffing, 'I thought I could too. I can't see any sign of smoke, though. When we're in the air, we'll soon know whether or not we have a fire. There's nothing we can do now. The captain wouldn't thank me for making him miss his slot.'

Much worse has been happening, though, continents away from deregulation. When the crew of a flight from Kisangani to Kinshasa in Zaire in 1984 discovered that the aircraft was overbooked, they lifted all the armrests and squeezed four passengers into every three seats. When the plane eventually took off, it was carrying seventy passengers above its maximum permitted load. The cowboy attitude of that crew might have passed unexposed but for the fact that a journalist from *Newsweek* was on board. Even so, no action was taken against the crew or airline.

Back in the late seventies, the flight-deck crew and cabin staff of a British charter Boeing 707 aircraft slept overnight in their plane at Palma, Majorca, after fog had closed the airport and the operators refused to pay for them to stay in a hotel. Next morning they took off tired, unshaven, unwashed and unfed. The passengers, who included myself, had spent the night in the airport building. After landing at Luton, the pilot told me, 'We are all wrecks. I was seeing double all the way back. It's lucky we landed on the real runway and not the mirage. If we'd been called upon to do anything out of the ordinary, no chance!' It would seem that, even without deregulation, tight profit margins inevitably lead to overtired aircrew, with all the consequent dangers.

In the late summer of 1989, a dossier from British charter pilots told of a crew who allowed their aircraft to run out of fuel at 30,000 feet. This crisis was the result of faulty manoeuvres which simultaneously starved of fuel both engines of a McDonnell Douglas MD83. Fortunately, the crew were able to re-start the engines in time to avert a crash. The report also told of pilots having only eighty minutes' training at the controls of jet airliners before being assigned to flying passengers, having flown propeller aircraft for all their previous careers.

For the consumer, like myself, flying ceased to be fun. Travel agents throughout the West were reporting a change of mood among even the most inveterate, laid-back flyers. People began asking themselves if their intended journey was really necessary. If the answer was yes, then many looked for alternative means of travel. A new motto was coined: *Don't fly, don't die.* In the fashion of so many American slogans, it struck a chord.

Flying would never be quite the same again. Deregulation and Lockerbie, and all their ramifications, had seen to that.

Despite the American experience, Mrs Thatcher and many of her government colleagues were far from disenchanted with the concept of deregulation. On the contrary, the 'Freedom of the Skies' philosophy seemed the quintessence of Thatcherism. There was no one more enthusiastic for deregulation in the United Kingdom than Lord Bethell, a Euro MP for London, though he and other supporters in both the European and Westminster parliaments accepted that it would not come before 1992.

One of Lord Bethell's political colleagues explained to me, 'Liberalization is the essential part of any free market economy. The air fares for European travel are extravagantly high, due entirely to agreed prices among the airlines. A "Freedom of the Skies" policy will be great for the consumer. There will be a proliferation of small companies who will be able to set fares according to their own viability. Of course the big airlines are against deregulation because they know that they will have to reduce their fares in order to remain competitive.

'The general mood is towards a free Europe in the air and this will come about as soon as possible after 1992, though the actual legislation will have to be passed by individual governments, based on a Euro policy. Legislation will have to be so strict that safety is in no way jeopardized.'

I seem to have heard all that somewhere before.

CONCLUSION

At the outset of my research, I was a true lover of long-distance flying. I can honestly say that, once airborne, I even enjoyed my flight from London Heathrow to the United States, with Pan Am, the morning after Lockerbie. I am sad to report, therefore, that my study of air safety has killed my appetite for the very experience which for so long I had counted a pleasure.

There are those, mostly with vested interests, who will continue to recite statistics as proof that flying is not becoming more perilous.

However, a graph demonstrating no significant yearly upward trend of deaths in air crashes is not in itself evidence that flying remains safe. Let us consider an analogy: as time pushes the last world war further into the recesses of history, it would be a dubious proposition that the earth is now a safer place just because we have been free for so long of conflict on a global scale; the threat from pollution and weapons of greater capability than ever before merely inflame the degree of danger.

The pioneering days of aviation have returned. Every time an old aircraft takes off, it is flying into the unknown. The airlines claim that old can be nearly as good as new with modern maintenance techniques, but no one can put hand on heart and swear to know for sure. We, the passengers, are paying to be guinea-pigs.

The skies are more crowded than ever before. Traffic-controllers are pushed beyond their limits.

Pilots are wilting under the strain.

Some maintenance crews are negligent almost to the point of criminality.

Some airliners are defective.

Dangerous goods are carried on almost every long-haul flight.

Terrorists have turned from hijacking to sabotage.

Drugs and drink have been introduced to flight-decks.

The curse of metal fatigue has returned to haunt almost every airline.

The cataclysm is waiting to happen.

But not everything is downbeat. Not so long ago, 'miracle' was the media's term for any air crash in which there was a survivor. Nowadays, something like 80 per cent of passengers survive crashes when they occur at low altitude, such as on take-off or landing. It is not uncommon for passengers to walk away completely unscathed, or with minor injuries, from the kind of wreckage one would consider tomb-like.

Wayne Williams, an advisor on air safety in the United States, discounted the 'miracle' notion. 'The idea that you can't survive an air crash is a major misconception. The fact that more and more people are walking away from crashes is no accident.'

Williams believed that new safety regulations, particularly those which directly resulted from the airplane fire at Manchester in 1985, had already saved many lives. He was specifically alluding to more fire-resistant furnishings inside aircraft, which gave passengers an extra couple of minutes in which to complete evacuation, and floor-level lighting.

Passengers have themselves become much more safety-conscious and are persistent with their questions at airports, particularly with reference to the section of the plane in which they have the best chance of survival should there be an accident. Unfortunately, it is a question without a definitive answer.

Passengers scrambled for seats as far back as possible in aircraft after the four survivors of a Japan Air Lines 747 crash in 1985 all came from Row 54. The proclivity to choose the back-end of planes was supported by the majority of experts, on the grounds that the rear was usually the furthest point from impact. But the chance of being killed or injured as a result of turbulence is commensurate with the distance from the aircraft's centre of gravity; hence, the most dangerous area of the plane is towards the tail section. However, in the fire at Manchester, most of the survivors were from the front rows, which, for a time, influenced passengers' preferences accordingly. The intelligence from one crash tends to be negated by the very next accident.

Inescapable, however, is the fact that there are survivors in six out of every ten air crashes, and where people are sitting proves to be a life-or-death factor.

Statistics have also hinted that the frequent air traveller is most at risk; that is, the person who does not bother to listen to the emergency drill before take-off. He or she does not believe it could ever happen to him or her and has no idea where the nearest exits are situated or where the life-saving gear is stored, should the plane have to ditch on water.

Reporting from Washington in August 1989 for the London *Evening Standard*, Jeremy Campbell wrote, 'The unsettling message to passengers nowadays is this: if you die in a plane crash, it may be your own silly fault.'

Experts stress that while waiting for take-off, passengers should be busily working out their escape route should an emergency be encountered, but people prefer to run from reality.

Clothing is an important consideration, too. Shorts should never be worn because they reduce protection from flames in the event of a fire. Synthetic fibres are more flammable than cotton and wool. Nylon stockings have been known to melt and burn. And high heels are tantamount to tripwires; stilettos can puncture rubber slides and dinghies.

Many passengers who die in survivable accidents have been knocked unconscious because they simply failed to adopt the crouching position for a crash-landing; head down and hands gripping knees or ankles. If you remain sitting upright, you are likely to be pitched headfirst into the back of the seat in front.

As Campbell wrote, 'Improvements in the design of aircraft have led to the remarkable spectacle of more and more people walking away from air accidents. The use of shoulder-harnesses and protective breathing devices could create more survivors still.

'But here is the irony. The airline industry opposed nearly all such improvements, giving in only in the face of a determined and well-informed public.

'Now that same public must educate itself in the art of a survival made possible by its own intelligent persistence.'

But sometimes safety is in the hands of the gods. Here is a pilot's own account of a flight from the Mediterranean to London which almost ended tragically during the freak storms of February 1990: 'As we descended into the clouds, the situation deteriorated rapidly. At 3000 feet in-bound on the Instrument Landing System localizer, we were experiencing westerly winds of 188 knots and we were encountering severe turbulence.

'When the first officer reported the wind to Air Traffic Control, the reply was, "Roger, understand westerly 88 knots." First officer: "Negative, 188 knots." ATC: "Good grief!"

'Both Flight Management Systems were repeatedly failing and recovering, and at various times both autopilot and the captain's Flight Director [electronic artificial horizon] were out of action. The ride down was very wild. At 700 feet, with violent turbulence and an apparent 130 knots negative wind sheer between that altitude and the ground, we commenced a go-around [overshoot]. During the go-around, virtually all the automatics failed again and the turbulence became extreme.

'Levelling at 3000 feet, flaps and gear up, but still in severe turbulence, we were now confronted with further problems: our bolt holes [diversion airports] began to look suspect. We determined only one diversion airfield was still just about okay, but were now on the limit of our fuel reserves. We elected to go.

'En route to the diversion, we had to cope with a combination of failed automatics, unfamiliar ATC clearances, monitoring the weather, to say nothing of liaison with the cabin crew and the very frightened passengers. We had about 30 minutes fuel available and we had to make it in and, with the weather deteriorating literally by the minute, it had to be the first time.'

In his book published in 1988, Laurie Taylor concluded; 'If a concerted and international safety programme is implemented it would be reasonable to expect the total number of accidents and fatalities to remain constant in an industry expected to achieve an annual growth rate of 7 per cent per annum. Such an achievement would make air travel safer than competing travel modes and ensure further growth in the future.

'The answer to the question "air travel, how safe is it?" must therefore be that it is safe in 1988 and will become safer each year if sufficient resources are committed to a co-ordinated and internationally implemented air safety programme.'

Everything hinges on *if* . . . and I am less optimistic than Laurie Taylor. I fear that sabotage and ageing aircraft will make the risk of flying in the 1990s unacceptable for millions.

By all accepted criteria, flying is still safe . . . but not to a satisfactory degree; there *is* a difference. And the worst, I fear, is still to come.

INDEX